SHORTLIST

Tokyo

WHAT'S NEW | WHAT'S ON | WHAT'S BEST

www.timeout.com/tokyo

Contents

Tokyo by Area

Essentials

Published by Time Out Guides Ltd
Universal House
251 Tottenham Court Road
London W1T 7AB
Tel: + 44 (0)20 7813 3000
Fax: + 44 (0)20 7813 6001
Email: guides@timeout.com
www.timeout.com

Managing Director Peter Fiennes
Editorial Director Ruth Jarvis
Deputy Series Editor Dominic Earle
Business Manager Gareth Garner
Editorial Manager Holly Pick
Assistant Management Accountant Ilja Krasnikova

Time Out Guides is a wholly owned subsidiary of Time Out Group Ltd.

© **Time Out Group Ltd**
Chairman Tony Elliott
Financial Director Richard Waterlow
Group General Manager/Director Nichola Coulthard
Time Out Magazine Ltd MD Richard Waterlow
Time Out Communications Ltd MD David Pepper
Time Out International MD Cathy Runciman
Production Director Mark Lamond
Group Marketing Director John Luck
Group Art Director John Oakey
Group IT Director Simon Chappell

Time Out and the Time Out logo are trademarks of Time Out Group Ltd.

This edition first published in Great Britain in 2007 by Ebury Publishing
A Random House Group Company
Company information can be found on www.randomhouse.co.uk
10 9 8 7 6 5 4 3 2 1

For further distribution details, see www.timeout.com

ISBN 13: 978184670 0446
ISBN 10: 1-84670-044-2

A CIP catalogue record for this book is available from the British Library

Printed and bound by Firmengruppe APPL, aprinta druck, Wemding, Germany

The Random House Group Limited makes every effort to ensure that the papers used in
our books are made from trees that have been legally sourced from well-managed and
credibly certified forests. Our paper procurement policy can be found on
www.rbooks.co.uk/environment.

Tokyo Shortlist

The **Time Out Tokyo Shortlist** is one of a new series of guides that draws on Time Out's background as a magazine publisher to keep you current with what's going on in town. As well as Tokyo's key sights and the best of its eating, drinking and leisure options, the guide picks out the most exciting venues to have recently opened and gives a full calendar of annual events. It also includes features on the important news, trends and openings, all compiled by locally based editors and writers. Whether you're visiting for the first time, or you're a regular, you'll find the *Time Out Tokyo Shortlist* contains all you need to know, in a portable and easy-to-use format.

The guide divides central Tokyo into nine areas, each of which contains listings for Sights & Museums, Eating & Drinking, Shopping, Nightlife and Arts & Leisure, with maps pinpointing all their locations. At the front of the book are chapters rounding up these scenes city-wide, and giving a shortlist of our overall picks in a variety of categories. We include recommended itineraries for days out, plus essentials such as transport information and hotels.

Our listings give phone numbers as they should be dialled within Tokyo. To ring from outside Tokyo, add the area code 03 to the front of the given eight-digit number. To dial from abroad, use your country's exit code, followed by 81 (the country code for Japan), followed by 3.

We have noted appropriate price categories by using one to four ¥ signs (¥ ¥¥¥¥), which represent budget, moderate, expensive and luxury. Major credit cards are accepted unless otherwise stated. We also indicated when a venue is NEW .

All our listings are double-checked, but places sometimes close or change their hours or prices, so it's best to call venues before visiting. Every effort has been made to ensure accuracy, but the publishers cannot accept responsibility for any errors that this guide may contain.

Venues are marked on the maps using symbols numbered according to their order within the chapter and colour-coded according to the type of venue they represent:

❶ Sights & Museums
❶ Eating & Drinking
❶ Shopping
❶ Nightlife
❶ Arts & Leisure

Map key	
Major sight or landmark	▭
Parks	▭
Hospitals/universities	▭
Post offices	✉
Temples	卍
Shrines	卅
Railway stations	▬
Subway stations	Ⓢ
Districts	GINZA
Ward	SHIBUYA-KU

Time Out Tokyo Shortlist

EDITORIAL
Editor Nick Coldicott
Copy Editor Simon Coppock
Proofreader Carol Baker

DESIGN
Art Director Scott Moore
Art Editor Pinelope Kourmouzoglou
Senior Designer Henry Elphick
Graphic Designer Gemma Doyle
Junior Graphic Designer Kei Ishimaru
Digital Imaging Simon Foster
Ad Make-up Jodi Sher
Picture Editor Jael Marschner
Deputy Picture Editor Tracey Kerrigan
Picture Researcher Helen McFarland

ADVERTISING
Sales Director/Sponsorship Mark Phillips
International Sales Manager
  Kasimir Berger
International Sales Consultant
  Ross Canadé
International Sales Executive
  Charlie Sokol
Advertising Assistant Kate Staddon

MARKETING
Marketing Manager Yvonne Poon
Sales & Marketing Director,
  North America Lisa Levinson
Marketing Designer Anthony Huggins

PRODUCTION
Production Manager Brendan McKeown
Production Co-ordinator Caroline Bradford
Production Controller Susan Whittaker

CONTRIBUTORS
This guide was researched and written by Tom Baker, Alexander Coidan, Tazlu Endo, Dan Grunebaum, James Hardy, Gordon Kanki Knight, Mike Kleindl, Julian Satterthwaite, Mark Schilling, Rob Schwartz, Richard Smart, Frank Spignese and Martin Webb. Thanks also to contributors to the *Time Out Guide to Tokyo*.

PHOTOGRAPHY
All photography by Fumie Suzuki, except page 12 Keizo Kioku; page 13 Suntory Museum of Art; pages 16, 17, 20, 21, 23, 37, 38, 39, 46, 47, 55, 79, 93, 143 Kazunari Ogawa; page 29 Suntory Hall; pages 31, 32, 33, 35, 36 JNTO; page 103 Masaya Yoshimura/ Nacasa & Partners Inc; pages 42, 50, 58, 62, 84, 86, 91 Karl Blackwell.

The following images were provided by the featured establishments/artists: pages 43, 69, 110, 169, 175.

Cover photograph: Overhead view of crosswalk. Credit: Jan Halaska/Photolibrary Group.

MAPS
JS Graphics (john@jsgraphics.co.uk).

Special thanks to the Japan National Tourist Organization, Mark Kobayashi, Masako Mizoguchi and Ikue Usami.

About Time Out

Founded in 1968, Time Out has expanded from humble London beginnings into the leading resource for those wanting to know what's happening in the world's greatest cities. As well as our influential what's-on weeklies in London, New York and Chicago, we publish more than a dozen other listings magazines in cities as varied as Beijing and Mumbai. The magazines established Time Out's trademark style: sharp writing, informed reviewing and bang up-to-date inside knowledge of every scene.

Time Out made the natural leap into travel guides in the 1980s with the City Guide series, which now extends to over 50 destinations around the world. Written and researched by expert local writers and generously illustrated with original photography, the full-size guides cover a larger area than our Shortlist guides and include many more venue reviews, along with additional background features and a full set of maps.

Throughout this rapid growth, the company has remained proudly independent, still owned by Tony Elliott nearly four decades after he started Time Out London as a single fold-out sheet of A5 paper. This independence extends to the editorial content of all our publications, this Shortlist included. No establishment has been featured because it has advertised, and no payment has influenced any of our reviews. And, for our critics, there's definitely no such thing as a free lunch: all restaurants and bars are visited and reviewed anonymously, and Time Out always picks up the bill.

For more about the company, see www.timeout.com.

Don't Miss

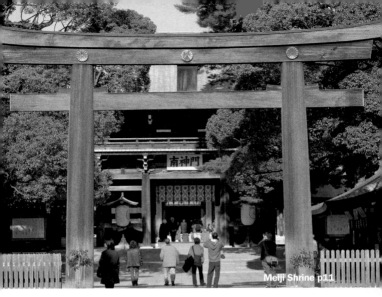
Meiji Shrine p11

Sights & Museums

Sightseeing in Tokyo is a little different from doing so in other major world cities, for the simple reason that – at first – there don't seem to be many sights to see. Flattened by an earthquake in 1923 and razed by fire bombing during World War II, Japan's capital has since been rebuilt again and again in a ceaseless churning of development and redevelopment. How do you get a handle on a city that continually erases its past?

Of course, the endless reinvention can be exciting, and is the motive force behind Tokyo's commitment to the cutting edge in everything from architecture to fashion and technology. But it can also be bewildering, even for a native. That 'great little place' someone told you about might be fresh rubble by the time you find it.

But getting lost is often the first step toward appreciating Tokyo's real charm – the infinite variety and invention of the human life that fills its myriad nooks and crannies. Wander the streets and there will always be something new to discover about the ingenious ways Tokyoites have found to live, love, eat, sleep and party.

If you really do get lost, don't worry. With little street crime and the world's best public transport, you're unlikely to come to much harm, and are never far from a train line to whisk you back to your hotel. (We have also included some common signs, complete with Japanese characters, on p189.)

Be our guest, book online.

Ancient art, modern museums

The defining elements of Tokyo's latest self-reinvention are the mixed-use mega-complexes that have sprung up over the last five years. Happily for the visitor, these often include a showpiece gallery or museum, as well as the obligatory retail, office and hotel facilities.

Driving the current wave of change is an economic recovery that means developers once again have cash to spare for the finer things in life. Better still, instead of blowing it on Old Masters, as would once have been the case, a newly confident Tokyo is investing in its own cultural heritage, as well as providing a forum for the most exciting contemporary art from Japan, Asia and around the world.

Numerous new venues have opened in recent years, and some of the very freshest are to be found in the Roppongi district – formerly the destination of choice for bar crawlers rather than gallery-goers, but now a symbol of the Tokyo's ability to regenerate.

There you'll find the Midtown development, which opened in March 2007. Its main tower is home to the Suntory Museum of Art (p104), designed by starchitect Kengo Kuma. He calls it a 'living room for the city', and it certainly makes a comfortable space for one of the country's best collections of traditional Japanese art. It's also one of the most foreigner-friendly museums in town – don't miss the excellent English-language earphone guides.

In the landscaped gardens of the same complex is the more challenging 21_21 Design Sight (see box p103) – a joint effort by veteran designer Issey Miyake and architect Tadao Ando. Designed to evoke origami with a structure

SHORTLIST

Best new
- 21_21 Design Sight (p100)
- National Art Center, Tokyo (p102)
- Suntory Museum of Art (p104)

Best outdoor
- Imperial Palace East Gardens (p90)
- Shinjuku Gyoen (p136)

Best views
- Tokyo City View (p102)
- Tokyo Metropolitan Government Building No.1 (p137)
- Tokyo Tower (p104)

Best people-watching
- Sunday afternoons in Ginza (p58)
- Weekends in Harajuku (p73)
- Shibuya crossing on a Friday evening (p116)

Best religious sites
- Asakusa Kannon (p53)
- Meiji Shrine (p73)
- Nogi Jinja (p102)

Best modern art
- Mori Art Museum (p102)
- National Museum of Modern Art (p90)
- Parco Museum of Art & Beyond (p119)
- Watari-um Museum of Contemporary Art (p81)

Best traditional art
- Idemitsu Museum of Arts (p87)
- Ukiyo-e Ota Memorial Museum of Art (p74)

Best offbeat museums
- Kite Museum (p90)
- Toto Super Space (p137)

Best nostalgia
- Edo-Tokyo Open-Air Architectural Museum (p161)
- Hanayashiki (p54)

DON'T MISS

Suntory Museum of Art p11

seemingly crafted from a folded concrete sheet, the exhibition space showed an idiosyncratic streak right from the start by opening with an exhibition on chocolate in art.

Midtown is new, but it's also a riposte to a nearby development that is only slightly older. Built around its landmark Mori Tower, Roppongi Hills set the blueprint for the new wave of developments. Many would argue that its Mori Art Museum (p102) is still the best private gallery in town. It's certainly the venue of choice for stylish curating and the latest in contemporary art. Perhaps more importantly, the destruction of Roppongi Hills has already been depicted in a Japanese disaster movie, and there's no greater honour than that.

Just down the road from these developments in Nogizaka, there's a new museum that – remarkably enough in today's climate – doesn't have a shopping centre attached. The National Art Center, Tokyo (p102), which opened a month

before Midtown, and is now the biggest museum in Japan. With no permanent collection to call its own, it will be interesting to see if curators can fill its cavernous spaces with consistently interesting shows.

Commerce, history, greenery

Another emblematic view of the modern Japanese capital can be had by stepping out of the west exit of Tokyo Station – exactly what many visitors do by chance when they get off the train from Narita Airport.

There you will find yourself ringed by skyscrapers, not one of which dates back more than five years. Formerly a drab office district, Marunouchi is now another leisure destination – and a lesson in how big, new commercial developments can actually revive a city centre, not drain it of life. Newest of the new towers is the Shin Marunouchi Building (April 2007) designed by Britain's Sir Michael Hopkins. It isn't a must-see, but it does make a decent place

DON'T MISS

to grab a bite to eat on your way to better sights, including the nearby Imperial Palace East Gardens (p90).

This last is the only public part of the Imperial Palace, which makes it an almost obligatory item on the tourist itinerary, but it's far from the best green space in the city. For two of the best parks, try the mix of Western and Japanese styles in Shinjuku Gyoen (p136) or the fully Japanese flavour of the Hama-Rikyu Detached Garden in Shiodome, near Ginza (1-1 Hama-Rikyu Teien, Chuo-ku).

Walking the streets

Tokyo is less a cohesive capital than a collection of distinct mini-areas separated by large belts of grey and beige. To experience the full press of Japanese humanity, try Shinjuku – home to the world's busiest railway station (about 3.3 million users daily) and the heart of Tokyo's government. It's also the place for a titillating (but generally safe) peek at Tokyo's underbelly, in the form of a walk round the

yakuza-run red-light district of Kabuki-cho. While you're there, stop by the impressive Hanazono Shrine, sitting incongruously next to the sleaze.

Shibuya and Harajuku are the places to see how teen Tokyo keeps up with the fashion of the week; Ginza is where they go when they've grown up, got married and moved in to serious chic – take a fat wallet if you want to do more than watch.

Tokyo's historic side remains an elusive quarry. Best bet, perhaps, is Asakusa with Asakusa Kannon (p53), the city's oldest temple. Here the back streets also offer a hint of the atmosphere of the *shitamachi* – Tokyo's largely vanished traditional downtown districts. For a walk around the area, see p46.

There are other places around town that offer a glimpse of old Tokyo. The Shitamachi Museum in Ueno (p150) is a quaint spot that recreates 19th-century life in downtown Tokyo and a 30-minute ride out of town will take you to the Edo-Tokyo Open-Air Architectural Museum (p161), where numerous classic residences and shops have been preserved in a spacious park.

But the truth is, Tokyo isn't defined by its heritage. The real city is made up of the innovations, the bizarre juxtapositions and the cacophony that comes with all the crowds. Look out for 'pet architecture', as funky young Japanese architects Atelier Bow-Wow have dubbed the tiny eccentric buildings that pop up on any vacant plot of land, no matter how small or weirdly shaped. Try the aural assault of a pachinko parlour. Enjoy the garish fun of a love hotel.

The bottom line is that discovery and adventure are pretty much inescapable. The secret to enjoying Tokyo is to surrender to all the mayhem and see what happens.

The best guides to enjoying London life

(but don't just take our word for it)

Roti

Eating & Drinking

Welcome to the dining capital of the world. With over 300,000 restaurants and bars, Tokyo offers an astounding panoply of choice – from the sleek lines of a high-rise designer spot to the smoke-in-the-eye sizzle of a yakitori joint.

It isn't a city that likes to stand still. Over the last several years Tokyo has been transforming itself (again) with the construction of huge metropolitan complexes in Roppongi, Marunouchi, Shiodome and Omotesando.

The most dramatic new face, Roppongi's Tokyo Midtown complex, embodies the essentials of Japanese design and style with its pale wood, hints of shoji screen and washi paper, flowing water, and leafy bamboo sprouting from interior pebbled gardens. It also showcases some great eating. The basement food court offers cheap chow in an attractive setting, but for a visual and culinary treat, head upstairs to Kafka (p108) for an unforgettable lunch of soba and champagne. Sir Terence Conran's latest offering, Botanica (5413 3282, www.conran-restaurants.jp), has snagged the prime fourth-floor garden terrace location overlooking Midtown's sculpture garden. Roti (p111) – the upmarket sister of a long-time local favourite – is also worth a visit.

Midtown's rival, the Roppongi Hills complex, also offers the full range of dining experiences, from chain coffee shop to the visual masterpiece of the counter-based

Mado Lounge

L'Atelier de Joël Robuchon (p105), which serves superb 'à la minute' dining at reasonable prices.

The city's other major revamp is taking place in Marunouchi. Amid the towers now overshadowing the lovely red-brick Tokyo Station are some terrific dining options. Both the Bar de España Muy (p92) and the remarkable Tapas Molecular Bar (p96) combine two trends – chic design and Spanish tapas. The recent explosive growth of tapas bars in Tokyo is a no-brainer. The Japanese have always had an *otsumami* (drinking snack) served with beer or sake. Now, instead of a saucer of peanuts or shreds of dried squid, the nibbles have been upgraded to wedges of Spanish omelette, gazpacho or Catalan-style beef tripe with white beans.

Away from the multi-billion yen renewal projects, some of Tokyo's less shouty neighbourhoods are bolstering their reputations too. One of the hippest, most laid-back areas is Naka-Meguro (p160), where a wide range of funky eateries draw in the city's bohemians. Wandering this riverside locale reveals myriad charming, independent bars, cafés and restaurants.

Designer dining

Design and style have always played a central role in Japanese cuisine – in the movement and utensils of the tea ceremony, in the elegant progression of a *kaiseki* banquet, even in the lowly toothpick, hand-cut and trimmed, with a rustic strip of bark still attached. With the economy rebounding, restaurateurs have looked to Tokyo's current crop of star interior designers – Yukio Hashimoto, Ryu Kosaka, Takashi Sugimoto – to help lure in the punters. The result: a city full of fanciful façades and inventive

interiors that span the spectrum from award-winning to throwaway kitsch. Recent eye-poppers include the bejewelled Dazzle (p63) and its downstairs partner WaZa (p67), Hashimoto's Azumitei (p62) and Sugimoto's Shunju Tsugihagi (p66).

More unabashed interiors are on the rise right across the city, thanks to the rampant growth of theme restaurants. You can now dine locked up in a jail cell, among vampires, inside a lotus blossom, in a medieval dungeon, before the Buddha, in a gothic cathedral or in the midst of a rainforest, among many other options. The best of these themed eateries is Asakusa's Ninja (2-14-3 Nagatacho, Chiyoda-ku, 5157 3936, www.ninja.tv).

Local fare

Sometimes what's new is that nothing has changed: Tokyo still offers superlative Japanese cuisine

---

SHORTLIST

Best new
- Kafka (p108)
- Roti (p111)
- Tapas Molecular Bar (p96)

Best sushi
- Fukuzushi (p107)
- Sushi Ouchi (p124)

Best tempura
- Kondo (p64)
- Ten-Ichi (p66)

Best noodles
- Kafka (p108)

Best French
- Les Saisons (p65)

Best bistrot
- Bistrot des Arts (p157)

Best interiors
- Dazzle (p63)
- Mandarin Bar (p95)
- Shunju Tsugihagi (p66)

Veggie heaven
- Gesshinkyo (p74)

Best views
- Bello Visto (p120)
- Mado Lounge (p108)
- New York Grill (p140)

Best standing bar
- Uogashi Nippon-ichi (p124)

Best hole-in-the-wall bars
- Albatross (p138)
- La Jetée (p139)
- Shot Bar Shadow (p140)

Best nostalgia
- Kamiya Bar (p56)
- Kissa Ginza (p158)

Best after hours
- Chandelier Bar/Red Bar (p120)

Best for couples
- High Tide (p108)
- Fonda de la Madrugada (p74)

of every kind. In contrast to most Japanese restaurants abroad, Tokyo's spots usually specialise in a single culinary strand. The sushi chefs make their daily dawn trek to the world's largest fish market in Tsukiji, just minutes from Ginza, while others prepare handmade soba, udon, oden and tofu. Meanwhile, *tempura* restaurants, *tonkatsu* and *kushiyaki* shops are heating up their oils; *teppanyaki*, *sukiyaki* and *shabu-shabu* specialists are slicing succulent cuts of beef, and *kaiseki* artisans, eel and blowfish specialists, *okonomiyaki* and *yakitori* cooks are doing their prep work.

Prices for local fare start at a rock-bottom ¥80 for a bamboo skewer of grilled chicken at a smoky *yakitori* stand and climb steadily in tandem with ambience and neighbourhood. But while Tokyoites might be lured by the latest budget-busting new options, we would be remiss if we didn't point you in the direction of several classic Tokyo joints where style is a loosened necktie and design is duct tape and last year's beer poster. Exemplars are Robata (p65) and Shin-Hinomoto (p65).

Recent years have seen a rise in the popularity of food from the southern Japanese islands of Okinawa. Cheap travel packages have lured Tokyoites into Pacific escapes, and they've returned with a taste for *goya* (bitter gourd) and *awamori* (the fiery southern version of shochu). Little Okinawa (p64) is a good place to taste why.

Drinking

There is no better way to end an evening of eating and drinking in Tokyo than with more drinking. There's certainly no shortage of opportunities. From festivals in temple grounds to outdoor hot springs (Seta onsen, 4-15-30 Seta, Setagaya-ku, 3707 8228, www.seta onsen.co.jp) and department store rooftops, alcohol is the lubricant that smoothes many social settings. There are joints catering to all tastes, from the ritzy, glitzy bars of Ginza to Shinjuku's warren of tiny drinking dens known as Golden Gai, where ten-seater counter bars cater to dedicated barflies.

One of the best ways to feel the pulse of Tokyo life is to spend a couple of hours in a standing bar. These *tachinomi* were once strictly male watering holes serving an open tin of sardines and a few hard-boiled eggs as nibbles. Now young professionals, male and female, fill these spots to unwind after work. You'll find much more appetising fare these days, as well as more extensive drinks menus, but the friendly, informal hum remains.

The only danger on the drinking scene is the hostess bar – or its tamer cousin, the 'snack pub'. Both such establishments will seat a staff member at your table who will drink merrily away on your tab. Prices are often unlisted and, if you're not a regular, you might be charged whatever the staff think they can get away with.

Etiquette

Dining out in Tokyo should cause little worry, but keep a few points in mind. Don't leave chopsticks sticking in your rice unless you're at a funeral. Don't pass food chopsticks to chopsticks for the same reason. In Japanese restaurants, the rice bowl is usually held in your hand when eating rice, not left on the table. Most importantly, any restaurant with tatami mats will expect you to remove your shoes. Tipping is not required anywhere.

We have included a menu reader, complete with Japanese characters and details of types of Japanese cuisine, on pp188-189.

Restir

Shopping

Tokyoites know how to shop, and they're getting better at it all the time. Above and beyond being an opportunity to buy rare crafts, manga or electronics, time spent shopping in Tokyo should be considered almost as an anthropological study.

Megaplexes rise up

A spate of large-scale, all-in-one consumer magnets in the Roppongi and Marunouchi districts has raised those areas' profiles and added several new spending options to the city, including in 2007 Tokyo Midtown (p112) and the Shin Marunouchi building.

Monocle magazine honcho Tyler Brûlé described Midtown as 'the new international benchmark for mixed-use developments', for its range of outlets and attention to detail. The interior is certainly impressive, using water and wood to create a remarkably serene atmosphere, and the tenants have clearly made the effort to keep up. Everything from the 7-11 convenience store to the basement food court blends seamlessly into the upmarket aesthetic.

But behind the sleek designs, the retail experiences are more conventional. Other than the dark, disco-like super-boutique Restir (p112), it's best to think of Midtown's shops as a diversion after visiting one of the eateries or the cultural attractions 21_21 Design Sight and the Suntory Museum of Art.

S H O R T L I S T

Best new shops
- Restir, in Tokyo Midtown (p112)
- Uniqlo UT (p80)

Best multi-label
- Loveless (p84)

Best urban fashion
- A Bathing Ape (p83)
- Billionaire Boys Club (p77)

Best manga
- Tora no Ana (p157)

Best for DJs
- Dance Music Record (p125)
- Technique (p127)

Best bargains
- RagTag (p70)

Best jewellery
- NIWAKA (p70)
- Tasaki Shinju (p71)

Flashiest façades
- Comme des Garçons (p83)
- Mikimoto (p68)
- Prada, in Aoyama (p81)

Best souvenirs
- Ginza Natsuno (p67)
- Nakamise Dori (p57)
- Oriental Bazaar (p80)

Best for kids
- Hakuhinkan (p67)
- LIMI feu prankster (p78)
- Sayegusa (p71)

Teen favourites
- 109 (p124)
- Laforet Harajuku (p78)

Best *depachika* (food halls)
- Isetan, in Shinjuku (p141)
- Mitsukoshi, in Ginza (p68)

Something quirky
- ranKing ranQueen (p127)

Similarly, in nearby Roppongi Hills (p112), unless you're looking for mainstream women's fashion, the shopping is best seen as a complement to a trip around the Mori Art Museum.

The Marunouchi area has undergone an equally dramatic makeover recently. The former business district has been revitalised by Mitsubishi Real Estate. The once-quiet Naka Dori is now a big, brand-lined boulevard that leads to the mixed-use Marunouchi Building (p96) – the first structure to flout a long-standing but unofficial rule preventing buildings from overlooking the Imperial Palace. A similar venture, the Shin Marunouchi Building (p98), opened virtually next door in 2007, and while the former is notable only for its restaurants, the latter offers a fascinating insight into the conservative tastes of the working women resident in the Kanto region, with its combination of bland boutiques and minimalist pâtisseries.

Tokyo's trendiest, most innovative fashion retailers still choose to be based in upscale Aoyama and the adjacent Harajuku district. A wander around the streets here will uncover any number of interesting stores, ranging from hip hop style source A Bathing Ape (p83) and cult newcomer Billionaire Boys Club (p77) to the spectacular high-end flagships of Comme des Garçons, Louis Vuitton and Prada. Directly opposite Comme des Garçons is the painfully trendy, dungeon-like fashion emporium Loveless (p84), with a large selection of up-and-coming home-grown brands. Meanwhile, local teens are served at the recently revamped fashion mall Laforet (p78), an earlier venture from the magnate behind Roppongi Hills.

Serious antiques freaks are also served in Aoyama, where a stroll along nearby Kotto Dori will take you to half a dozen of the city's longest established dealerships.

Youth central

A one-stop ride from Harajuku station is Shibuya, where fast-fashion mecca 109 (p124) is an essential destination, whether you're looking for the fashion of the week or simply watching those that are. Nearby manga and anime mega-store Mandarake (B2F Beam Bldg, 31-2 Udagawacho, Shibuya-ku, 3477 0777, www.mandarake.co.jp) is the most central option for geek goods. More committed fans need to head to Akihabara (p155), where the area known for its electronics is fast becoming a haven for *otaku* (geek) culture in all its forms – everything from homemade manga to multimillion yen sex dolls is on offer. And the electronics are still

in plentiful supply, with several multi-storey emporiums competing for your attention here.

Across town, in Nakano on the Chuo line, sits the other great home of all things anime: the Nakano Broadway shopping centre (3387 1610, www.nbw.jp). This shabby, time-worn arcade is home to several branches of Mandarake and Fujiya Avic, where you can pick up classic manga, collectable figures and bootlegs of the geek variety.

Spend, spend, spend!

Tokyo's most famous consumer destination is Ginza, a name so widely known as a synonym for luxurious consumer experiences that small towns across the nation have named their shopping streets after it. Premium department stores and European luxury brands dominate the landscape. The important foreign fashion behemoths are all represented, satisfying the never-diminishing local appetite for brand-emblazoned bags, but the best reason to check them out is their dramatic façades. Mikimoto (p68), Chanel and Maison Hermès (p60) all have photo-worthy stores that play up to Tokyo's taste for whimsy.

The back streets of Ginza are worth exploring, with dozens of interesting little shops purveying traditional crafts, kimono, samurai swords and the like. One must here is Japanese paper specialist Kyukyodo (p68), whose Ginza store, with its landmark arched brick entrance, proffers seasonal gift cards and lots of small and moderately priced items (boxes, notebooks, picture frames) made from colourful washi.

Foodies should head for the basements of the department stores, known as *depachika*, where vast arrays of gourmet delights offer visual and olfactory stimulation. The nation's leading confectioners are all here, vying to assist you in your souvenir search. Try *wasanbon*, a delicately flavoured powdered sugar tablet, or azuki bean *yokan* cakes. You'll also find an extensive selection of green tea, exquisitely wrapped.

Turntable treats

In Tokyo at least, vinyl is alive and kicking. Shibuya is renowned for its devotion to wax, catering largely to the house and hip hop crowds with new and vintage discs. Shinjuku is the place to look for rock and alternative, with scores of tiny shops clustered around Otakibashi Dori – the main road that heads north from Shinjuku station's west exit. Shinjuku is also the main home of domestic chain Disk Union (p141), each of whose numerous branches specialises in a particular genre – from punk to funk, from jazz to heavy metal. In both Shibuya and Shinjuku, many of the specialist stores are tucked away in apartment buildings, with street-side sandwich boards alerting you to their existence. These diminutive outlets are usually pricier than other shops, but the owners are die-hard fans who source global vinyl, so the selection tends to be first-rate.

Hours

Opening times are inching ever longer. The standard is still 10am or 11am until 8pm daily, but many shops in the busiest areas, such as Shibuya, Harajuku or Shinjuku, now stay open as late as 10pm. Independent shops, especially the traditional or craft-oriented ones, may close for one day, usually Monday or Wednesday. Most shops stay open on national holidays, but it's wise to call ahead to check.

DON'T MISS

Tokyo Midtown p20

Velours

Nightlife

Tokyo's lively nightlife benefits from the city's extortionate cab prices and early closing public transport: if you're out in Tokyo at 1am, you're out until sunrise. Thus most clubs are open until dawn and parties can be as busy at 4am as they were at midnight.

The 'Big Three' of Tokyo clubland are Ageha, Womb and Yellow, all of which featured in *DJ* magazine's 50 best clubs of 2007. The pick of the three is still Womb (p132), with its great Shibuya location and a towering main room decked with superb lighting and sound. But it's a temple for über-serious clubbers, so check the schedule before turning up. Scene veteran Yellow (p114) offers a broader, more accessible range, with a soft spot for deep house.

Although they test the limits of their capacity at times, the ambience is great. Ageha (p162), however, is hit or miss. Its cavernous interior offers twice the capacity of Yellow and Womb combined, and a far-flung location that means only committed clubbers will make it, so the venue needs a blockbuster line-up to draw a decent crowd. When it does, even the overbearing security team can't dampen the mood.

International superstars are still the story at the megaclubs, but Tokyo now has the confidence to support homegrown talent. Local DJs and producers, often little known outside Japan, offer some of the city's best nights. Towa Tei (formerly of Deee-Lite), Masanori Morita (Studio Apartment) and Shinichi Osawa (Mondo Grosso) are some of the biggest local names and can be found at venues large and small. Among the new clubs energising the scene, Velours (p85) has had most success, winning the hearts of the see-and-be-seen set.

For all-night partying without the formalities, Roppongi is the place. Famed for its sleaze and hedonism, the area is markedly tamer than it used to be (a number of top spots have lost their licences), but it's still Tokyo's most popular night out. Legendary meat markets Heartland (p108), Muse (p114) and Gas Panic (p114) epitomise the scene, but venue-hopping is simple – just follow your ears.

Jazz

Tokyo's jazz scene is still world-class. The massive, corporate Blue Note (p85) and its funk- and soul-focused new sister, the Cotton Club (p99), host the stars, but with short sets and sky-high prices. A fresher, more friendly face on the jazz-and-dining scene is JZ Brat (p129), a spacious, comfortable venue with diverse line-ups. Shinjuku Pit Inn (p146) is good for cutting-edge improvisation, and you'll find the city loaded with jazz bars and coffee shops playing great vinyl.

Gay Tokyo

Shinjuku's Ni-chome, heart of the gay scene, is a party district of around 200 gay bars. Advocates Café (p144) is a huge hit in the warmer months with outdoor, street-corner drinking; at other times, the most fun is found at Arty Farty (p145), affectionately known as Arthur's. Here gay, bi and straight punters dance to a wonderful electro, disco and house remixes. Ni-chome nightlife is said to be next for Tokyo governor Shintaro Ishihara's clampdown on fun, but for now the party is in full swing, even mid-week.

S H O R T L I S T

Best new
- Ovo (p161)
- Seco Bar (p132)

Best superclub
- Womb (p132)
- Space Lab Yellow (p114)

Best intimate
- Loop (p130)
- Organ Bar (p131)
- Room (p131)

Best avant-garde
- Super-deluxe (p115)

Best sound system
- Ageha (p162)

Best reggae
- Open (p145)

Best jazz
- Hot House (p40)
- JZ Brat (p129)
- Shinjuku Pit Inn (p146)

Best punk
- Antiknock (p144)
- Gig-antic (p129)

Best hip-hop
- Club Bar Family (p128)
- Shibuya Nuts (p132)

Best nightlife areas
- Roppongi (p112)
- Shibuya (p128)
- Shinjuku (p144)

Best gay
- Advocates Café (p144)
- Arty Farty (p145)

Best event
- Medvacances, at La Fabrique (p129)
- Real Grooves, at Yellow (p114)
- Sterne, at Womb (p132)

Best live venue
- Club Quattro (p129)

Best for a giggle
- J-pop Café (p129)

DON'T MISS

Uplink Factory p30

WHAT'S BEST
Arts & Leisure

Catering to an eclectic audience of over 30 million people, greater Tokyo has enough cultural offerings to keep the visitor busy for a lifetime and then some. Notwithstanding their worker bee image, Japanese are voracious consumers of culture, with a wide range of tastes that run from austere Noh theatre to the crass pleasures of Disneyland and on to the experimental dance form butoh. The good news for travellers is that Japan, unlike during the boom years of the Bubble era, is now relatively affordable. The recently weak yen makes Tokyo good value in comparison to big-city rivals such as New York or London.

Performance

Japan is home to a lively domestic theatre circuit, and the colossal Gekidan Shiki translates Broadway hits into Japanese – but you didn't come to Japan to see *Cats* in Japanese, did you? The main allure for visitors is either Japan's cutting-edge contemporary dance scene, or its kitschy, over-the-top, all-female Takarazuka revue.

The avant-garde postwar dance form butoh is starkly removed from Western contemporary dance, with white body paint, shaved heads and torturously slow movements creating a bizarre spectacle. Tatsumi Hijikata scandalised Japan with his invention of this

DON'T MISS

SHORTLIST

Flashiest new venue
- Cerulean Tower Noh Theatre (p132)

Best traditional theatre
- Kabuki-za (p72)

Best concert halls
- Casals Hall (p99)
- Suntory Hall (p115)

Best dance companies
- For butoh, Dairakudakan (left)
- For ballet, K-Ballet Company (p28)

Best avant-garde
- Die Pratze Dance Festival and Mentally Shocking Arts Collection (p28)

Best kitsch
- Tokyo Takarazuka Gekijo (p72)

Best for kids
- Disneyland and DisneySea at Tokyo Disney Resort (p162)

Best karaoke venue
- Lovenet (p114)

Best street festival
- Awa Odori in Koenji (p35)

Best expos
- Tokyo Game Show (p35)
- Tokyo International Anime Fair (p32)

Best arthouse cinemas
- Cinema Rise (p133)
- Iwanami Hall (p99)
- National Film Centre (p72)

Best cineplex
- Toho Cinemas Roppongi Hills (p115)

Underground culture
- Shinjuku Loft Plus One (p146)

Most relaxing
- Edo-style bathhouse Oedo Onsen Monogatari (p159)

'dance of darkness' in the late 1950s, but butoh can now be judged Japan's greatest contribution to contemporary performing arts.

World-famous troupes Sankai Juku and Dairakudakan stage large performances at venues such as the ambitious Setagaya Public Theatre (4-1-1 Taishido, Setagaya-ku, 5432 1526, http://setagaya-pt.jp/en/) several times a year, while Dairakudakan also presents smaller-scale pieces on a more regular basis at its home in Tokyo's suburban college district of Kichijoji.

Butoh and contemporary performance art can also be seen at the New National Theatre, Tokyo (1-1-1 Honmachi, Shibuya-ku, 5352 9999, www.nntt.jac.go.jp) or at the Die Pratze black box theatres in Azabu (1-26-6 Higashi-Azabu 2F, Minato-ku, 5545 1385, www.geocities.jp/azabubu) and

Kagurazaka (2-12 Nishi-Gokencho, Shinjuku-ku, 3235 7990), which often play home to performances by leading butoh choreographers such as Maruboshi Ko.

If you time your visit right, you can also take in one of Japan's performing arts festivals, including Die Pratze's Dance Festival or its Mentally Shocking Arts (MSA) Collection, both intriguing and sprawling platforms for some of Japan's most avant-garde and often rather baffling stage undertakings.

Speaking of baffling stage undertakings, Takarazuka features an all-woman, oft-moustachioed cast performing campy revues. This popular performance form was created in 1913 by tycoon Ichizo Kobayashi to attract the punters to his resort near Osaka. A peculiar expression of Japan's fixation with androgynous performers, it can nowadays be sampled at the Tokyo Takarazuka Gekijo (p72), recently rebuilt and reopened in Hibiya.

Classical ballet also draws a devoted audience in Japan, with the country has been churning out world-class dancers including Testuya Kumakawa, who returned from his position as soloist with the Royal Ballet in London a few years ago and now makes waves with his K-Ballet Company. The Tokyo Ballet and the Asami Maki Ballet regularly perform the dependable Stravinsky classics, while the Leningrad State Ballet's annual winter tours have become an institution.

Classical sounds

The glory years of the Bubble provided Tokyo with numerous monuments to high-cultural ambition, including soaring structures such as Tokyo Opera City (3-20-2 Nishi-Shinjuku, Shinjuku-ku, 5353 0770, www.operacity.jp), the adjacent New National Theatre, Tokyo (1-1-1 Honmachi, Shibuya-ka, 5352 9999, www.nntt.jac.go.jp), Suntory Hall (p115) and Triphony Hall (1-2-3 Kinshi, Sumida-ku, 5608 1212, www.triphony.com), to complement already extant halls such as Tokyo Bunka Kaikan (5-45 Ueno Koen, Taito-ku, 3828 2111, www.t-bunka.jp) and Orchard Hall (p133).

Tokyo claims more concerts and more venues than any city in the world. Since it opened its ears to classical music in the 19th century, it has welcomed a steady stream of star conductors and soloists from overseas, and has now produced its own legitimate luminaries – from conductor Seiji Ozawa to violinist Midori.

Greater Tokyo has no less than five symphony orchestras, including the Tokyo Symphony Orchestra, the New Japan Philharmonic Orchestra and the NHK Symphony Orchestra, while the Fujiwara Opera Company and the New National Theatre, Tokyo, stage their own, occasionally innovative, opera productions.

Traditional theatre

No trip to Japan would be complete without taking in the fearsome masks, silken costumes, precise choreography and exotic music of kabuki, Noh or bunraku. You probably won't have a clue what's going on, but then neither does most of the native audience.

Said to have originated with female shrine attendant Okuni, who led her female company in performances in Kyoto, kabuki ('unusual' or 'shocking') quickly became the most popular form of theatre in the 17th century. Concerns over the sex trade that developed around kabuki led to a ban on women performers in 1629, and female roles are now played by *onnagata*, male actors who specialise in portraying a stylised feminine beauty.

The venerable Kabuki-za (p72) in Ginza is the place to take in kabuki. English-language programmes and earphone guides make it accessible to foreigners, as does the detailed information about each month's performance given on its website.

In recent years, actor/director Ichikawa Monnosuke has adapted kabuki for a generation weaned on Hollywood with his flashy 'Super Kabuki' performances. Traditionalists have held their noses, but that hasn't stopped the masses from making them a hit.

Japan's oldest theatre form, Noh, emerged from 14th-century Shinto and Buddhist religious festivals. It was intended both to educate and to entertain. Characterised by the startling masks worn by its principal actors, noh plays explore metaphysical themes. The weighty nature of the dramas is relieved by short interludes of comedic kyogen.

The National Noh Theatre (4-18-1 Sendagaya, Shibuya-ku, 3230 3000, www.ntj.jac.go.jp/english/index.html), the National Theatre (p99) and the newer Cerulean Tower Noh Theatre (p132), in a skyscraper in Shibuya, all offer regular noh performances. The National Theatre is probably the most English-friendly, with English programmes and earphone guides available for many performances.

Unlike the otherworldly noh, bunraku was developed by commoners during the Edo period (1600-1868), taking its name from the Bunraku-za organised in Osaka in the 19th century. Bunraku puppets are a half to two-thirds

Suntory Hall

human-size and learning to operate them demands decades of study. The National Bunraku Theatre is in Osaka, but bunraku performances are staged at the National Theatre.

Entertainment

Again highlighting the easy coexistence of tradition and modernity in Japan, Tokyo's diverse entertainment options run from ancient fire-walking ceremonies to garish sports centres and everything in between.

For hunters of tradition, colourful festivals take place regularly in Tokyo, with parades of portable shrines, costumed participants, ornate floats and boozy revellers. At the other of the spectrum, Tokyoites entertain themselves with karaoke – usually in private rooms with a group of friends. Karaoke venues are pretty easy to spot at almost any station, but our pick is Lovenet (p114)– where stylishly themed rooms and a superior menu elevate the warbling experience.

There are avant-garde venues, such as Shibuya's cult Uplink Factory, and gleaming corporate bastions such as the ever-popular Tokyo Disneyland and its adjacent DisneySea (p162). And Canada's Cirque du Soleil, which is set to receive its own US$200 million permanent home in suburban Tokyo in autumn 2008.

Sports

Many of Japan's top baseball stars have departed for richer pastures in the US Major Leagues, but taking in a match at either Tokyo Dome (1-3-61 Koraku, Bunkyo-ku, 5800 9999, www.tokyo-dome.co.jp) or Jingu Stadium (13 Kasumigaoka-machi, Shinjuku-ku, 3404 8999) can provide an intriguing lesson in how the Japanese have recast the game to suit their own culture. Beginning

with the introduction of games that end in a tie, the contrasts with American pro ball extend to the stands, where fans cheer on cue and jump up and down in tightly choreographed routines.

The 2002 Japan–South Korea World Cup fanned the fires of football in Japan, and matches involving Tokyo teams FC Tokyo and Tokyo Verdy 1969 can be watched in the west of the city at the Ajinomoto Stadium (376-3 Nishimachi, Chofu, 0424 40 0555, www.ajinomotostadium.com), which the teams share. In the wake of the World Cup and with the loss of Japan's baseball stars, football is giving baseball a run for its money as Japan's most popular sport.

But it's the loincloth-clad giants of sumo that are the oversized lure for visiting sports fans. Mongolian wrestlers Asashoryu and Hakuho are currently lording it over the domestic competition, which makes these interesting days indeed for the tradition-drenched, 2,000-year-old sport. Three of sumo's six annual 15-day tournaments take place at Tokyo's Ryogoku Kokugikan (1-3-28 Yokoami, Sumida-ku, 3623 5111) in January, May and September, while in downtimes it's possible to visit sumo stables to watch wrestlers' morning practice sessions.

Tickets

The city's leading ticket agency, Ticket Pia (0570 029 111, http://t. pia.co.jp), deals with concerts, shows, sporting events, films and pretty much anything else that you can buy a ticket for. They have branches in many department stores and their telephone operators can often handle English enquiries. Most branches of convenience store chain Lawson (www2.lawsonticket. com) have ticket vending machines, but navigation is in Japanese.

Calendar

Sanja Festival p34

January

1 New Year's Day (Ganjitsu)
Japan's most important annual holiday sees large crowds at temples and shrines for the first visit of the year.

1 Emperor's Cup Final
www.jfa.or.jp/eng
The showpiece event of Japan's domestic football season.

2 New Year Congratulatory Visit (Ippan Sanga)
Imperial Palace
Seven times during the day, from 9.30am to 3pm, the Emperor addresses his subjects from the palace balcony.

6 Tokyo Metropolitan Fire Brigade Parade (Dezome-shiki)
Tokyo Big Sight
An acrobatic display put on by the Preservation Association of the old Edo Fire Brigade.

2nd Sun-4th Sun New Year Grand Sumo Tournament (Ozumo Hatsu Basho)
Kokugikan
www.sumo.or.jp/eng/index.html
The first of the year's three major sumo tournaments (*basho*) held in Tokyo.

2nd Mon **Coming of Age Day (Seijin no Hi)**
Those turning 20 in this financial year head to shrines in their best kimonos and suits for blessings.

Jan/Feb **Chinese New Year**
Yokohama Chinatown
www.chinatown.or.jp/info/schedule.html
Dragon dancers weave their way along the streets of Yokohama Chinatown.

Late Jan-early Feb **Toray Pan Pacific Open Tennis Tournament**
Tokyo Metropolitan Gymnasium
www.toray-ppo.co.jp/web/pc/
A women's indoor tennis tournament, usually well attended by big names.

February

Ongoing Chinese New Year (see Jan); Toray Pan Pacific Open Tennis Tournament (see Jan)

3 Setsubun
Celebrate the last days of winter by hurling soybeans to cries of 'demons out, good luck in' at homes and shrines.

14 Valentine's Day
Women give chocolate to men in the local take on the romantic festival.

Mid Feb-mid Mar
Plum-blossom viewing
The white blooms are celebrated less
energetically than the cherry blossoms.

March

Ongoing Plum-blossom
viewing (see Feb)

3-4 **Daruma Fair**
Shrines sell red Daruma dolls, modelled after Zen monk Bodhidharma.

2nd Sun **Fire-Walking
Ceremony (Hi-watari)**
Kotsu Anzen Kitosho
www.takaotozan.co.jp.
Monks and others traverse hot coals.

14 **White Day**
Guys give chocolate to girls.

17 **St Patrick's Day Parade**
Omotesando
www.inj.or.jp

Late Mar **Tokyo International
Anime Fair**
Tokyo Big Sight
www.tokyoanime.jp/en/
The world's largest anime fair, with
trade booths, stage shows and awards.

Late Mar-early Apr **Cherry-
blossom viewing (Hanami)**
Picnics under petals. See box right.

Late Mar-early Apr
Tokyo Motorcycle Show
Tokyo Big Sight
www.motorcycleshow.org
A three-day expo of the latest models
from Japan and abroad, as well as some
great classics.

April

Ongoing Cherry-blossom viewing
(see Mar); Tokyo Motorcycle
Show (see Mar)

Early Apr **Art Fair Tokyo**
Tokyo International Forum
www.artfairtokyo.com
This three-day fair is the largest
in Japan, featuring everything from
ukiyo-e to avant-garde work.

Early Apr **Start of the
baseball season**

Mid Apr **Horseback Archery
(Yabusame)**
Sumida Park, Asakusa
Mounted riders dressed as samurai
fire at stationary targets while galloping
at full speed.

29-early May **Meiji Jingu Spring
Festival (Haru no Taisai)**
Meiji Shrine
Free performances of traditional enter-
tainment at the large shrine.

Sanno Festival p34

Cheery blossom

How to be happy in *sakura* season.

Like youth, like happiness, like life itself, Japanese cherry blossoms are utterly glorious while we have them... and disappear all too soon. No wonder their sudden profusion each spring inspires countless poems – not to mention *hanami* (flower-viewing) parties. You may gaze on these pale pink flowers and contemplate mortality, or get sloshed and toast their short-lived beauty with friends, who on a bright spring day in a crowded Tokyo park may include anyone who happens to be nearby. Haiku poet Issa (1763-1828) understood this when he wrote: 'Cherry blossoms above / The people below / Are strangers no more.'

The largest number of former strangers can be found at Ueno Park (next to Ueno Station), which has over a thousand cherry trees and many times that number of *hanami*-goers. The park is also home to several art museums.

Inokashira Park (south of Kichijoji station) has hundreds of blossoming trees arranged around a small lake. Rental boats on the lake are said to be cursed, with couples who use them doomed to break up. But that doesn't stop many from trying their luck.

Yoyogi Park (Yoyogi station) has a few hundred blossoming trees, including one standing alone on an island in a pond. Broad lawns provide some elbow room, and with the park's reputation for attracting performers, cosplayers ('costume role-players') and other eccentrics, this is often the best spot for human scenery.

Shinjuku Gyoen (Shinjukugyoen-mae station) has 1,500 trees of 75 cherry varieties on its spacious grounds, but is the only park on this list to charge admission (¥200). A more serious threat to cherry-blossom revelry ought to be the park-wide ban on alcohol, but at *hanami* time the rule becomes virtually unenforceable.

If boozing amid gravestones doesn't seem too morbid, Aoyama Cemetery (Nogizaka station) is another popular *hanami* spot. Several hundred trees are dotted between the graves, which include the final resting places of many of Tokyo's noted expats.

Cherry blossoms usually peak in March or April, depending on the weather. Once they come, they don't stay long, usually fluttering to the ground in under a week. So as soon as they appear, grab a picnic blanket, some refreshments, and make a beeline for the pink trees. When the blossoms are out, you should be too.

Pink screens

Tokyo's Lesbian & Gay Film Festival.

It started in 1992 when some gay activists borrowed a small conference room to show films. From this humble beginning, the Tokyo International Lesbian and Gay Film Festival (www.tokyo-lgff.org) has grown to be one of the largest such events in Asia, with around 7,000 people attending over several days in 2006. The 2007 event was set to be even bigger, with 22 programmes playing in 32 time-slots in July at Spiral (p81) and the nearby Tokyo Women's Plaza.

More than a dozen countries are represented each year, often with the official support of their governments. The embassies of Spain, Canada, Israel and France have been particularly helpful, according to one organiser – 'but never the US Embassy'. Japan's Cultural Affairs Agency recently lent its support, but the event is still run entirely by volunteers.

Entries range from low-budget shorts to slick features, with many of the local contributions cheap cinéma-vérité works. Ryosuke Hashiguchi, director of the well-received *Hush!* (2001), is a rare example of an openly gay Japanese filmmaker finding mainstream success.

The 'boys' love' genre, a distinctly Japanese phenomenon of gay male romances aimed at straight women, was set to make its festival debut with a special edition of *Sukitomo* (2007), a film about beautiful young boxers.

Movies are shown with both Japanese and English subtitles.

29-5 May **Golden Week**
A string of national holidays, among them the birthday of the late Emperor Hirohito, that together form one of Japan's most popular holiday periods.

May

Ongoing Meiji Jingu Spring Festival (see Apr); Golden Week (see Apr)

Mid May **Kanda Festival**
Kanda Myojin Shrine
www.kandamyoujin.or.jp
One of Tokyo's 'Big Three' festivals, held in odd-numbered years, with a gala procession of floats and martial arts demonstrations.

Mid May **Thai Festival**
Yoyogi Park
www.thaifestival.net
A weekend of Thai food and culture.

3rd weekend **Sanja Festival**
Asakusa Shrine
Tokyo's largest annual festival.

Late May **Design Festa**
Tokyo Big Sight
www.designfesta.com
Two-day showcase of hundreds of young artists and performers.

June

Mid June **Sanno Festival**
Hie Shrine
Another of Tokyo's Big Three festivals, this one held on even numbered years, with floats and costume parades.

July

9-10 **Ground-Cherry Market (Hozuchi-ichi)**
Senso-ji, Asakusa
Prayers at Senso-ji on these days are said to carry the equivalent of 46,000 days' worth at other times. A ground-cherry market also takes place.

Mid July **Tokyo International Lesbian & Gay Film Festival**
www.tokyo-lgff.org
Annual pink film festival that lasts around five days. See box left.

Last Sat in July **Sumida River Fireworks**
The oldest, biggest and most crowded of Tokyo's summer firework events.

August

13-15 **Obon**
Buddhist festival for departed souls.

15 **War-End Anniversary**
Many politicians mark this day with contentious visits to Yasukuni Shrine.

3rd weekend **Azabu-Juban Noryo Festival**
www.azabujuban.or.jp
Taiko drums and traditional dancing.

Last Sat **Asakusa Samba Carnival**
Thousands of brilliantly plumed dancers shake their stuff in Asakusa.

Last weekend **Awa Odori**
Koenji
Street carnival, Japanese style.

September

3rd Mon **Respect for the Aged Day**
Public holiday honouring the elderly.

Late Sept **Tokyo Game Show**
Makuhari Messe
http://tgs.cesa.or.jp
The biggest computer and video-game show on the planet.

Late Sept **Moon Viewing (Tsukimi)**
Parties held to view the harvest moon.

Late Sept-mid Oct
Art-Link Ueno-Yanaka
http://artlink.jp.org
Art fair staged in galleries, shops and temples of Ueno and Yanaka.

Sept-Oct **Takigi Noh**
Outdoor performances of Noh drama at shrines, temples and parks spread across the city.

October

Ongoing Art-Link Ueno-Yanaka (see Sept); Takigi Noh (see Sept)

Sumida River Fireworks

Early Oct **CEATEC Japan**
Makuhari Messe
www.ceatec.com/index.html
Consumer gadgets and communication technology fair. Digital Nirvana.

Early Oct **Japan Tennis Open**
Ariake Tennis Forest
Japan's most important international tennis tournament.

2nd Mon **Sports Day**
Public holiday commemorating the 1964 Olympics.

Late Oct-early Nov
Tokyo Motor Show
Makuhari Messe
www.tokyo-motorshow.com
Cars and motorbikes feature in odd-numbered years, commercial vehicles in even ones.

Late Oct-early Nov **Tokyo International Film Festival**
www.tiff-jp.net
The largest film festival in Japan, screening over 300 films.

November

Ongoing Tokyo Motor Show
(see Oct); Tokyo International
Film Festival (see Oct)

3 Culture Day/Meiji Jingu Grand Autumn Festival (Reisai)
Meiji Shrine
The largest festival at Meiji Shrine,
featuring traditional music, theatre and
horseback archery.

15 Seven-Five-Three Festival (Shichi Go San)
Kids aged three, five or seven visit their
local shrine in their finest outfits.

Nov Tori no Ichi Fair
Chokoku-ji/Otori Jinja, Asakusa
www.torinoichi.jp
The city's largest fair for Kumade – the
expensive and gaudily decorated
bamboo rakes are reputed to bring
prosperity and good fortune.

Late Nov Autumn Leaves (Koyo)
The spectacular colours of maple
and gingko trees transform many of
Tokyo's parks and gardens.

Late Nov Japan Cup
Tokyo Racecourse
Highlight of the horse-racing calendar.

December

Mid Dec FIFA Club World Cup
www.fifa.com
A new football tournament involving
the league champion clubs from each
of the six continents.

14 47 Ronin Memorial Service (Ako Gishi-sai)
Nihonbashi/Sengaku-ji
A costumed parade in Nihonbashi and
a formal ceremony at Sengaku-ji mark
the famous revenge attack by 47
masterless samurai.

17-19 Battledore Market (Hagoita Ichi)
Ornate paddle-shaped bats are sold
at temples across the city. Asakusa
Kannon Temple has the largest fair.

23 Emperor's Birthday (Tenno Tanjobi)
A public holiday and one of only two
days each year (the other is 2 January),
when members of the public are
permitted to enter the inner grounds of
the Imperial Palace.

28-31 Year End
The last official day of work in Japan
is 28 December.

Battledore Market

Itineraries

J-pop Café p40

Into the Music

Forget the 'big in Japan' years when fading stars and one-hit-wonders found inexplicable fame eastside – these days international A-listers are referencing Tokyo trends (Gwen Stefani), launching local brands (Pharrell Williams), collaborating with Japanese bands (Kanye West) or just churning out neon skyline videos (Madonna, among others). The cultural flow between Japan and the West is pretty equal now, and for music-loving visitors this is a great time to sample the passionate and diverse scenes. This itinerary takes you through a music-related mix of sightseeing, shopping, dancing and, of course, a little bit of singing.

You're going to be out late, so aim for a relaxed 11am start at **Harajuku station**. And make it a weekend, when the bridge beside the station is a gathering point for the teenage Harajuku girls who, as Gwen Stefani sang, 'have got the wicked style'. The mix of goths, punks, schoolgirls and superheroes sits somewhere between cool and bizarre, and this weekly expression of youthful exuberance has become a major tourist attraction, with a photo alongside the girls a modern must-have souvenir.

Just around the corner, close to the entrance to **Yoyogi park**, you'll find a local rockabilly crew using tarmac as their dancefloor most weekends. Some of these ladies and gents clearly date back to the original rockabilly years, but their enthusiasm seems undimmed. They've been joined by a younger generation that takes its fashion and moves every bit as seriously.

The area between Yoyogi park and the edge of Shibuya is also a popular spot for buskers, and the acts – most of them hoping to be discovered – could be anything

from a cappella pop stars to skiffle groups. There might also be stand-up comedians, performance artists or breakdance crews practising their skills.

After a blast of local talent, head back past Harajuku station until you see the narrow pedestrianised street **Takeshita Dori**, usually heaving with masses of teens out wandering with their friends. The narrow thoroughfare is lined with stores such as Closet Child (1-6-11 Jingumae, 3403 4106, www.closet-child.com) and Mari's Rock (1-8-3 Jingumae, 3423 0069, www.maris-rock.co.jp), outfitters to the Harajuku girls. The side streets are also crammed with quirky clothes shops and jewellery stores, worth a peek even if just out of anthropological interest. At the lower end of Takeshita Dori, cross the main road (Meiji Dori) and take the next right, which leads to Pharrell Williams' Billionaire Boys Club/Ice Cream Store (p77), easily identifiable by the traditional ice-cream cart in the window. You can

only buy these clothes in a handful of locations around the world, and this is the futuristic and funky flagship. Pharrell's collaborator, legendary local DJ/designer Nigo, has his own flagship A Bathing Ape store downstairs, where you'll find even more urban attire.

A short walk down Meiji Dori, or one stop on the Yamanote line, leads to **Shibuya**, where visitors are greeted with two massive LCD screens playing the latest J-pop videos. Musically, Shibuya is all about dance music. Besides being the home to many of the city's very best clubs, the area is a DJ's fantasy, with the greatest concentration of vinyl outlets in the city. Technique (p127), Dance Music Record (p125) and the five buildings that comprise Cisco (p124) are the big draws here, but wander the surrounding streets and you'll uncover myriad more. For vinyl freaks this is dangerous territory, where afternoons can slip by unnoticed. The Quintrix Disc Lounge (10-1 Udagawa-cho,

Shibuya-ku, 6415 6678, www.
quintrix.jp) stands out from its
peers by selling CDs and running a
fully-stocked café/bar at the back.
If you can stomach their relentless
trance this early in the day, take a
coffee, herb tea or beer break here.

Next stop: nostalgiaville.
A couple of blocks away, in the
basement of the **Quattro building**
are Get Back and Gimme Shelter,
a pair of stores dedicated to the
original Britrock legends. Get Back
is the more impressive of the two,
offering Fab Four-related goodies
including vintage magazines,
inflatable dolls, a full-size Yellow
Submarine jukebox and New York-
era Lennon action figures. With
admirable thoroughness, even
Ringo's solo years are represented
in the music section. The Rolling
Stones-related Gimme Shelter
has a smaller range of goods, but
you can pick up some T-shirts or
rare presses of the classics. The
basement also houses a ticket shop
for upcoming rock and pop gigs.

Now for something more
contemporary. Cross the street
to the massive **Beam building**
and head up to the seventh floor
for the J-pop Café (p129). This
indigenous take on pop is an
acquired taste, but the saccharin
sounds account for around 60 per
cent of Japan's music industry,
have a big following all around
Asia and are beginning to break
into Australia and the US market.
J-pop is the sound of anime and
video-game soundtracks, and its
rise on the global scene is closely
tied to the success of those formats.

The spacious J-pop Café is
a fun place to hear some of the
latest tracks. The main room
loosely follows the dining club
concept, and two or three times
a week baby-faced songstresses
perform to a young crowd of pop
fans. Unlike its fellow dining clubs

(Blue Note, Cotton Club and so on),
at J-pop Café everything is priced
for the pockets of an adolescent
audience. But ours is just a flying
visit, so head instead for the
surprisingly urbane lounge bar,
where the pop gets pumped through
speakers while you relax with a
drink. If the music appeals, you'll
find flyers for all the city's upcoming
J-pop gigs on your way out.

For dinner, head north for some
jazz. Although Tokyo is home to
around 50 jazz clubs, there's one
special spot 15 minutes away in
Takadanobaba on the Yamanote
line. The **Hot House** (Liberal
Takadanobaba B1F, 3-23-5
Takadanobaba, Shinjuku-ku, 3367
1233, www2.vc-net.ne.jp/~winning/
menu/hothouse/hothouse.html) is
surely the world's smallest jazz
club, struggling to cram in a dozen
listeners. It can't fit quartets and
doesn't need amps, but this is one
place that proves biggest isn't
always best. The venue's unique

ITINERARIES

atmosphere, akin to a jam session in a living room, persuades some eminent musicians to perform here, almost nose-to-nose with their audience. The food is simple Japanese fare, handed from kitchen to customer by whoever happens to be seated in the middle. The Hot House is the only spot on the itinerary that demands a reservation, and be sure to show up in time for the 8.30pm start – if you're late, there might be a pianist blocking the entrance.

How to round off a day of music in Tokyo? If you're travelling solo and still have the energy, you're in a world-class party city with such superclubs as Yellow (p114) and Womb (p132) at your disposal. On a Friday or Saturday night they'll be bursting with fellow clubbers. For groups, now is the perfect time to try the essential Japanese pastime: karaoke. The easiest option is to head for Shinjuku and get nabbed by one of the touts that hover around **Yasukuni Dori**. They'll drag you to one of the big, cheap chains such as Big Echo or Karaoke-Kan (as featured in *Lost in Translation*), where you'll get a private lounge in which to drink and croon until the sun rises. A more stylish option is Lovenet (p114) in Roppongi, a collection of themed lounges where you can perform your drunken rendition of 'Total Eclipse of the Heart' in relative luxury. The Morocco Suite is a cosy two-person cave with a mattress and low table, perfect for amorous couples; the deep-red Kiss Suite is, curiously, designed to hold four singers; while the most popular room of all is the Aqua Suite, where you can exercise your tonsils from a six-seater jacuzzi. The food here is a cut above the karaoke box norm, with a good selection of Italian and Asian dishes. Lovenet stays open until 5am, which ought to be enough singing for anyone.

Technique p39

青山製図専門学校

Aoyama Technical College p45

ITINERARIES

Adventures in Architecture

Tokyo isn't always beautiful, but the city's architecture has never lacked a wild and creative streak. Mix liberal planning laws with a native love of novelty and the end result is an architectural playground, by turns flamboyant, eccentric and plain crazy. Things slowed down during Japan's long period in the economic doldrums, but recovery is again turning Tokyo into one of the most exciting destinations in contemporary architecture.

This walk will guide you around some notable recent additions to the city, ending with a curiosity from the previous decade. It can be done in two or three hours if all you need is a quick glance. But since most of the buildings you will see are galleries or shops, the walk can last as long as it takes you to sate your appetite for art and retail therapy.

Begin by taking the Hibiya or Oedo subway line to Roppongi. Long notorious as a centre of sleaze, this district is fast turning into an upscale entertainment and shopping mecca. The trend began in 2003 when the Roppongi Hills mega-complex established the blueprint for new Japanese developments – a mix of shops, entertainment, offices and hotel space, all with an upmarket flavour and on a monumental scale.

Roppongi Hills' central Mori Tower has become an iconic city landmark, but since March 2007 it has been literally overshadowed by the nearby **Tokyo Midtown** (p112) – a new development with a landmark tower that is, not

National Art Center, Tokyo

coincidentally, ten metres taller and currently the highest in the city.

A short, well-signposted walk from the station's exit 8, the tower is a stylish but conventional piece of commercial design by American giants Skidmore, Owings & Merrill. They say the whole development is based on a traditional Zen garden, but you'll need a vivid imagination to spot it. Stock up on coffee and snacks at one of Midtown's many food outlets before following the signs to the first real highlight of the walk for architecture spotters: **21_21 Design Sight** (see box p103) by Tadao Ando.

Located in Midtown's pleasant landscaped gardens, which bring to mind Singapore or Vancouver more than Tokyo, Design Sight is an exhibition space created by Ando in conjunction with veteran designer Issey Miyake. Composed of two sharp trapezoids, it appears to have been made from a single folded sheet of concrete. You will need to pay for entry to the current exhibition to explore the gallery

spaces located in its sunken courtyard, but even from outside the building is characteristically sober and elegant work from the reigning superstar of Japanese architecture.

Coming out of Design Sight, turn right and head back to the main road, where you should see a sign for the Oakwood Premier Midtown Residences. Cross over, keep going, and at the end of the street is the next stop: **National Art Center, Tokyo** (p102), which opened in January 2007.

Together with the Mori Art Museum in Roppongi Hills and the Suntory Museum of Art in Midtown, this is the final point of what's being called the Roppongi 'art triangle'. Designed by Kisho Kurokawa – an elder statesman of Japanese architecture and unsuccessful 2007 candidate for Tokyo mayor – the first thing you notice about the NACT is its bulk. In fact, the bulging façade gives the impression that its 14,000 square metres (150,000 square feet) of gallery space is ready to burst right out. This is the largest museum in Japan, and exploring its concurrent exhibitions can take a full day.

The exhibition spaces are vast but standard white cubes, which means the highlight for building buffs is the public atrium, which you can enter for free. Behind Kurokawa's wave of glass and steel lies an immense space punctuated with inverted concrete cones that seem to have been plunged into the earth point-first. Stop for a bite to eat in Paul Bocuse's French restaurant (p106), sat on top of the tallest cone, if it's not overrun with ladies who lunch.

Exiting the NACT, follow the signs to its west gate. From there, cross the road to **Aoyama Cemetery**, which stands opposite. This maze of overgrown stone paths is home to some of Tokyo's most distinguished deceased, and offers a beautiful refuge from the relentless bustle of downtown. If it's an alfresco lunch you're after, this is the spot for a secluded picnic. Alternatively, take your time exploring the cemetery's many paths, including the area for foreigners towards the north-west corner. If you are here at the right moment in spring, the cemetery becomes one of the best places in Tokyo to view the cherry blossom (see box p33).

At the main crossroads in the centre of the cemetery take the road towards its western edge. Head out of the grounds and keep going in the same direction until you reach a crossroads signposted 'Minamiaoyama 4', at which point turn right. After a couple of minutes, you'll find the decade's most talked about architectural arrival: the **Prada** store (2003).

Designed by Swiss duo Herzog and de Meuron, creators of Tate Modern in London, the store is an astonishing sight from any angle. From the outside it's a black steel lattice filled with bulging glass panes. Inside, it's a series of interlocking planes ('floor' seems too prosaic) and funky spaces. Even if it's familiar from a thousand glossy mag articles, it doesn't disappoint in reality.

After leaving Prada, turn left and walk to the next crossroads. Cross over and continue in the same direction. You'll be walking along Omotesando – one of Tokyo's most chi-chi shopping streets, and a veritable theme park for state-of-the-art retail architecture.

Among the highlights, about 100 metres down on your left, is **Tod's** store (2004) by Toyo Ito. Perhaps the only building to give Prada a run for its money in the stylishness stakes, Tod's zigzagging concrete beams evoke the trunk and branches of the trees that frame it. Further down on the same side is the **Louis Vuitton** store (2002) by Jun Aoki, taking its inspiration from a stack of the luxury brand's famed trunks.

By far the most controversial work here, however, is the **Omotesando Hills** development, which stands opposite. Yet another concrete creation by Tadao Ando, many feel the low-rise structure is not his most inspiring work, though the ingenious spiral layout of the interior brings to mind a retail version of the Guggenheim.

The real reason for the controversy, however, is the fact that the building replaced the much-loved Dojunkai apartments – post-war social housing that later became a hive of small boutiques. One unit of the old Dojunkai remains at the top end of Omotesando Hills, so decide for yourself whether preservation would have been preferable to progress.

Leaving Omotesando Hills, cross the road and turn right, continuing down the slope as far as the Chanel store. There turn left into a small alleyway, which is the beginning of Cat Street (p78). The long street is lined with small boutiques aimed at trendy teens, but for architecture fans the highlight will be the black rhomboid of the **hhstyle.com** store – yet another work by the ubiquitous Ando.

At the end of Cat Street, bear left along the main road until you reach the messy sprawl of Shibuya station. Entering the station, follow signs to the Hachiko exit and you come out at one of Tokyo's iconic views – Shibuya crossing.

The landmark here, and a symbol of Japan's fascination with technology, is the **Q-Front** building (Research Institute of Architecture, 1999). It stands diagonally across from the station. Stand and watch for a moment and you will see vast images sliding across its façade: the skin of the building is also a screen composed of thousands of individual LEDs.

For the last stop on this walk, continue along the side of Shibuya station, keeping the tracks on your left and the Tokyu Plaza on your right. Cross over the main junction using the overhead walkways and follow the tracks along an uninviting road. When you draw level with the end of the railway platforms, you should see an office block with incongruously classical columns. Turn right there and after a minute or two you'll spot our unmistakably Japanese finale.

Aoyama Technical College is the oldest work on your route, having been completed in 1990. Designed by Makoto Sei Watanabe, it looks like a piece of Japanese anime given three-dimensional form. Nicknamed the 'Gundam building' after a popular Japanese cartoon series about fighting robots, it looks as though it could spring menacingly into life at any moment. Knobs, blobs, pipes and spikes are joined in a seemingly random explosion of parts. Bright colours and a playful distortion of perspective complete the effect. It will strike some as a postmodern throwback, but love it or loathe it, one glance and you'll know you can't be anywhere else in the world but Tokyo.

ITINERARIES

Tod's

Asakusa Kannon Temple

Vintage Tokyo

Asakusa is famous as the home of Tokyo's oldest temple. But for two centuries, the area was better known as a lively if indecorous entertainment district, home to cinemas, kabuki, gambling dens and 'operas' with dancing girls. Most of the entertainment venues have been relocated, but Asakusa remains offbeat and charming. The area is flat, pedestrian-friendly and easily navigable, so a leisurely day can be spent, with the major sights tackled in a few hours. Asakusa is by no means Tokyo's best-kept secret, though, so be prepared for hordes at the weekend.

This itinerary shows both faces of Asakusa: its solemn temples and its lively diversions. It starts at **Asakusa Station**. From the station take Exit 1, which emerges on Kaminarimon Dori close to the first stop for the day, the eight-pillared **Kaminarimon**. Despite

appearances, this gate, framed by the gods of wind and thunder, and featuring a four-metre-tall (13-foot) lantern is less than 50 years old – a gift from Konosuke Matsushita, the founder of Panasonic, to replace an oft-destroyed gate first built in 942; it burnt down most recently in 1945.

Kaminarimon marks the beginning of **Nakamise Dori** (p57), a bustling row of tiny shops, most offering tacky souvenirs but a few giving visitors the chance to buy traditional foods and goods, including rice crackers and folding fans. But hold on to your yen for now, because the journey will take in more authentic shops a little later. At the end of the long, straight Nakamise Dori you'll see **Asakusa Kannon Temple** (p53) loom into view.

The temple has stood here since 628, although the building was frequently destroyed and rebuilt, most recently after World War II. The temple is reputed to hold (it has never actually displayed it) a small golden statue of bodhisattva Kannon. The statue is said to have been found by two men fishing in the nearby Sumida river. They gave it to the local priest, who built Senso-ji to house it.

Before entering the temple 'purify' yourself by washing your hands and wafting Japanese incense over you. Then walk up the stairs and grab the rope to ring the bell (this alerts the deities to your presence), throw five yen into the *saisen bako* – a slatted box – then bow twice, clap twice (just to make sure the gods really are paying attention) and pray. After one more post-prayer bow, head back down the stairs. To your right will be **Gojuno-to**, a five-storey pagoda built in 1973. Entry to the pagoda is restricted to relatives of people whose souls are enshrined there, so view it from outside.

Now it's time for some fun. Head between the temple and pagoda, past the statue of 19th-century nurse Uryu Iwako – Japan's Florence Nightingale, who treated the war-wounded and built an orphanage – and the tomb of samurai poet (and guidebook writer) Toda Mosui. Turn right, then left and you're at **Hanayashiki** (p54) – Japan's oldest funfair, which features a rollercoaster built in 1953. The quaint park has rides, food and activities for all ages. You need a certain sense of nostalgia to appreciate Hanayashiki, but you won't have to endure Disney-length queues. Avoid filling up on candy floss, because we'll soon have lunch.

Before we take in a traditional restaurant, however, we will visit a little museum that is close the hearts of those living in Asakusa, the **Edo-Shitamachi Traditional Crafts Museum** (p53). Head west from the

Sometaro p48

gates of Hanayashiki and turn right into Hisago Dori; cross one street and you will find the museum on the left side of the street.

Asakusa is in the Taito-ku area, which prides itself on maintaining old traditions, including arts and crafts. In 1996 this museum opened, not only to display work by local artisans, but also to show people how such pieces are created. Every weekend, craftworkers demonstrate how to make items including the guitar-like shamisen, Igashi Ningyo dolls and ornate wood carvings. Before heading upstairs to the displays, take a pamphlet that describes the items you will see.

When you've had your fill, it's time to eat. Turn right out of the museum, walk back down Hisago Dori and continue straight ahead when it meets Rokku Broadway. Rokku Broadway is one of the few parts of Asakusa where you'll still see businessmen hurrying into strip clubs and down-on-their-luck gamblers puffing cigarettes down to the filter. Let's keep moving.

ITINERARIES

Carry on down Rokku Broadway until you reach Kaminarimon Dori and turn right. Cross Kokusai Dori and head up the side street just to your right. A couple of hundred metres along the street, on your right, you'll see **Sometaro** (p56), a low, wooden restaurant fronted by a low bamboo fence. Open the sliding door, slip off your shoes and wait to be shown to your table.

Sometaro serves working-class fare – noodles with beef, seafood or vegetables – which you cook on a hotplate in your table. Try to arrive before 12.30pm to beat the crowds. If you can't work out what to do, the English-speaking staff are happy to help; if you'd rather have someone else do the hard work, opt for *osomeyaki* (noodle, cabbage, egg, minced beef, fish and dried shrimp). It's a dish that originates in Hiroshima and is so difficult to prepare that the staff take over. Each dish is shared, and people will often order more than a dish per head. Wash the food down with a cold beer or grapefruit sour (shochu with fresh grapefruit).

Hunger sated, it's time to check out Asakusa's hidden temple. To find it, turn right as you leave the restaurant, first left, then right at the next street for the front gates.

The current **Tokyo Honganji** is a relatively new structure, built in 1953. However, if not for the perseverance of the faithful, nothing would be here. The temple was burnt down or badly damaged eleven times between 1612 and 1945. As with Asakusa Kannon, you can pray here, but you might prefer to simply enjoy the silence.

Batteries recharged? Head back down Kaminarimon Dori, until you reach Kaminarimon. Turn left into Nakamise Dori, then take the first left. This is where you'll find the **Kanesou** knife shop (1-18-12 Asakusa, Taito-ku, 3844 1379,

www.kanesoh.com), visited by chefs and barbers seeking the perfect tool for the job since 1873. If a knife isn't top of your souvenir list, head east to Kannon Dori for sweet treats at **Izumiya** (1-1-6 Asakusa, Taito-ku, 3841 8385, www.asakusa.gr.jp/nakama/ izumiya) and dry sake at **Daimasu Sake Bar** (p54), which is tucked away on a lane running between Kannon Dori and Nakamise Dori.

From Kannon Dori you can take a stroll down to the Sumida River to see Asakusa's much-loved **Azuma Bridge** and, across the river, French designer Philippe Starck's outlandish **Flamme d'Or** (p56) – a black, windowless building with a giant golden sculpture on top that is fondly known as the Golden Turd.

If Starck's building isn't enough to make your head spin, it's time to head to the last stop of the day, the **Kamiya Bar** (p56). Situated close to the bridge on the corner of Kaminarimon Dori and Umamichi Dori, Kamiya, which opened in 1880, was Japan's first Western-style bar. It would appear last to have been given a lick of paint at about the same time, and while the bar prides itself on being Western, the method of obtaining drinks is anything but. Before being shown to your table you must buy tokens with which you pay for your drinks – the most popular of which is Denki Bran (literally 'electric brandy'), a drink devised by this bar and now sold across the city. This notorious hangover inducer – concocted from brandy, gin, wine and curaçao – tastes far better than it sounds. Each table at Kamiya seats about a dozen people, and whether you're alone or in a group, the chances are that by the end of the night you will have befriended a resident of this charming if faded area of Tokyo.

Tokyo by Area

Asakusa Kannon Temple p53

Asakusa

Long before Roppongi and Shibuya figured on anybody's radar of interest, Asakusa was *the* place for entertainment in Tokyo. For a couple of centuries up until around 1940, this area adjacent to the eastern bank of the Sumida river was far and away the most exciting and dynamic part of town. It's a fine example of *shitamachi*, the low-lying districts of the city where the commoners lived cheek by jowl until Tokyo's population began drifting westwards in the aftermath of the Great Earthquake of 1923 and fire bombing in World War II. With this westward shift, Asakusa became increasingly peripheral to mainstream city life.

Today a sense of faded grandeur hangs over the area. For the visitor the greatest appeal lies in the **Asakusa Kannon Temple**.

It is this temple complex and its environs that have helped make Asakusa one of Tokyo's prime tourist attractions.

Also known as Senso-ji, Asakusa Kannon is Tokyo's oldest temple, with origins, so the remarkably precise story has it, dating to 18 March 628. That was when two brothers fishing on the Sumida river caught a five-centimetre (two-inch) golden statue in their net. Clearly lacking wisdom, they threw the statue back into the river twice, only for it to reappear both times. At this point they twigged that something out of the ordinary was happening, and took the statue to the village chief. He enshrined it in his house, and in 645 a hall was built for this image of Kannon, the Buddhist goddess of mercy, on the spot where today's temple stands.

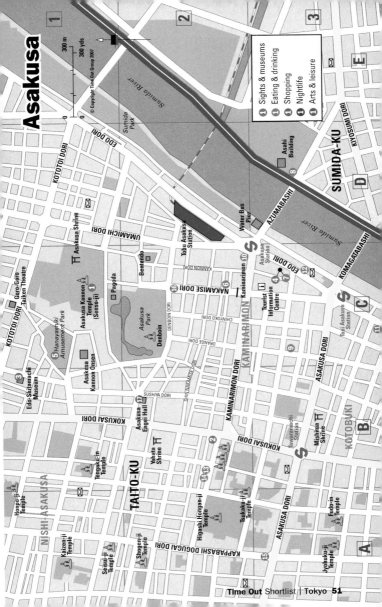

Asakusa

Legend:
- Sights & museums
- Eating & drinking
- Shopping
- Nightlife
- Arts & leisure

300 m
300 yds

© Copyright Time Out Group 2007

Sumida River

Sumida Park

KOTOTOI DORI

EDO DORI

UMAMICHI DORI

Asakusa Shrine

Guro-Guro Taiken Theatre

Edo-Shitamachi Museum

Hanayashiki Amusement Park

Asakusa Kannon Temple (Senso-ji)

Pagoda

Bentendo

Asakusa Park

Denboin

Asakusa Kannon Onsen

KOKUSAI DORI

TAITO-KU

NISHI-ASAKUSA

Hongo-ji Temple

Kaizen-ji Temple

Sesku-ji Temple

Shogen-ji Temple

Tangaku-in Temple

Yahata Shrine

Asakusa Engei Hall

SUSHIYA DORI

KAMINARIMON DORI

Higashi Hongan-ji Temple

Tsukaki-ji Temple

KAPPABASHI DOGUGAI DORI

ASAKUSA DORI

Kuramaebashi Station

Mishima Shrine

KOTOBUKI

Fudo-in Temple

Jyohuku-ji Temple

Tobu Asakusa Station

KANNON DORI

NAKAMISE DORI

DENBOIN DORI

ORANGE DORI

CHINYOKO DORI

KAMINARIMON

Kaminarimon

Tourist Information Centre

Asakusa Station

EDO DORI

Toei Asakusa Station

Water Bus Pier

AZUMABASHI

Sumida River

Asahi Building

SUMIDA-KU

KIYOSUMI DORI

KOMAGATABASHI

The complex also houses a Shinto shrine, **Asakusa Jinja**, established in 1649 to honour the two fishermen and the village headman.

In later years, Asakusa thrived due to its proximity to Yoshiwara, the biggest area of licensed prostitution in Edo (as Tokyo was originally known). Seeking refreshment before the evening's activities, Yoshiwara's clientele headed for Asakusa. The area's entertainment ranged from magicians to comedians to performing monkeys. The area also flourished as the centre of kabuki, a vastly popular form of entertainment whose actors were idolised like rock stars.

Nowadays, Asakusa is popular for its olde-worlde charms, having resisted the rampant development that characterises most of Tokyo. As well as **Hanayashiki**, its quaint theme park, and the many restaurants and drinking dens, Asakusa also offers two great souvenir shopping opportunities. For the more touristy stuff, **Nakamise Dori** has a plethora of all the most obvious gifts – from chopsticks to kimonos. A few streets away is the restaurant industry's wholesale district, **Kappabashi Dori**, where an enormous range of lacquerware and utensils awaits.

A recommended itinerary for exploring Asakusa is on p46.

Sights & museums

Asakusa Kannon Temple (Senso-ji) & Asakusa Jinja

2-3-1 Asakusa, Taito-ku (temple 3842 0181/shrine 3844 1575). Asakusa station (Asakusa, Ginza lines), exits 1, 3, 6, A4. **Open** *Temple & shrine 6.30am-5pm daily. Grounds 24hrs daily.* **Admission** *free.* **Map** p51 C1 ❶
Tokyo's most popular temple is a vivid reminder of the Edo era. The main gate, Kaminarimon, leads to a bustling street of stalls offering everything from rice

crackers to geisha wigs. At the far end, in the temple grounds proper, are a five-storey pagoda (the second-highest in Japan), the stunning Main Hall, with gold-plated Gokuden shrine inside, and Asakusa Jinja, the starting point of the Sanja festival. A huge bronze incense burner stands in front of the Main Hall, billowing smoke that's reputed to have curative powers. Watch for visitors ushering the smoke towards a troubled part of their body.

Drum Museum (Taiko-kan)

Miyamoto Unosuke Shoten, Nishi-Asakusa Bldg 4F, 2-1-1 Nishi-Asakusa, Taito-ku (3842 5622/www.tctv.ne.jp/members/taikokan). Tawaramachi station (Ginza line). **Open** 10am-5pm Wed-Sun. **Admission** ¥300; ¥150 reductions; free under-6s. No credit cards. **Map** p51 B2 ❷
With a clay drum from Mexico, a Sri Lankan *udekki* and hundreds of other drums from around the world, this interactive museum is a fine place to visit. Find your own rhythm by banging on many of them (a blue dot means it's allowed, a red one means it's not).

Edo-Shitamachi Traditional Crafts Museum

2-22-13 Asakusa, Taito-ku (3842 1990). Asakusa station (Asakusa, Ginza lines), exit 1. **Open** 10am-8pm daily. **Admission** free. **Map** p51 B1 ❸
This smart, modern museum offers exhibitions and demonstrations of traditional Japanese crafts from local artisans. Occasional lessons are geared towards beginners who fancy trying their hand at the ancient techniques.

Gallery ef

2-19-18 Kaminarimon, Taito-ku (3841 0442/www.tctv.ne.jp/get2-ef). Asakusa station (Asakusa line), exit A5; (Ginza line) exit 2. **Open** noon-7pm Mon, Wed-Sun. **Map** p51 C3 ❹
The beamed ceilings and lacquered floors of this extremely rare example of a 19th-century earth-walled warehouse are tough competition for the contemporary art that is shown here. The shows are mainly by lesser-known

Hanayashiki

but interesting Japanese artists, with some international names joining in. There's a nice café too (listed below).

Hanayashiki

2-28-1 Asakusa, Taito-ku (3842 8780/www.hanayashiki.net/first.html). Asakusa station (Asakusa, Ginza lines), exit 3. **Open** 10am-6pm Mon, Wed-Sun. **Admission** ¥900; ¥400 reductions. No credit cards. **Map** p51 C1 **⑤**

A quaint amusement park that's been in business since 1885. There are around 20 rides, more appealing for nostalgia than thrills, including Japan's oldest steel-track rollercoaster and a haunted house. Most have been upgraded over the years, but their scope is limited due to the park's small size.

Eating & drinking

Daimasu Sake Bar

1-2-8 Asakusa, Taito-ku (5806 3811/ www.e-daimasu.com/sakebar/english. html). Asakusa station (Asakusa line), exit A4; (Ginza line), exit 1. **Open** noon-midnight daily. **Bar**. English menu. **Map** p51 C2 **⑥**

As the name says, Daimasu serves sake. The setting is surprisingly modern for this area, but the range of over 100 indigenous potions fits right in with Asakusa's traditional scene. A 'sake sommelier' can help you decide.

ef

2-19-18 Kaminarimon, Taito-ku (3841 0114/gallery 3841 0442/www.gallery-ef.com). Asakusa station (Asakusa line), exit A5; (Ginza line), exit 2. **Open** *Café* 11am-7pm Mon, Wed, Thur, Sat; 11am-2am Fri; 11am-10pm Sun. *Bar* 6pm-midnight Mon, Wed, Thur, Sat; 11am-2am Fri; 11am-10pm Sun. *¥*. No credit cards. **Café/bar**. **Map** p51 C3 **⑦**

This retro café hangout is a welcome attempt to inject a little Harajuku cool into musty Asakusa. Duck into the low entrance at the back, and suddenly you're out of 1950s Americana and into tatami territory, with admittance to the main exhibits up a steep set of traditional wooden steps. A nice place to relax after traipsing the temples.

Moby Dick for dinner

For a real power lunch while you're in Tokyo, tuck into the world's largest mammal. It might be another PR shot in the foot by Japan, but whales are back on the political agenda and some restaurant menus. So if your moral compass points to trying the most exotic dish around, here's a quick guide to the politics, the restaurants and the taste.

The Japanese Fisheries Agency tells us that whales eat too many fish, that they are not endangered and that the Japanese have a rich tradition of whaling, dating back at least to the seventh-century Kojiki, their oldest historical text. They paint anti-whaling nations as cultural imperialists, and press the International Whaling Commission to lift the 1986 moratorium on commercial whale hunting. This has all proved convincing locally: a November 2006 Yahoo Japan poll had 90 per cent of respondents (a huge 19,000 people) supporting a return to commercial whaling. In the meantime, Japan undertakes 'scientific whaling' each year in a protected area of the Antarctic, analysing the populations then selling on the meat.

While local opinion supports whaling, local tastebuds have been harder to convince. Some supermarkets offer whale flesh, and there are dedicated restaurants, but the meat is more novelty than delicacy. The mammal was more popular in the post-war period, when food was scarce and the giant creature was an efficient source of protein. Consumption peaked in 1962, declining in popularity as tastier alternatives became more readily

available. In 2006, a record 6,000 tons of the 'scientific whaling' stock went unsold.

For now, the contentious meat is more a political topic than a culinary one, which is why whale restaurants greet foreign diners nervously and try to pre-empt complaints by flagging up their contentious ingredient. For those wishing to try the big mammal, Nishi Asakusa's **Ichimon** (pictured) is the friendliest option. The young English-speaking staff of this informal eaterie are happy to talk you through the menu, which offers a variety of whale species, parts and styles of cooking. The speciality is raw whale, served on the bone, to be scraped off with the seashell provided.

And the taste? Well, that would spoil the surprise, but don't worry – it's nothing like chicken.

■ Ichimon (3-12-6 Asakusa, Taito-ku, 3875 6800, www.asakusa-ichimon.com/honten/info.html)

TOKYO BY AREA

Flamme d'Or

Asahi Super Dry Hall 1F-2F, 1-23-16 Azumabashi, Sumida-ku (5608 5381/ www.asahibeer.co.jp/restaurant/azuma/ flamdoll1.html). Asakusa station (Asakusa line) exit A5; (Ginza line), exits 4, 5. **Open** *June-Aug* 11.30am-11pm daily. *Sept-May* 11.30am-10pm daily. **¥**. **German**. English menu. **Map** p51 D3 **8**

One of Tokyo's quirkier landmarks, the golden object atop Philippe Starck's ultra-modern building looks like giant golden faeces. The interior is also distinctive: oddly shaped pillars, tiny porthole windows and sweeping curved walls covered in soft grey cushioning. But for all the fancy design, the atmosphere is somewhat sterile. There's a choice of German-style bar snacks and Asahi draught beers.

Hatsuogawa

2-8-4 Kaminarimon, Taito-ku (3844 2723). Asakusa station (Asakusa, Ginza lines), exits 1, 2, 3, A3, A4. **Open** noon-2pm, 5-8pm Mon-Sat; 5-8pm Sun. **¥¥**. No credit cards. **Eel**. **Map** p51 C3 **9**

Stones, plants, bamboo latticework and a white *noren* (shop curtain) mark the entrance to this venerable eel shop. The *unaju* box set is delicious, but you should also try *kabayaki* – skewered eel with the rice served separately.

Kamiya Bar

1-1-1 Asakusa, Taito-ku (3841 5400/ www.kamiya-bar.com). Asakusa station (Asakusa line), exit A5; (Ginza line), exit 3. **Open** 11.30am-10pm Mon, Wed-Sun. No credit cards. **Bar**. **Map** p51 C2 **10**

Established in the late 1800s, Kamiya is a legendary drinking spot. It's the oldest Western-style bar in Tokyo and it's also one of the friendliest. The crowds certainly don't come for the decor (think Formica tables and too bright lighting), but the atmosphere – loud, smoky and occasionally raucous – is typical of this working-class neighbourhood. Try the house Denki Bran (Electric Brandy) – a sweet blend of wine, gin, brandy and curaçao that's a lot nicer than it sounds.

Komagata Dojo

1-7-12 Komagata, Taito-ku (3842 4001/www.dozeu.co.jp). Asakusa station (Ginza, Asakusa lines), exit A1. **Open** 11am-9pm daily. **¥¥**. **Traditional Japanese**. English menu. **Map** p51 C3 **11**

You dine here much as you would have a century ago – sitting on thin cushions at low tables that are little more than polished planks on the rush-matting floor. The menu revolves around *dojo* – small, plump, eel-like fish served (in ascending order of delectability) as *nabe* hot-pots, *yanagawa* (in a runny omelette) or *kabayaki* (grilled, like eel). Not gourmet, but an absolute institution.

Mugitoro

2-2-4 Kaminarimon, Taito-ku (3842 1066/www.mugitoro.co.jp). Asakusa station (Asakusa, Ginza lines), exits A1, A3, A4. **Open** 11.30am-10.30pm daily (last orders 9pm). **¥¥**. **Yam**. **Map** p51 C3 **12**

The speciality at this Japanese restaurant is rice cooked with barley and served with a bowl of grated yam (so gooey it must be healthy). There are lots of other options too, ranging from simple lunches to full evening meals.

Sometaro

2-2-2 Nishi-Asakusa, Taito-ku (3844 9502). Tawaramachi station (Ginza line), exit 3. **Open** noon-10pm daily. **¥¥**. No credit cards. **Okonomiyaki**. English menu. **Map** p51 B2 **13**

Comfort food in a funky wooden shack that's an easy walk from the tourist sights. It can get incredibly sweaty in summer, but when you're sitting round the *okonomiyaki* pan, the intimate atmosphere is wonderfully authentic.

Vin Chou

2-2-13 Nishi-Asakusa, Taito-ku (3845 4430). Tawaramachi station (Ginza line), exit 3. **Open** 5-10.30pm Mon, Tue, Thur-Sat; 4-9.30pm Sun. **¥¥¥**. **Yakitori**. **Map** p51 B2 **14**

This five-star yakitori shop is an offshoot of the nearby French bistro La Chèvre. This explains why it offers charcoal-grilled Bresse chicken, quail

Kappabashi Dori

and a fine range of wines and cheese. Casual and simple, this is some of the best food in the neighbourhood.

Shopping

Kappabashi Dori
Tawaramachi station (Ginza line), exit 1; or Asakusa station (Asakusa, Ginza lines), exits 1, 2, 3, A4. **Open** varies. **Map** p51 A3 ⑮
An area devoted to wholesale kitchenware shops, this is the place for low-cost lacquerware, rice cookers, knives, grills, or anything else you need to set up a restaurant, including the realistic plastic food replicas that are displayed in restaurant windows. The shops run along Shinbori Dori, from the corner of Asakusa Dori; look for the giant chef's head on the top of the Niimi store.

Nakamise Dori
www.asakusa-nakamise.jp. Asakusa station (Asakusa, Ginza lines), exits 1, 3, A4. **Open** 8am-8pm daily. No credit cards. **Map** p51 C2 ⑯

This avenue of stalls and tiny shops leading up to the entrance to Senso-ji temple sells all sorts of Japanese souvenirs, some dating back to the Edo era. It also sells traditional snacks like *kaminari-okoshii* (toasted rice crackers) and *ningyo-yaki* (red bean-filled buns moulded into humorous shapes). A great place for souvenir shopping.

Arts & leisure

Asakusa Engei Hall
1-43-12 Asakusa, Taito-ku (3841 6545/www.asakusaengei.com). Tawaramachi station (Ginza line), exit 3. **Performances** 11.40am-4.30pm; 4.40-9pm. **Admission** ¥2,500. **Map** p51 B2 ⑰
Unless you're fluent in Japanese, there's little chance of following the *rakugo* – Japan's old-time comic story-telling show, but the atmosphere alone is worth the admission price. Narrators in traditional garb kneel on stage and mime, making use of folding fans, to illustrate their tales.

Ginza

Throughout the recent economic slump, when all around were tightening their purse strings, Tokyo's fanciest district carried on regardless. Ginza is, was and always will be the epitome of Tokyo extravagance. Ladies saunter the wide streets dressed head to toe in luxury brands, shopping for more of the same. Come nightfall, come the politicians and businessmen on bottomless expense accounts to quaff overpriced drinks poured by kimono-clad staff. For the rest of us there's *Ginbura* ('Ginza strolling'), a tour of the numerous small art galleries that dot the area, or a day of high culture at the **Kabuki-za**.

Committed shoppers can choose from over 10,000 shops crammed into Ginza's eight main blocks (*chome*), many of them selling goods at boom-era prices. Tiny shops selling traditional items such as kimonos, *wagashi* (Japanese sweets) and *go*-boards sit quietly amid an increasing number of big brand flagships from the likes of Gucci, Cartier and Chanel. Competition between these luxury heavyweights has seen them commission stores with spectacular façades, and the exteriors of **Mikimoto**, Hermès, Chanel and Louis Vuitton are all worth a look for design fans.

For visitors wishing merely to window-shop, Ginza's unusually wide pavements offer a less congested experience than most of Tokyo. From noon each weekend it gets even easier, because cars are banished from the main street, Chuo Dori, creating what is known as *hokousha tengoku* (pedestrian

Ginza

Legend:
- 🔴 Sights & museums
- 🔴 Eating & drinking
- 🔴 Shopping
- 🔴 Nightlife
- 🔴 Arts & leisure

© Copyright Time Out Group 2007

KYOBASHI

National Film Centre

Kyobashi Station

CHUO-KU

Tsukiji Station

MARONNIER DORI

TSUKIJI

MATSUYA DORI

E

SHOWA DORI

CHUO-DORI

TOKYO EXPRESSWAY

HARUMI DORI

Ginza 1-chome Station

Meidi-ya

Tiffany

Matsuya

Kabuki-za

D

Printemps Ginza

Mitsukoshi

Matsuzakaya

GINZA

Higashi-Ginza Station

Nissan Gallery

Wako

HARUMI DORI

San-ai Building

Ginza Station

To Tsukiji Fish Market

Tokyo TIC

Tokyo Kotsu Kaikan Bldg

Seibu

Sony Building

GINZA DORI / CHUO DORI

Yamaha Hall

C

Tokyo International Forum

Yurakucho Station

Yurakucho Hankyu

Sukiyabashi Hankyu

NAMIKI DORI

Shiseido

Hakuhinkan

Yurakucho Station

MARUNOUCHI-NAKA DORI

SOTOBORI DORI

Moat

Idemitsu Museum of Art

Theatres

YURAKUCHO

Hibiya Station

Hibiya Chanter

Tokyo Takarazuka Theatre

Yamanote Line

B

Shimbashi Station

SHINBASHI

Nissei Theatre

Imperial Hotel

Mizuho Bank

A

Hibiya Hospital

Hibiya Park

CHIYODA-KU

HIBIYA DORI

Uchisaiwaicho Station

150 m

150 yds

Kasumigaseki Station

Hibiya Public Hall

heaven). Cafés spill out on to the road, lending the area a relaxed, almost European feel.

Sights & museums

Galleria Grafica Tokyo

Ginza S2 Bldg 1 2F, 6-13-4 Ginza, Chuo-ku (5550 1335/www2.big.or.jp/~adel/grafica.html). Ginza station (Ginza, Hibiya, Marunouchi lines), exit A3. **Open** 11am-7pm Mon-Sat. **Map** p59 C/D3 ❶
Galleria Grafica's ground floor is a rental space for up-and-coming artists, but the second floor is home to fine works by the likes of Picasso, Miró, Giacometti, Matisse and Man Ray; it concentrates mainly on a variety of prints and lithographs.

Gallery Koyanagi

1-7-5 Ginza, Chuo-ku (3561 1896). Ginza station (Ginza, Hibiya, Marunouchi lines), exit A13; or Ginza-Itchome station (Yurakucho Line), exit 7. **Open** 11am-7pm Tue-Sat. **Map** p59 D1 ❷
This long-standing gallery may have a reputation for photography, but that's been by chance rather than design. It still represents photographer Hiroshi Sugimoto, as well as animation queen Tabaimo, and works with notable foreign artists such as Thomas Ruff and Sophie Calle.

Ginza Graphic Gallery

DNP Ginza Bldg 1F, 7-7-2 Ginza, Chuo-ku (3571 5206/www.dnp.co.jp/gallery). Ginza station (Ginza, Hibiya, Marunouchi lines). **Open** 11am-7pm Mon-Fri; 11am-6pm Sat. **Map** p59 C3 ❸
One of Japan's largest printing companies presents contemporary design and graphics here. Japanese designers are prominent, but major international talents appear from time to time.

INAX Gallery

INAX Ginza Showroom 9F, 3-6-18 Kyobashi, Chuo-ku (5250 6530/www.inax.co.jp/Culture/gallery/1_tokyo.html). Ginza-Itchome station (Yurakucho line), exit 7; or Kyobashi station (Ginza line),
exit 2. **Open** 10am-6pm Mon-Sat. Closed 1wk Aug. **Map** p59 E1 ❹
Major ceramics-maker INAX runs an architecture bookshop on the ground floor and two galleries upstairs. One gallery hosts emerging artists with a craft edge, while the other deals with exhibitions of traditional craft techniques from around the world.

Komparu-yu

8-7-5 Ginza, Chuo-ku (3571 5469). Ginza station (Ginza, Hibiya lines), exit A2. **Open** 2-11pm Mon-Fri; 2-10pm Sat. **Map** p59 C3 ❺
Ritzy Ginza is the unlikely home of this tiny old bathhouse, which dates back to Edo days. There are two baths – *atatakai* (hot) and *nurui* (lukewarm); lukewarm is hot enough for most. After an afternoon of Ginza strolling, try an olde-worlde soak.

Maison Hermès

Maison Hermès 8F Forum, 5-4-1 Ginza, Chuo-ku (3289 6811). Ginza station (Ginza, Hibiya, Marunouchi lines), exit B7. **Open** 11am-7pm Mon, Tue, Thur-Sun. **Map** p59 C2 ❻
The rounded glass-block walls of this beautiful, Renzo Piano-designed building filter daylight and magnify neon at night. The gallery on the eighth floor holds shows of Japanese and international contemporary art and crafts, organised according to annual themes.

Metropolitan Police Department Museum

Matsushita Denko Tokyo Honsha Bldg B2-2F, 3-5-1 Kyobashi, Chuo-ku (3581 4321/www.keishicho.metro.tokyo.jp/index.htm). Kyobashi station (Ginza line), exit 2. **Open** 10am-6pm Tue-Sun. **Admission** free. **Map** p59 E1 ❼
With a reputation somewhere between inept and corrupt, Japan's police force needs more than this drab collection of artefacts to turn things around. The absence of anything relating to modern crime-fighting might alarm more than reassure visitors, and the most exciting exhibit is an arcade-style gaming machine that turns out to be no more than a safe-driving simulator. Still, kids

might enjoy dressing as mini officers, sitting on a Kawasaki police motorbike and meeting mascot Pipo-kun.

Nishimura Gallery

Nihombashi Nikko Bldg 3F, 2-10-8 Nihonbashi, Chuo-ku (5203 2800/www. nishimura-gallery.com). Nihonbashi station (Ginza, Tozai lines), exit B1. **Open** 10.30am-6.30pm Tue-Sat. **Map** p59 C2 ⑧

Tadanori Yokoo, Chieko Oshie and David Hockney are among the artists, both Japanese and international, appearing here.

Shiseido Gallery

Tokyo Ginza Shiseido Bldg B1, 8-8-3 Ginza, Chuo-ku (3572 3901/www. shiseido.co.jp/gallery/html). Shinbashi station (Yamanote line), Ginza exit; (Asakusa line), exit A3; (Ginza line), exit 1. **Open** 11am-7pm Tue-Sat; 11am-6pm Sun. **Map** p59 C3 ⑨

Run by cosmetics giant Shiseido, this is more of a *Kunsthalle* than a commercial gallery. It hosts group and solo shows by contemporary artists such as Masato Nakamura and Roman Signer, as well as occasional retrospectives (Man Ray, for instance) and fashion-related shows. The gallery is located in the basement of the company's Ricardo Bofill-designed headquarters.

Tokyo Gallery

Daiwa Shunya Bldg 7F, 8-10-5 Ginza, Chuo-ku (3571 1808/www. tokyo-gallery.com). Shinbashi station (Yamanote line), exit A3; (Ginza line), exit 1. **Open** 11am-7pm Mon-Fri; 11am-5pm Sat. **Map** p59 C3 ⑩

Tokyo Gallery shows modern and contemporary Japanese, Chinese and Korean artists. It opened a Beijing branch in 2003.

Vanilla Gallery

6-10-10 Ginza 4F, Chuo-ku (5568 1233/www.vanilla-gallery.com). Ginza station (Ginza, Hibiya, Marunouchi lines), exit A3. **Open** noon-7pm Mon-Fri; noon-5pm Sat. **Map** p59 C3 ⑪

A tiny space tucked in a time-worn backstreet building, Vanilla is Tokyo's only gallery dedicated to erotic art.

Wacoal Ginza Art Space

Miyuki No.1 Bldg B1, 5-1-15 Ginza, Chuo-ku (3573 3798/www.wacoal.co.jp/ company/artspace). Ginza station (Ginza, Hibiya, Marunouchi lines), exit C2. **Open** 11am-7pm Mon-Fri; 11am-5pm Sat. Closed 1wk Aug, 2wks Dec-Jan. **Map** p59 C2 ⑫

It's sponsored by lingerie-makers Wacoal, but the exhibits here focus on contemporary art in fabric, ceramics and other media.

Dazzle p63

Hajime

Eating & drinking

Azumitei

NEW *Ginza Inz 1 Bldg 2F, 3-1 Saki Ginza-Nishi, Chuo-ku (5524 7890/ www.azumi-food.com/ginza/index. html). Yurakucho station (Yamanote, Yurakucho lines), Sukiyabashi exit.* **Open** 5-11pm daily. **¥¥¥**. **Sukiyaki**. Map p59 C1 🔞

This sleek, modern restaurant specialises in premium sukiyaki and shabu-shabu, prepared with finely marbled beef from Japanese wagyu steers. The full-course dinners (¥6,300 and up) make a great introduction to contemporary Japanese cuisine, but you can also order à la carte. Try to nab one of the semi-private booths in the centre of the restaurant.

Bangkok Kitchen

Ginza Corridor, 8-2 Saki Ginza, Chuo-ku (5537 3886). Ginza station (Ginza, Hibiya, Marunouchi lines), exit C1 or Shinbashi station (Yamanote line), Ginza exit; (Asakusa line), exit A3; (Ginza line), exit 3. **Open** 11am-3pm, 5.30-11.15pm Mon-Fri; 5.30-11.30pm Sat, Sun. **¥¥**. **Thai**. Map p59 B2 🔞

Contemporary Bangkok touches down in the heart of Ginza. Thai noodles, fiery curries, pungent soups and spicy Isaan specialities are all prepared with finesse. The kitchen crew and most of the waiters are Thai, so the ambience is as authentic as the flavours.

Bar Ginza Panorama

Ginza Hachikan Bldg 8F, 8-4-5 Ginza, Chuo-ku (3289 8700/www.ginza-panorama.com/bar). Shinbashi station (Yamanote, Asakusa, Ginza lines), Ginza exit. **Open** 6pm-3am Mon-Sat; 6pm-11pm Sun. **Bar**. Map p59 B3 🔞

Don't be fooled by the name: there's no sign of a panoramic view here. Instead, you'll find an immaculate Japanese interior with plenty of softly lit wood and stone. Plus, rather incongruously, a model train chugging around the bar. See box p79.

Bird Land

Tsukamoto Sozan Bldg B1F, 4-2-15 Ginza, Chuo-ku (5250 1081). Ginza station (Ginza, Hibiya, Marunouchi lines), exit C6. **Open** noon-1.30pm, 5-10pm Tue-Fri; 5-9pm Sat. **¥¥¥**. **Yakitori**. English menu. Map p59 C2 🔞

Upmarket yakitori (grilled chicken skewers), served with imported beer and fine wines. Grill master Wada Toshihiro uses top-quality, free-range bantam chickens that are so tasty you can enjoy their meat raw as sashimi. It's a small, popular place, so make a reservation if you can.

Cabaret
Ginzazetton Bldg B1F, 5-14-15 Ginza, Chuo-ku (5148 3601/www.zetton.co. jp/j/restaurant/cabaret/cabaret.htm). Higashi-Ginza station (Asakusa, Hibiya lines), exit 4. **Open** 8pm-5am Mon-Sat. **Bar**. Map p59 D3 ⓱

Descend the red velvet-draped spiral staircase and… that's pretty much where the cabaret theme ends. But you'll find yourself in the sleek basement of Zetton, a Korean/Japanese restaurant in the backstreets of Ginza. Be warned, though: a seat at the bar costs ¥500, while a spot on the sofa carries a hefty ¥1,500 charge.

Le Café Doutor Ginza
San'ai Bldg 1F, 5-7-2 Ginza, Chuo-ku (5537 8959). Ginza station (Ginza, Hibiya, Marunouchi lines), exits A1, A3. **Open** 7.30am-11pm Mon-Fri; 8am-11pm Sat; 8am-10pm Sun. **¥**. No credit cards. **Café**. Map p59 D2 ⓲

The most impressive branch of the cheap 'n' cheerful chain that proliferated across Tokyo during the recession-hit 1990s is remarkably affordable for its location – on the landmark Ginza Yonchome crossing. Streetside tables or the highly prized upstairs window seats provide perfect views of the bustling Ginza crowds outside. The coffee is Doutor's standard fare, but the sandwiches are a slight step upmarket.

Café Fontana
Abe Bldg B1, 5-5-9 Ginza, Chuo-ku (3572 7320). Ginza station (Ginza, Hibiya, Marunouchi lines), exits B3, B5. **Open** noon-11pm Mon-Fri; 2-11pm Sat; 2-7pm Sun. **¥**. No credit cards. **Café**. Map p59 C2 ⓳

A typically genteel Ginza basement establishment, but one where the individually served apple pies come in distinctly non-dainty proportions. Each steaming specimen contains a whole fruit, thinly covered in pastry, then doused thoroughly in cream.

Café Paulista
Nagasaki Centre, 8-9-16 Ginza, Chuo-ku (3572 6160/www.paulista. co.jp). Ginza station (Ginza, Hibiya, Marunouchi lines), exits A3, A4, A5. **Open** 8.30am-10pm Mon-Sat; noon-8pm Sun. **¥**. No credit cards. **Café**. Map p59 C3 ⓴

This Brazilian-themed Ginza establishment was founded back in 1914. The all-natural beans are imported directly from Brazil, keeping blend coffee prices down to ¥498, a bargain for the area. Low leather seats, plants and wall engravings catch the eye amid a general brown-and-green motif.

Dazzle
NEW *Mikimoto Ginza 2 8/9F, 2-4-12 Ginza, Chuo-ku (5159 0991/www.huge. co.jp). Ginza station (Ginza, Hibiya, Marunouchi lines), exit C8.* **Open** *Restaurant* 5.30-10.30pm daily. *Bar* 5.30pm-1am daily. **¥¥¥¥**. **Fusion**. Map p59 D2 ㉑

Dazzle's remarkable interior lives up to its immodest name. This eatery in the Mikimoto 2 building is a glittering, cavernous space dominated by a massive, glass-fronted wine cellar. So what if the fusion food – think oysters, foie gras and grilled fish – is overambitious and priced high for what you get? Come for the setting.

Hajime
Iraka Ginza Bldg B1F, 6-4-7 Ginza, Chuo-ku (5568 4552/www.ginza-hajime.com). Ginza station (Ginza, Hibiya, Marunouchi lines), Sotobori Dori exit. **Open** 6pm-3am Mon-Fri; 6-11pm Sat. **Bar**. Map p59 C2 ㉒

Hajime looks like an old apartment from the outside but is actually a sleek designer bar. Yellow light gives the tiny basement space a warm glow. The menu focuses on wines – both grape and rice varieties. This being Ginza, there's a ¥1,000 seating charge.

Ki No Hana
4-13-1 Ginza, Chuo-ku (3543 5280). Higashi-Ginza station (Asakusa, Hibiya lines), exit 5. **Open** 10am-8pm Mon-Fri. **¥**. No credit cards. **Café**. Map p59 D3 ㉓

The pair of signed John Lennon cartoons on the walls is the legacy of a chance visit by the former Beatle one afternoon in 1978. With its peaceful atmosphere, tasteful floral decorations, herbal teas and lunchtime vegetarian curries, it's easy to understand Lennon's choice. Apparently, the over-awed son of the former owner also preserved the great man's full ashtray, including butts. Alas, he kept this wonderful object as a personal memento, so it isn't on display here.

Kondo

Sakaguchi Bldg 9F, 5-5-13 Ginza, Chuo-ku (5568 0923). Ginza station (Ginza, Hibiya, Marunouchi lines), exits A3, A4. **Open** noon-8.30pm Mon-Sat. **¥¥¥. Tempura.** English menu. **Map** p59 C2 ㉔

Chef Fumio Kondo and his assistants deliver a wonderful succession of exquisite morsels of golden, batter-fried seafood and vegetables. A kimono-clad waitress hovers, repeatedly replacing the paper mats that absorb excess oil. Kondo is a tempura artist of the old school, but you'll discover his restaurant is less formal (and more affordable) than other traditional tempura shops. The view over the Ginza rooftops is another treat.

Lion Beer Hall

7-9-20 Ginza, Chuo-ku (3571 2590/www.ginzalion.jp). Ginza station (Ginza, Hibiya, Marunouchi lines), exit A4. **Open** 11.30am-11pm Mon-Sat; 11.30am-10.30pm Sun. **Bar.** **Map** p59 C3 ㉕

This 1930s beer hall, part of the Sapporo Lion chain, is a tourist attraction in itself. The tiled and wood-panelled interior looks as if it's been transplanted from Bavaria, and a menu laden with sausages adds to the effect. There is also a cheap and cheerful restaurant upstairs serving both Japanese and Western dishes.

Little Okinawa

8-7-10 Ginza, Chuo-ku (3572 2930/www.little-okinawa.co.jp). Shinbashi station (Yamanote line), Ginza exit; (Asakusa line), exit A3; (Ginza line), exit 3. **Open** noon-1.30pm, 5pm-3am Mon-Fri; noon-1.30pm, 4pm-midnight Sat, Sun. **¥¥. Okinawan.** English menu. **Map** p59 C3 ㉖

This cheerful, busy hole-in-the-wall serves the foods of Japan's southernmost islands. Among the more accessible dishes are deep-fried chips of *goya* (bitter gourd), *jimami-dofu* (a creamy peanut mousse) and *rafuti* (delectable, slow-simmered pork belly). Once you've had a few shots of *awamori*, the rice-based, rocket-fuel hooch native to Okinawa, you'll be ready to tackle the more exotic offerings, among them *mimiga* (gelatinous pig's ear) and *umi-budo* (crunchy seaweed).

Ohmatsuya

Ail d'Or Bldg 2F, 6-5-8 Ginza, Chuo-ku (3571 7053). Ginza station (Ginza, Hibiya, Marunouchi lines), exit B9. **Open** 5-10pm Mon-Sat. **¥¥¥¥. Traditional Japanese.** English menu. **Map** p59 C2 ㉗

Ohmatsuya serves the foods of rural Yamagata prefecture, but it does so in a swish style appropriate to the Ginza location. The decor is faux rustic, with wooden beams and farmhouse furniture. Every table has a charcoal fireplace on which fish, vegetables, mushrooms and delicious wagyu beef are grilled as you watch. The rest of the menu features plenty of wild mountain herbs and fresh seafood from the Japan Sea coast, not to mention some of the best sake in the country.

Oshima

Ginza Core Bldg 9F, 5-8-20 Ginza, Chuo-ku (3574 8080). Ginza station (Ginza, Hibiya, Marunouchi lines), exits A3, A4. **Open** 11am-10pm daily. **¥¥¥. Traditional Japanese.** **Map** p59 D3 ㉓

Oshima offers traditional food from the Kaga (Kanazawa) area, expertly prepared and beautifully presented. There's a wide range of set meals, including tempura, *shabu-shabu* and *nabe* (hot-pot) courses. The 'ladies' afternoon lunch (*kaiseki*)', served after 2pm, is a bargain.

Shunju Tsugihagi p66

Robata

1-3-8 Yurakucho, Chiyoda-ku (3591 1905). Hibiya station (Chiyoda, Hibiya, Mita lines), exit A4. **Open** 5-11pm daily. ¥¥. No credit cards. **Izakaya**. **Map** p59 B2 ㉙

This venerable *izakaya* provides one of the most charming dining experiences in central Tokyo. Perch yourself on one of the wooden seats and pick from the freshly prepared dishes arrayed in huge bowls on the giant counter. The food is a curious mix of Japanese and Western – salads, pork in cream sauce, tofu and tomato-based veggie stews.

Les Saisons

Imperial Hotel 2F, 1-1-1 Uchisaiwaicho, Chiyoda-ku (3539 8087). Hibiya station (Chiyoda, Hibiya, Mita lines), exits A5, A13; or Yurakucho station (Yamanote, Yurakucho lines), Hibiya exit. **Open** 7-10am, 11.30am-3pm, 5.30-10pm daily. ¥¥¥¥. **French**. **Map** p59 B2 ㉚

Always one of Tokyo's top French restaurants, the Imperial Hotel's flag-ship eatery has hit a peak with the arrival of Thierry Voisin (formerly of Les Creyères in Reims). The dining room is ample and luxurious, the service supremely professional, the wine cellar extensive, and Voisin's haute cuisine outstanding (especially his autumn *gibiers*). Classic heavyweight dining.

Shin-Hinomoto

2-4-4 Yurakucho, Chiyoda-ku (3214 8021). Yurakucho station (Yamanote, Yurakucho lines), Hibiya exit. **Open** 5pm-midnight daily. ¥¥. No credit cards. **Izakaya**. English menu. **Map** p59 C2 ㉛

Tucked under the Yamanote line tracks and shuddering every time a train passes overhead, Shin-Hinomoto delivers the classic *izakaya* experience. That means it's cramped, boisterous and smoky, and serves a good range of cheap, honest grub with plenty of sake and *shochu* to wash it down. What makes it unique is that the master of the house is an English expat.

Shunju Tsugihagi

Nihon Seimei Bldg B1F, 1-1-1 Yurakucho, Chiyoda-ku (3595 0511/www.shunju.com/ja/restaurants/tsugihagi). Hibiya station (Chiyoda, Hibiya, Mita lines), exit A13. **Open** 11.30am-2.30pm, 5-11pm Mon-Sat; noon-2.30pm, 5-9.30pm Sun. **¥¥¥. Izakaya.** English menu. **Map** p59 B2 ㉜

The newest and largest member of the ever-reliable Shunju group conforms to a tried-and-tested modern-*izakaya* formula. On offer is everything from home-made tofu and country-style vegetable dishes to premium seafood and grilled meats. Be warned: it's all pricier than at other branches of Shunju, reflecting the upscale ambience and neighbourhood.

Ten-Ichi

6-6-5 Ginza, Chuo-ku (3571 1949/ www.tenichi.co.jp). Ginza station (Ginza, Hibiya, Marunouchi lines), exits C3, B6. **Open** 11.30am-9.30pm daily. **¥¥¥¥. Tempura.** English menu. **Map** p59 C2 ㉝

You won't find better tempura than at Ten-Ichi. The atmosphere is tranquil and pampering, the tempura light and aromatic. A full-course meal also includes sashimi, salad, rice and dessert. This Ginza flagship is the most refined member of the restaurant chain (it regularly hosts visiting dignitaries and film stars), but other branches all guarantee similar quality.

Ten-Ichi Deux

Nishi Ginza Depato 1F, 4-1 Ginza (3566 4188). Yurakucho station (Yamanote line), Ginza exit; (Yurakucho line), exit A7; or Ginza station (Ginza, Hibiya, Marunouchi lines), exits C5, C9. **Open** 11am-10pm daily. **¥. Tempura.** English menu. **Map** p59 C2 ㉞

This smart-casual offshoot of the reputable Ten-Ichi chain specialises in light (and rather more affordable) tempura-based meals accompanied by simple side dishes. The *ten-don* (tempura prawns on a rice bowl) makes a small but satisfying snack.

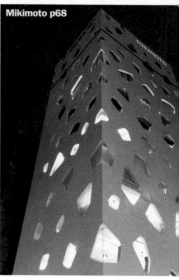

Mikimoto p68

WaZa

NEW *Mikimoto Ginza 2 7F, 2-4-12 Ginza, Chuo-ku (5524 5965/www.dynac-japan.com/waza). Ginza station (Ginza, Hibiya, Marunouchi lines), exit C8.* **Open** 11.30am-2.30pm, 5-11.30pm daily. **¥¥¥**. **Continental**. Map p59 D2 ⑮
Sitting in the landmark Toyo Ito-designed Mikimoto Ginza 2 building, WaZa is a stylish, intimate spot serving confident, contemporary dishes. The menu focuses on charcoal-grilled meat and chicken, pot-au-feu, cheese fondue and lots of fresh vegetables. The set lunches, with self-service salad, soup and coffee, are especially good value.

Shopping

Akebono

5-7-19 Ginza, Chuo-ku (3571 3640/ www.ginza-akebono.co.jp/top.html). Ginza station (Ginza, Hibiya, Marunouchi lines), exit A1. **Open** 9am-9pm Mon-Sat; 9am-8pm Sun. Map p59 C2 ⑯
This small but lively shop offers a wide variety of traditional Japanese sweets, which changes with the seasons. The Akebono range is also available from many department stores.

Familiar

New Melsa Bldg B1F, 5-7-10 Ginza, Chuo-ku (3574 7111/www.familiar. co.jp). Ginza station (Ginza, Hibiya, Marunouchi lines), exit A2. **Open** 11am-8pm Mon, Tue, Thur-Sun. Map p59 C3 ⑰
The children's goods here are appropriately upscale for the area. Familiar handles everything from clothes, shoes and umbrellas to desks, beds, strollers and skincare. Prices are hefty, but quality is high.

Ginza Kanematsu

6-9-9 Ginza, Chuo-ku (3573 0077/ www.ginza-kanematsu.co.jp). Ginza station (Ginza, Hibiya, Marunouchi lines), exit A4. **Open** 11am-9pm Mon-Sat; 11am-8pm Sun. Map p59 C3 ⑱
The Ginza branch of the Kanematsu chain specialises in stylish shoes for

men and women. Westerners will find the sizes are larger than usual for a Japanese footwear shop.

Ginza Natsuno

6-7-4 Ginza, Chuo-ku (3569 0952/ www.e-ohashi.com/natsuno/index. html). Ginza station (Ginza, Hibiya, Marunouchi lines), exit A5. **Open** 10am-8pm Mon-Sat; 10am-7pm Sun. Map p59 C3 ⑲
Japanese chopsticks make affordable and easily portable souvenirs, so make a beeline for this shop and its amazing, eclectic collection. Ginza Natsuno's premises are small, but there's plenty to choose from.

Hakuhinkan

8-8-11 Ginza, Chuo-ku (3571 8008/ www.hakuhinkan.co.jp). Shinbashi station (Yamanote line), Ginza exit; (Asakusa line), exit A3; (Ginza line), exit 1. **Open** 11am-8pm daily. Map p59 C3 ⑳
One of the city's biggest and best-known toy shops is a multi-storey showcase for the wacky, the cuddly and the cute, all with a Japanese twist. The basement is the headquarters of the Licca-chan Club (the Japanese equivalent of Barbie). There is a tax-exemption counter on the fourth floor.

Ito-ya

2-7-15 Ginza, Chuo-ku (3561 8311/ www.ito-ya.co.jp). Ginza station (Ginza, Hibiya, Marunouchi lines), exit A13. **Open** 10am-7pm Mon-Sat; 10.30am-7pm Sun. Map p59 D2 ㊶
A huge, bustling stationary store specialising in Japanese paper, Ito-ya's range is conventional but comprehensive. The main shop (Ito-ya 1 Bldg) sells standard stationery and calligraphic tools, while the annex (Ito-ya 3 Bldg) – directly behind it – has the *washi* paper.

Kimuraya

4-5-7 Ginza, Chuo-ku (3561 0091/ www.kimuraya-sohonten.co.jp). Ginza station (Ginza, Hibiya, Marunouchi lines), exits A9, B1. **Open** 10am-9.30pm daily. No credit cards. Map p59 D2 ㊷

Kimuraya's claim to fame is that it was the first in Tokyo to sell *anpan* – bread rolls filled with adzuki-bean paste. Break up a Ginza shopping trip with a visit to this venerable shop to try them for yourself.

Kyukyodo

5-7-4 Ginza, Chuo-ku (3571 4429/ www.kyukyodo.co.jp). Ginza station (Ginza, Hibiya, Marunouchi lines), exit A2. **Open** 10am-7.30pm Mon-Sat; 11am-7pm Sun. **Map** p59 C2 ❸

Japanese paper specialist Kyukyodo opened its first shop in Kyoto in 1663 and supplied incense to the Imperial Palace during the Edo period. The shop moved to Tokyo in 1880 and is still run by the Kumagai family that founded it. This branch in Ginza, with its distinctive arched brick entrance, sells incense, seasonal gift cards and lots of moderately priced items (boxes, notebooks, picture frames) made from colourful *washi* paper.

Matsuya

3-6-1 Ginza, Chuo-ku (3567 1211/ www.matsuya.com). Ginza station (Ginza, Hibiya, Marunouchi lines), exits A12, A13. **Open** 10am-8pm daily (but closing time varies by month). **Map** p59 D2 ❹

A department store notable for having in-store boutiques from the triumvirate of famous Japanese fashion revolutionaries: Yohji Yamamoto, Issey Miyake and Comme des Garçons, all situated on the third floor, along with a tax exemption and overseas delivery counter. Traditional Japanese souvenirs are on the seventh floor.

Matsuzakaya

10-1 Ginza, Chuo-ku (3572 1111/ www.matsuzakaya.co.jp/ginza/index. html). Ginza station (Ginza, Hibiya, Marunouchi lines), exits A1-A4. **Open** 10.30am-7.30pm Mon-Wed, Sun; 10.30am-8pm Thur-Sat. **Map** p59 C3 ❺

The main Matsuzakaya store is actually in Ueno, but the most convenient branch for shopaholics is this one, located on Ginza's main drag near

Mitsukoshi and Matsuya. Well-heeled souvenir shoppers can pick up a kimono on the sixth floor. The annex contains a beauty salon, art gallery and even a ladies' deportment school.

Meidi-ya

2-6-7 Ginza, Chuo-ku (3563 0221/ www.meidi-ya-store.com). Ginza-Itchome station (Yurakucho line), exit 8. **Open** 10am-9pm Mon-Sat; 10am-8pm Sun. **Map** p59 D2 ❻

This central branch of a city-wide chain boasts an attractive array of imported foods from all over the world and an impressive wine cellar. The store also holds regular themed fairs at discount prices.

Mikimoto

NEW *2-4-12 Ginza, Chuo-ku (3562 3130/www.mikimoto.com). Ginza station (Ginza, Hibiya, Marunouchi lines), exit A9.* **Open** 11am-7pm daily. **Map** p59 D2 ❼

This second flagship store for cultured pearl brand Mikimoto was designed by Toyo Ito. Its amazing pink façade is a favourite with tourists. The astronomically priced creations inside aren't.

Mitsukoshi

4-6-16 Ginza, Chuo-ku (3562 1111/ www.mitsukoshi.co.jp). Ginza station (Ginza, Hibiya, Marunouchi lines), exits A7, A8, A11. **Open** 10am-8pm daily. **Map** p59 D2 ❽

The oldest surviving department store chain in Japan (it was founded way back in 1673), Mitsukoshi has its gargantuan flagship store in Nihonbashi. This more accessible Ginza branch sits on Yon-chome crossing, just opposite Wako. It sells womenswear and accessories on the first five floors, menswear on the sixth and household goods on the seventh. Head down to the B3 floor for toys, childrenswear and the tax-exemption counter.

Mujirushi Ryohin

3-8-3 Marunouchi, Chiyoda-ku (5208 8241/www.muji.net). Yurakucho station (Yamanote line), Kyobashi exit; (Yurakucho line), exit A9. **Open** 10am-9pm daily. **Map** p59 D1 ❾

Mika Ninagawa

Japan's red-hot young director.

Born in Tokyo in 1972, Mika Ninagawa is a multi-award winning photographer known for her vivid sense of colour. In February 2007 she branched out into film, with her first feature *Sakuran*, a period drama about a feisty feudal-era worker in Tokyo's fabled Yoshiwara brothel district. A surprise smash, with dedicated fans turning up in glam kimonos as worn by the cast, *Sakuran* made Ninagawa the leader of a growing cohort of Japanese women directors. In person, she is a ball of verbal energy, firing off lengthy answers with sub-clauses to sub-clauses, making an interview less an interaction than an inundation.

What made you take on Sakuran *as your first feature?*
I really liked the original manga. (Writer Moyoco) Anno is very accurate in her depictions of women. There were aspects of the psychology of the Yoshiwara prostitutes I couldn't understand, but as I studied the records of the period, I learned that a lot of their feelings were the same as those of women today. That's when I thought that perhaps I could do this.

Did you start with the visuals, or did the story come first?
If a film is just beautiful, it's no different from a promo video. The visuals were my lowest priority, actually. I had confidence that I could make them look good, so I sort of shunted them aside and concentrated on the script.

Yoshiwara, of course, had its dark side, being a place where women were bought and sold.
Yes, but the *oiran* (top-ranking prostitutes) were like superstars. The kimonos and accessories they wore became fashionable in society at large. In that sense, they were idols. The biggest indication (of their social status) was that *oiran* sat in the place of honour. If they didn't like a client, they didn't have to take him to her bed. And once a client had chosen an *oiran*, he couldn't play with *oiran* from other brothels. I thought that system was very interesting. Of course, it was a form of prostitution, but conditions were very different from now. I didn't particularly want people to feel sorry for them. I wanted to show their daily lives.

Are you going to continue making films?
Yes, but next I want to do a contemporary story. I'm sure that would be easier.

TOKYO BY AREA

Kabuki-za p72

Better known simply as Muji, this is the original no-brand designer brand. Ginza's is the biggest Tokyo outlet of the all-purpose, one-stop shop that went on to conquer London and Paris.

Nail Bee

Keitoku Bldg 3F, 3-3-14 Ginza, Chuo-ku (5250 0018/www.nailbee. com). Ginza station (Ginza, Hibiya, Marunouchi lines), exit C8. **Open** 11am-8pm daily. **Map** p59 D2 ⑤⓪
Tokyo's leading nail salon has been serving the international community's beauty needs for over a decade. In addition to manicures and nail art, Nail Bee offers facials, massages, waxing, pedicures and eyelash perms.

NIWAKA

2-8-18 Ginza, Chuo-ku (3564 0707/ www.niwaka.com). Ginza station (Ginza, Hibiya, Marunouchi lines), exit A13. **Open** 11am-8pm daily. **Map** p59 D2 ⑤①
NIWAKA's elegant, nature-inspired designs are created by a team of artisans in workshops in Kyoto. The sleek jewellery comes in platinum or white, pink or yellow gold, and there is

also a made-to-order service that enables customers to design their own sparkling creation.

RagTag

3-3-15 Ginza, Chuo-ku (3535 4100/ www.ragtag.jp/shop/ginza.html). Ginza station (Ginza, Hibiya, Marunouchi lines), exit C8. **Open** 11am-8pm daily. **Map** p59 D2 ⑤②
A six-storey second-hand clothing shop that deals only in the biggest brands for ladies and gents. Ginza's fickle fashionistas keep the store stocked with barely worn garments from recent catwalk collections, as well as great value watches and jewellery.

Restir

4-2-2 Ginza, Chuo-ku (5159 0595/ www.restir. com). Ginza station (Ginza, Hibiya, Marunouchi lines), exit C8. **Open** 11.30am-8.30pm Mon-Sat; 11am-8pm Sun. **Map** p59 C2 ⑤③
This mega-boutique offers one of the most luxurious fashion shopping experiences in Tokyo. Besides a VIP room and live DJ, it also offers high-quality customer service, with a reasonable level of spoken English. The high-end

brands include more than a few home-grown labels. An equally dazzling sister store is located in Roppongi's Midtown complex (p112).

Sayegusa

7-8-8 Ginza, Chuo-ku (3573 2441/ www.sayegusa.com). Ginza station (Ginza, Hibiya, Marunouchi lines), exit A2. **Open** 10.30am-7.30pm daily. **Map** p59 C3 ❺❹

Purveyors of finery for small fry since 1869, Sayegusa is housed in a four-storey Meiji-era building and offers top-of-the-range baby and children's clothing and accessories. The second basement floor has a made-to-order clothing service. Expect impeccable service and gut-churning prices.

Sony Building

5-3-1 Ginza, Chuo-ku (3573 2563/ www.sonybuilding.jp). Ginza station (Ginza, Hibiya, Marunouchi lines), exit B9. **Open** 11am-7pm daily. **Map** p59 C2 ❺❺

This eight-floor building – a notable Ginza landmark – contains showrooms for Sony's world-famous products, including the AIBO robot hound, PlayStation 3, VAIO, Cyber-Shot and Handycam. The building also contains a number of cafés and restaurants, and even an English pub.

Tanagokoro

1-8-15 Ginza, Chuo-ku (3538 6555/ www.tanagokoro.com). Ginza-Itchome station (Yurakucho line), exits 7, 9. **Open** 11am-8pm Mon-Fri; 11am-7pm Sat, Sun. **Map** p59 D1 ❺❻

This shop, whose name means 'palm of the hand', sells *binchotan*, a highly refined form of Japanese charcoal that can purify, dehumidify and deodorise a room's air. If you can't wait until you get home to try, you can indulge in the curative powers of *binchotan's* fragrance in the basement healing room.

Tasaki Shinju

5-7-5 Ginza, Chuo-ku (3289 1111/ www.tasaki.co.jp). Ginza station (Ginza, Hibiya, Marunouchi lines), exit A2. **Open** 10.30am-7.30pm daily. **Map** p59 C2 ❺❼

Known, with good reason, as the Jewellery Tower, each floor of this huge building is devoted to a particular jewellery theme. The museum on the fifth floor is also worth a look.

Uniqlo

5-7-7 Ginza, Chuo-ku (3569 6781/ www.uniqlo.co.jp). Ginza station (Ginza, Hibiya, Marunouchi lines), exit A2. **Open** 11am-9pm daily. **Map** p59 C2/3 ❺❽

Uniqlo is the chain store that revolutionised retail in Japan with bargain-priced basic clothing. But the brand is in the process of going upmarket, and to that end it opened a huge flagship store in Ginza last year, designed by resident Tokyo architect duo Klein Dytham. The façade is a matrix of 1,000 illuminated cells, which form Tetris-style patterns.

Wako

4-5-11 Ginza, Chuo-ku (3562 2111/ www.wako.co.jp). Ginza station (Ginza, Hibiya, Marunouchi lines), exits A9, A10, B1. **Open** 10.30am-6pm Mon-Sat. **Map** p59 D2 ❺❾

This prestigious department store boasts a grand exterior and landmark clock tower that graces most stock images of Ginza. The distinguished look continues inside, where a hushed ambience surrounds the fine jewellery, porcelain, crystal and designer apparel.

Nightlife

Someday

1-20-9 Nishi Shinbashi, Minato-ku (3506 1777/www.someday.net). Shinbashi station (Yamanote, Asakusa, Ginza lines), Karasumori exit. **Open** Shows from 7.45pm daily. **Admission** ¥2,500-¥3,700. **Map** p59 A3 ❻⓪

Someday specialises in big-band and Latin groups. The atmosphere isn't particularly notable, though the crowd is always knowledgeable and enthusiastic. There's an extensive (and expensive) selection of whisky, along with the usual Japanese snacks and small pizzas to satisfy any hunger pangs.

Arts & leisure

Ciné Pathos

4-8-7 Ginza, Chuo-ku (3561 4660/
www.cinema-st.com/road/r005.html).
Ginza station (Ginza, Hibiya,
Marunouchi lines), exit A6.
Map p59 D3 **61**

A three-screener that looks grotty from
the outside, but redeems itself with a
cosy interior and a schedule of the kind
of soon-to-be-videos that most commercial cinemas don't bother with. It
also screens classic revivals.

Ciné Switch Ginza

Ginza-Hata Bldg B1F, 4-4-5 Ginza,
Chuo-ku (3561 0707/www.cineswitch.
com). Ginza station (Ginza, Hibiya,
Marunouchi lines), exit B2. **Map**
p59 C/D2 **62**

A good spot to take in some Japanese
and European films, so long as your
language skills hold up.

Hibiya Chanter Ciné

1-2-2 Yurakucho, Chiyoda-ku (3591
1511/www.chantercine.com). Hibiya
station (Chiyoda, Hibiya, Mita lines),
exit A5. **Map** p59 B2 **63**

A comfy three-screen cinema showing
plenty of independent European and
American films.

Hibiya Yagai Ongakudo

1-3 Hibiya Koen, Chiyoda-ku (3591
6388). Kasumigaseki station (Chiyoda,
Hibiya, Marunouchi lines), exits B2, C4.
Map p59 A2 **64**

In use since 1923, this outdoor theatre
in Hibiya Park puts you at the mercy
of the weather, and umbrellas are not
allowed, but turn up on a nice day and
enjoy one of Tokyo's few open-air
venues. Unfortunately, it's an ode to
concrete, including the seats.

Kabuki-za

4-12-15 Ginza, Chuo-ku (information
3541 3131/box office 5565 6000/
www.shochiku.co.jp/play/kabukiza/
theater/index.html). Higashi-Ginza
station (Asakusa, Hibiya lines), exits
A3, A6. **Map** p59 D3 **65**

Japan's number-one *kabuki* theatre.
Matinées start around 11am and

evening performances around 4.30pm.
The shows can last up to five hours,
but you can buy tickets to watch just
one act from the fourth floor; these go
on sale from one hour beforehand and
often sell out. The English-language
audio guide is invaluable.

National Film Centre

3-7-6 Kyobashi, Chuo-ku (5777 8600/
www.momat.go.jp). Kyobashi station
(Ginza line), exit 1; or Takaracho
station (Asakusa line), exit A4.
Open 11am-6.30pm daily. No
credit cards. **Map** p59 E1 **66**

Part of the National Museum of
Modern Art, this venue has two cinemas, a gallery, a library and a café. Its
mission is to research and preserve
film, and the centre holds a collection
of 19,000 titles. Fans throng to its two
cinemas for series focusing on, for
example, DW Griffith or Korean films
from the 1960s. Visitors can also check
out the library of film books on the
fourth floor or film-related exhibitions
on the seventh.

Shinbashi Embujo

6-18-2 Ginza, Chuo-ku (3541 2600/
www.shochiku.co.jp/play/index.html).
Higashi-Ginza station (Asakusa, Hibiya
lines), exit A6. **Map** p59 D3 **67**

Ichikawa Ennosuke's 'Super-Kabuki',
a jazzed-up, modernised version of the
real thing, is staged here in April and
May (and at the Kabuki-za in July).
Samurai dramas are performed during
the rest of the year.

Tokyo Takarazuka Gekijo

1-1-3 Yurakucho, Chiyoda-ku
(5251 2001/http://kageki.hankyu
.co.jp/english/index.html). Yurakucho
station (Yamanote, Yurakucho lines),
Hibiya exit; or Hibiya station (Chiyoda,
Hibiya, Mita lines), exit A13. **Map**
p59 B2 **68**

Gender-bending kitsch is the order of
the day at the home of Takarazuka.
This all-female musical revue perform
in Japanese, and unlike the Kabuki-za,
there's no English audio guide. But you
won't feel you need it; just soak up the
flamboyant fun.

Takeshita Dori p80

Harajuku & Aoyama

Harajuku

When they were building **Meiji Jingu**, Tokyo's largest Shinto shrine, they couldn't have imagined that the surrounding area would develop into a youth fashion mecca of the quirkiest order. A stretch of pavement just in front of the shrine's main entrance is where the *cosplayers* gather each weekend, dressed as gothic nurses or twisted Lolitas or straightforward cartoon characters, striking poses for the tourist cameras. The source of many of their threads is **Takeshita Dori**, the congested artery of teenybop culture that leads from Harajuku station into the heart of 'Ura-Hara', the trendier back-streets that house many of the city's hippest urban labels. It's

no coincidence that Pharrell Williams and Nigo chose this area for their new streetwear stores **Billionaire Boys Club** and **Ice Cream Store**.

Sights & museums

Meiji Shrine & Inner Garden

1-1 Yoyogi-Kamizonocho, Shibuya-ku (3379 5511/www.meijijingu.or.jp). Harajuku station (Yamanote line), Omotesando exit; or Meiji-Jingumae station (Chiyoda line), exit 2. **Open** *Shrine & Inner Garden* Spring & autumn 5.10am-5.50pm daily. Summer 5am-6.30pm daily. Winter 6am-4.10pm daily. *Meiji Shrine Garden* Mar-Oct 9am-5pm daily. Nov-Feb 9am-4pm daily. **Admission** *Shrine & Inner Garden* free. *Meiji Shrine Garden* ¥500. *Treasure house* ¥200. No credit cards. **Map** p75 A1 ❶

Opened in 1920, the shrine is dedicated to Emperor Meiji – whose reign (1868-1912) coincided with Japan's modernisation – and his consort, Empress Shoken. The main building dates from 1958, and is an impressive example of the austere style and restrained colours typical of Shinto architecture. Just off the main path to the shrine, through the wooded Inner Garden, are two entrances to another garden, the little-visited Meiji Jingu Gyoen.

Ukiyo-e Ota Memorial Museum of Art (Ota Kinen Bijutsukan)

1-10-10 Jingumae, Shibuya-ku (3403 0880/www.ukiyoe-ota-muse.jp). Harajuku station (Yamanote line), Omotesando exit; or Meiji-Jingumae station (Chiyoda line), exit 5. **Open** 10.30am-5.30pm Tue-Sun. Closed from 27-end of mth. **Admission** ¥700; ¥500 reductions. No credit cards. **Map** p75 C2 **②**

The late Seizo Ota, chairman of Toho Mutual Life Insurance, began collecting *ukiyo-e* prints after he saw that Japan was losing its traditional art to Western museums and collectors. Temporary exhibitions drawn from his 12,000-strong collection often include works by popular masters such as Hiroshige and Hokusai.

Eating & drinking

L'Artémis

2-31-7 Jingumae, Shibuya-ku (5786 0220/http://r.gnavi.co.jp/g853800). Harajuku station (Yamanote line), Omotesando exit; or Meiji-Jingumae station (Chiyoda line), exit 5. **Open** 11am-9pm daily. **¥¥¥. French. Map** p75 D1 **③**

L'Artémis showcases the excellent skills of Yusuke Nakada, one Tokyo's most able young chefs (and a protégé of Regis Marcon). His ¥3,990 Menu Pétillant includes his signature smoked-salmon salad (with poached egg and caviar) and superb scrambled egg with *uni* (urchin). The tables are a bit cramped, but at prices this low who really cares?

Fonda de la Madrugada

Villa Bianca B1, 2-33-12 Jingumae, Shibuya-ku (5410 6288/www.fonda-m. com). Harajuku station (Yamanote line), Omotesando exit; or Meiji-Jingumae station (Chiyoda line), exit 5. **Open** 5.30pm-2am Mon-Thur, Sun; 5.30pm-5am Fri, Sat. **¥¥. Mexican.** English menu. **Map** p75 C1 **④**

This basement hacienda has some of the best Mexican food in Tokyo, and the most authentic atmosphere too. Chugging on a bottle of Dos Equis, serenaded by mariachi singers, with tortillas and chicken in mole sauce cooked and served by Latinos... you could almost be in Cancún.

Fujimamas

6-3-2 Jingumae, Shibuya-ku (5485 2262/ www.fujimamas.com). Harajuku station (Yamanote line), Omotesando exit; or Meiji-Jingumae station (Chiyoda line), exit 4. **Open** 11am-11pm daily. **¥¥. Fusion.** English menu. **Map** p75 C2 **⑤**

Chef Mark Vann and his polyglot crew produce confident and accessible East-West fusion cuisine in a converted two-storey wooden Japanese house that once saw use as a tatami workshop. The servings here are large and the prices reasonable, if you take the swanky address into account. The well-stocked bar draws a gregarious mix of locals and expats.

Gesshinkyo

4-24-12 Jingumae, Shibuya-ku (3796 6575/www.bs-n.co.jp/men/15.html). Harajuku station (Yamanote line), Omotesando exit; or Meiji-Jingumae station (Chiyoda line), exit 5. **Open** 6-10pm Mon-Sat. Closed 2nd Sat of month. **¥¥¥¥.** No credit cards. **Zen. Map** p75 C2 **⑥**

Tanahashi-san, who is the master of Gesshinkyo, studied *shojin ryori* – an 800-year-old style of vegetarian cooking – with Zen nuns in Kyoto, but has gone on to develop his own unorthodox, vegetable-intense version. The interior is classy and intimate, but the food is rough-hewn, intense on the palate (the green *sansho* pepper sorbet is a good example) and very satisfying.

Harajuku & Aoyama

To Aoyama Cemetery

200 m
200 yds

© Copyright Time Out Group 2007

GAIEN-NISHI DORI

AOYAMA DORI

MINAMI-AOYAMA

Omotesando Station

Anniversaire Building

Mizuho Bank

To Kotto Dori

MEIJI DORI

Omotesando Hills

OMOTESANDO

Oriental Bazaar

JINGUMAE

MEIJI DORI

Togo Shrine

Takeshita Dori

Meiji-Jingumae Station

To Shibuya

Yamanote Line

Harajuku Station

Meiji Shrine Inner Garden

SHIBUYA-KU

Yoyogi Park

INOKASHIRA DORI

JINNAN

National Gymnasium

KOEN DORI

NHK Hall

HK Broadcasting Centre

| Sights & museums |
| Eating & drinking |
| Shopping |
| Nightlife |
| Arts & leisure |

Meiji Shrine p73

Hannibal Deux

*Harajuku Miwa Bldg B1F, 3-53-3
Sendagaya, Shibuya-ku (3479 3710/
www.hannibal.cc). Harajuku station
(Yamanote line), Omotesando exit;
or Meiji-Jingumae station (Chiyoda
line), exit 5.* **Open** *5.30-11pm daily.*
¥¥. Tunisian. **Map** p75 C1 **7**

Chef Mondher Gheribi's Tunisian
home cooking adds another dimension
to this cosmopolitan area of Tokyo. He
draws on influences from right across
the Mediterranean at Hannibal Deux,
but his best dishes are those that hail
from his homeland. These include his
mechoui salad, roast chicken stuffed
with banana and herbs, and the home-
made *khobz* bread served with a red-
hot harissa sauce.

Kurkku Kitchen

*2-18-21 Jingumae, Shibuya-ku
(5414 0944/www.kurkku.jp/english/
kitchen.html). Harajuku station
(Yamanote line), Omotesando exit;
or Meiji-Jingumae station (Chiyoda
line), exit 5.* **Open** *11.30am-2pm,
6-10pm Tue-Sun.* **¥¥. Grill.** English
menu. **Map** p75 D1 **8**

The centrepiece of an ambitious project
that marries quality food with green
thinking and contemporary architecture, Kurkku Kitchen bases its French-
Japanese hybrid cuisine on a range of
organic produce and meat. Most of the
food is cooked over a charcoal grill, and
it's all delectable.

Montoak

*6-1-9 Jingumae, Shibuya-ku (5468
5928/www.montoak.com). Harajuku
station (Yamanote line), Omotesando
exit; or Meiji-Jingumae station (Chiyoda
line), exit 4.* **Open** *11am-3am daily.*
Bar. **Map** p75 C2 **9**

The staff, clientele and décor will all be
hipper than thou, but who cares? This
is a wonderfully comfortable, ultra-
stylish spot to rest your feet after hours
traipsing the shops of Harajuku.
Considering the plum location on
Omotesando, the layout is surprisingly
spacious and the menu affordable.

Nabi

*Accordy Jingumae B1, 2-31-20,
Jingumae, Shibuya-ku (5771 0071/
www.nabi-tokyo.com). Harajuku station*

(Yamanote line), Takeshita exit; or Meiji-jingumae station (Chiyoda line), exit 5. **Open** 11.30am-1am Mon-Sat; 6pm-midnight Sun. **¥¥. Korean.** **Map** p75 D1 ⑩

The chic interior was designed by the Idee group. The menu has a strong emphasis on organic vegetables and medicinal herbs, and the seasonings are applied with a light hand. This is modern Korean cooking for the hip, late-night Harajuku crowd.

Shopping

Aizu Tulpe

1-13-14 Jingumae, Shibuya-ku (5775 0561). Harajuku station (Yamanote line), Meiji-Jingumae exit; or Meiji-Jingumae station (Chiyoda line), exit 3. **Open** 9am-11pm daily. **Map** p75 B2 ⑪

Aizu Tulpe is a boon for anyone who wishes to do some late-night shopping and a dazzling introduction to the fascinating world of Japanese cosmetics and medicine. The two floors are filled with every conceivable kind of beauty and health product.

Billionaire Boys Club/ Ice Cream Store

NEW *4-28-22 Jingumae, Shibuya-ku (5775 2633/www.bbcicecream.com). Meiji-Jingumae station (Chiyoda line), exit 5.* **Open** 11am-7pm daily. **Map** p75 C2 ⑫

A collaboration between hip-hop hot-shot Pharrell Williams and A Bathing Ape fashion mogul Nigo, clothing label Billionaire Boys Club and sneaker brand Ice Cream have side-by-side shops on Propeller Street, one of Harajuku's hippest strips. High-quality sneakers, T-shirts, sweatshirts, parkas, shirts, jackets and jeans in bold colours and designs are all available.

BørneLund

Hara Bldg 1F, 6-10-9 Jingumae, Shibuya-ku (5485 3430/www. bornelund.co.jp). Harajuku station (Yamanote line), Omotesando exit; or Meiji-Jingumae station (Chiyoda line), exit 4. **Open** 11am-7.30pm daily. **Map** p75 C2/3 ⑬

No electric or 'character' toys are sold at this small shop, which specialises in imported wooden toys. You can touch and play with most of the items on display. Sofas and nursing/nappy-changing facilities are also provided.

CA4LA

6-29-4 Jingumae, Shibuya-ku (3406 8271/www.ca4la.com). Harajuku station (Yamanote line), Omotesando exit; or Meiji-Jingumae station (Chiyoda line), exit 4. **Open** 11am-8pm daily. **Map** p75 C2 ⑭

Japan's trendiest hat-maker. The flagship of CA4LA (pronounced 'ka-shi-la') offers a vast selection of headwear – from woolly bobble hats to pink panamas. Prices are very reasonable.

Cat Street

Harajuku station (Yamanote line), Omotesando exit; or Meiji-Jingumae (Chiyoda line), exit 4. **Open** varies. **Map** p75 C2 ⑮

Running for about half a mile perpendicular to each side of Omotesando, Cat Street is the spiritual home of Tokyo's vibrant street fashion culture. While the strip has been steadily heading upmarket over the past few years, it is still the main conduit for funkily dressed teens on shopping sprees in Tokyo. Highlights include the Tadao Ando-designed edifice housing the Armani Casa interior brand, and collectable figure store Pook et Koop.

Fuji Torii

6-1-10 Jingumae, Shibuya-ku (3400 2777/www.fuji-torii.com). Harajuku station (Yamanote line), Omotesando exit; Meiji-Jingumae station (Chiyoda line), exit 4; or Omotesando station (Chiyoda, Ginza, Hanzomon lines), exit A1. **Open** 11am-6pm Mon, Wed-Sun. Closed 3rd Mon of mth. **Map** p75 C2 ⑯

Fuji Torii sells a wide variety of Japanese antiques (screens, ceramics, sculptures), as well as its own original artwork and crafts.

Kiddyland

6-1-9 Jingumae, Shibuya-ku (3409 3431/www.kiddyland.co.jp). Harajuku station (Yamanote line), Omotesando exit; or Meiji-Jingumae station (Chiyoda line), exit 4. **Open** 10am-9pm daily. Closed 3rd Tue of mth. **Map** p75 C2 ⑰

Kiddyland is a Tokyo institution. The main Harajuku shop is a noisy, heaving maze of mascots, dolls, cuddly toys, furry toys, action figures, Disney, Kitty, Doraemon, Godzilla and more. Warning: this much cuteness can damage your mental health.

Laforet Harajuku

1-11-6 Jingumae, Shibuya-ku (3475 0411/www.laforet.ne.jp). Harajuku station (Yamanote line), Takeshita exit; or Meiji-Jingumae station (Chiyoda line), exit 5. **Open** 11am-8pm daily. **Map** p75 C2 ⑱

One of teenage Tokyo's hallowed sites, this multi-level emporium contains numerous small boutiques selling clothes and accessories aimed at young wearers of garish, eccentric fashion. Exhibitions and multimedia events are also held here.

LIMI feu prankster

6-7-12 Jingumae, Shibuya-ku (5464 2025/www.limifeu.com). Harajuku station (Yamanote line), Omotesando exit; or Meiji-Jingumae (Chiyoda line), exit 4. **Open** noon-9pm daily. **Map** p75 C3 ⑲

Tokyo's antidote to frilly, cutesy clothes for toddlers, LIMI feu prankster showcases the children's line of Limi Yamamoto, daughter of fashion paragon Yohji. The whippersnappers can be left in a padded play area while mum and dad rummage their way through the funky threads. Mother-of-two Limi has a keen sense of what trendy Tokyo mums want their children to be wearing, and this store is proving to be a big hit.

Neighborhood

4-32-5 Jingumae, Shibuya-ku (3401 1201). Harajuku station (Yamanote line), Omotesando exit; or Meiji-Jingumae station (Chiyoda line), exit 4. **Open** noon-8pm daily. **Map** p75 C2 ⑳

'Death from Above' declare the red neon signs outside this minimalist urban fashion shop. Inside are men's jackets, shirts, jeans and accessories with a biker or military influence.

Drinking games

Forget about boring darts and pool in Tokyo's hobby bars.

If you thought Scalextric was fun as a kid, try it with added booze at **Kyosho** (p83; pictured). From 5pm to 9pm, customers at this model racing shop can head into the back room and sip import beers while they send mini vehicles round the carpeted track. It makes a fun finale to a day of fashion-hunting – or a great crèche to dump any reluctant shoppers.

In neighbouring Shibuya, **Bar Tube** (p120) caters to that most modern hobby – browsing YouTube. The bar is a cosy third-floor joint that attracts a young Shibuya crowd who cue up their favourite YouTube videos for the bar's large screen. Opening hours are limited, but how long does anyone want to spend watching YouTube?

The **Nakame Takkyu Lounge** (p161) in Naka-Meguro is a legend on Tokyo's drinking scene, partly because it's so hard to find. From the station, cross the street, stay right of the tracks, take the second right after the canal and its on the second floor of the building beside the carpark (head upstairs and ring the bell). The interior is textbook chic lounge bar, apart from the centrepiece ping pong table. Standards of play slip as the night progresses, unless you're owner Sekino who beats all comers no matter the hour. There's a sizeable range of snacks and simple dishes to keep your stamina up, or shochu (a vodka-like spirit) to do the opposite.

Meanwhile, over in Ginza, a more nostalgic – and serene – experience awaits anyone who had a train set in their childhood. The refined **Bar Ginza Panorama** (p62) has an authentic Japanese interior, with plenty of wood and tasteful calligraphy adorning the walls. It also has a fully functioning model railway chugging around the central bar, with alternative rolling stock displayed in cabinets nearby. It's hands-off hobby play here, but customers can request their preferred stock.

From the sublime... to the maid café. Not only can the patrons of Akihabara's **@home café** (p155) indulge their hobby of eyeing up young girls dressed as saccharin-cute maids, but for just ¥500 they can enjoy three minutes of 'master' (customer) versus maid sessions of blackjack, Pop-up Pirate, Othello, Crocodile Dentist or one of several other games. Masters who get the best of their maids win a coin for the novelty-dispensing gumball machine. Oh, and the maids are also there to serve beer.

Oriental Bazaar

5-9-13 Jingumae, Shibuya-ku (3400 3933). Harajuku station (Yamanote line), Omotesando exit; Meiji-Jingumae station (Chiyoda line), exit 4; or Omotesando station (Chiyoda, Ginza, Hanzomon lines), exit A1. **Open** 10am-7pm Mon-Wed, Fri-Sun. **Map** p75 C2 **㉑**

Probably the best-known gift shop in Tokyo, this is a useful one-stop outlet for almost everything: dolls, china, kimonos, *yukata*, woodblock prints, furniture, antiques and books on Japan. Ideal for stocking up on presents and souvenirs in one easy trip. Prices are generally moderate and staff speak good English.

Override 9999

5-17-25 Jingumae, Shibuya-ku (5766 0575/www.ovr.jp). Harajuku station (Yamanote line), Omotesando exit; or Meiji-Jingumae station (Chiyoda line), exit 4. **Open** 11am-8pm daily. **Map** p75 C3 **㉒**

Eye-catching headgear, as worn by the young bucks prowling Harajuku.

Takeshita Dori

(www.harajuku.jp/takeshita). Harajuku station (Yamanote line), Takeshita exit; or Meiji-Jingumae station (Chiyoda line), exit 2. **Map** p75 A1 **㉓**

Takeshita Dori is an ever-congested little lane lined with hip-hop boutiques, retro toy shops, gothic and *cosplay* clothing emporiums, stalls selling photos of fresh-faced 'idols' to star-struck schoolgirls, and plenty more from the cheaper end of urban pop culture. Come to look, not to buy.

Uniqlo UT

NEW *6-10-8 Jingumae, Shibuya-ku (5468 7313/http://ut.uniqlo.com/store). Harajuku station (Yamanote line), Omotesando exit; or Meiji-Jingumae station (Chiyoda line), exit 4.* **Open** 11am-9pm daily. **Map** p75 C2 **㉔**

Uniqlo's T-shirt store opened in mid 2007 with shelving that mimics vending machines. The T-shirts are 'dispensed' in plastic capsules, although you still have to fork over your yen to a regular human being. The range of designs is impressive, as are the guest designers, including Kim Jones, Terry Richardson, Peter Saville and Nobuyoshi Araki.

Nightlife

Astro Hall

New Wave Harajuku Bldg B1F, 4-32-12 Jingumae, Shibuya-ku (3401 5352/ www.astro-hall.com). Harajuku station (Yamanote line), Takeshita exit; or Meiji-Jingumae station (Chiyoda line), exit 5. **Map** p75 C2 **㉕**

When it opened in 2000 this was the venue of choice for many local indie bands, and it's been holding steady ever since. Some foreign acts trying to break Japan also play here. Very intimate and well laid out.

Crocodile

New Sekiguchi Bldg B1F, 6-18-8 Jingumae, Shibuya-ku (3499 5205/ www.music.co.jp/~croco). Harajuku station (Yamanote line), Omotesando exit; Shibuya station (Yamanote, Ginza, Hanzomon lines), Miyamasusaka (east) exit; or Meiji-Jingumae station (Chiyoda line), exit 4. **Map** p75 B3 **㉖**

Although Crocodile bills itself as a modern music restaurant, it's best to skip the food and stick to the sounds. The venue presents anything from salsa to country, rock and jazz, plus combos of any of these.

Eggman

1-6-8 Jinnan, Shibuya-ku (3496 1561/ www.eggman.jp). Shibuya station (Yamanote, Ginza, Hanzomon lines), Hachiko exit. **Map** p75 A3 **㉗**

Eggman is a Shibuya institution. Most nights you'll find local bands playing, particularly those with one eye on a record deal, so you should be able to catch some upcoming talent. It hosts all strands of the rock genre.

Aoyama

Like Ginza and the upwardly mobile Marunouchi, Aoyama is big brand heaven. **Christian Dior**, **Ralph Lauren**, **Louis Vuitton** and **Tod's** are all represented, but

Prada, with its Herzon & de Meuron-designed bubble-glass high-rise, is still the highlight of the area. And things only got better, or worse, depending on your point of view, with the opening of the Tadao Ando-designed **Omotesando Hills** in 2005. The brainchild of the corporation behind multi-use mini-city Roppongi Hills (p112), the far smaller Omotesando version is almost entirely devoted to retail, with flashy fashion brands such as YSL and Dolce & Gabbana hogging the bulk of the floorspace. Unless you're heading to one of the posh eateries inside, this monument to Mammon is best experienced from the other side of the street, preferably after dark when the glass panels of its façade emit their chameleon-like ambient glow.

Despite the prevalence of top-tier fashion names, Aoyama is distinctly more accessible than Ginza, with a better nightlife to boot. The tree-lined avenue Omotesando runs through the heart of Harajuku and Aoyama, blurring the boundaries between the teen haven and its grown-up neighbour.

Sights & museums

Gallery 360°

2F, 5-1-27 Minami-Aoyama, Minato-ku (3406 5823/www.360. co.jp). Omotesando station (Chiyoda, Ginza, Hanzomon lines), exit B4. **Open** noon-7pm Tue-Sun. **Map** p75 D3 ㉘
This well-located space emphasises works on paper and multiples by the likes of Lawrence Wiener and Takashi Homma, as well as examining work by Fluxus, Buckminster Fuller and others.

Nadiff

Casa Real B1F, 4-9-8 Jingumae, Shibuya-ku (3403 8814/www.nadiff. com). Omotesando station (Chiyoda, Ginza, Hanzomon lines), exit A2. **Open** 11am-8pm daily. **Map** p75 D2 ㉙

The city's best art bookstore (the flag-ship shop in a chain) has a small gallery showing hot young Japanese artists, often in order to promote their latest book.

Spiral

Spiral Bldg 1F, 5-6-23 Minami-Aoyama, Minato-ku (3498 1171/www.spiral.co. jp). Omotesando station (Chiyoda, Ginza, Hanzomon lines), exit B1. **Open** 11am-8pm daily. Closed 1wk Aug, 1wk Dec-Jan. **Map** p75 D3 ㉚
A ramp spirals around the circular open space at one end of this Fumihiko Maki-designed building, hence its name. A wide range of fashion, art and design shows appears here. There's also a café, bar, interior goods store and record/CD shop.

Watari-Um Museum of Contemporary Art

3-7-6 Jingumae, Shibuya-ku (3402 3001/www.watarium.co.jp). Gaienmae station (Ginza line), exit 3. **Open** 11am-7pm Tue, Thur-Sun; 11am-9pm Wed. **Admission** ¥1,000; ¥800 reductions. No credit cards. **Map** p75 E1/2 ㉛
Mario Botta designed this small art museum for the Watari family in 1990. It holds four exhibitions a year, some of which originate at the museum, while others are brought in from abroad. There's a good art bookshop and a pleasant café in the basement.

Eating & drinking

Le Bretagne

4-9-8 Jingumae, Shibuya-ku, Shibuya-ku (3478 7855/www.le-bretagne.com). Omotesando station (Chiyoda, Ginza, Hanzomon lines), exit A2. **Open** 11am-11pm Mon-Sat; 11am-10pm Sun. **¥¥. French.** English menu. **Map** p75 D2 ㉜
Owner Bertrand Larcher is a native Breton, so it's no surprise that his buck-wheat galettes are authentically tasty. The sweet crêpes are excellent too. So close to swanky Omotesando, Le Bretagne's homely wood-clad interior makes a welcome break from fashion-store façades.

Prada p81

Crayon House Hiroba

*3-8-15 Kita-Aoyama, Minato-ku
(3406 6409/www.crayonhouse.co.jp).
Omotesando station (Chiyoda line),
exit A1; (Ginza, Hanzomon lines),
exit B2.* **Open** 11am-10pm daily. **¥**.
Wholefoods. Map p75 D3 ㉝
Sitting next to a natural food shop,
Crayon House is not exclusively vegetarian, but it does serve up a good
selection of wholesome and well-
prepared dishes, many of them made
with organic ingredients. The place
consists of two mini-restaurants:
Hiroba, offering Japanese food, and
Home, offering Western dishes.

Fumin

*Aoyama Ohara Bldg B1F, 5-7-17
Minami-Aoyama, Minato-ku (3498
4466). Omotesando station (Chiyoda,
Ginza, Hanzomon lines), exit B1.*
Open 11.45am-2.30pm, 6-9.30pm
Mon-Fri; 11.45am-2.30pm, 6-9pm
Sat, Sun. Closed 1st Mon of mth.
¥¥. No credit cards. **Chinese**.
Map p75 E3 ㉞

This much-loved Chinese restaurant
serves home-style cooking, full of
flavour and in generous servings. The
negi (spring onion) wonton, *kaisen
gyoza* (seafood dumplings) and house
special Fumin noodles are so popular
you'll inevitably have to wait in line.

Ghungroo

*Seinan Bldg 2F, 5-6-19 Minami-
Aoyama, Minato-ku (3406 0464/
www.ghungroo-jp.com). Omotesando
station (Chiyoda, Ginza, Hanzomon
lines), exit B1.* **Open** 11.30am-
10.30pm Mon-Thur; 11.30am-11pm
Fri; noon-11pm Sat; noon-9.30pm
Sun. **¥¥**. **Indian**. English menu.
Map p75 D3 ㉟
The closest you can get in Tokyo to an
upscale British-style Indian curry
house, Ghungroo is divided into two
rooms, the inner chamber being the
more inviting. The menu contains few
surprises, but the chicken dishes and
okra curry are especially good. As with
most Indian cooking in Japan, the rice
is Japanese-style short grain.

Harem

*CI Plaza B1, 2-3-1 Kita-Aoyama,
Minato-ku (5786 2929/www.harem.
co.jp). Gaienmae station (Ginza line),
exit 4.* **Open** *11.30am-2.30pm, 5.30-
11pm daily.* ¥¥. **Turkish**. English
menu. **Map** p75 E2 ⑯
After a gap of a year, Harem has made
a welcome return. The atmosphere
here is more refined than at most of
Tokyo's mom-and-pop Turkish eateries, and so is the cuisine. Among the
standouts: the excellent meze, *imam
bayildi* (aubergine) and *hunkar geben-
di* ('His Majesty's favourite') lamb.
Food fit for a sultan.

Kyosho

*Omotesando Hills B3F, 4-12-10
(5785 0280/www.kyoshoshop.com).
Omotesando station (Chiyoda, Ginza,
Hanzomon lines), exit A2.* **Open**
5-9pm daily. **Bar**. **Map** p75 D3 ⑰
Kyosho is a model racing shop whose
back room features a test track with a
bar attached (p79).

Maisen

*4-8-5 Jingumae, Shibuya-ku (3470
0071/http://members.aol.com/maisen
pr). Omotesando station (Chiyoda,
Ginza, Hanzomon lines), exit A2.* **Open**
11am-10pm daily. ¥¥. **Tonkatsu**.
English menu. **Map** p75 D2 ⑱
The main branch of this *tonkatsu* chain
is built around a converted bathhouse.
If you're able to get a seat in the huge
and airy dining room in the back, you'll
notice the telltale signs of the building's
origins: soaring ceilings and a small
garden pond. You can't go wrong with
any of the set meals offered here; standard *rosu katsu* or lean *hire katsu* are
especially good choices.

Natural Harmony Angolo

*3-38-12 Jingumae, Shibuya-ku (3405
8393). Gaienmae station (Ginza line),
exits 2, 3.* **Open** *11.30am-2.30pm,
6-10pm Tue-Sun.* ¥. No credit cards.
Wholefoods. English menu. **Map**
p75 E1 ⑲
This is still Tokyo's best natural-food
restaurant. The no-smoking venue
boasts a simple, wood-clad interior and

an additive-free menu. The food, which
is mostly in a Japanese vein, is tasty,
and although some fish is served, the
ethos is strongly vegetarian.

Pure Café

*5-5-21 Minami-Aoyama, Minato-ku
(5466 2611/www.pure-cafe.com).
Omotesando station (Chiyoda, Ginza,
Hanzomon lines), exit B3.* **Open**
8.30am-10pm daily. ¥. No credit
cards. **Vegetarian**. English menu.
Map p75 E3 ⑳
Pure Café melds its health-conscious,
near-vegan principles with a bright,
contemporary interior (it's part of the
Aveda holistic spa complex). The
menu offers a mix of East and West,
along with organic wines and beer.
Pure Café's early opening hours make
it just the place for a healthy breakfast.

Shopping

A Bathing Ape

*5-5-8 Minami-Aoyama, Minato-ku
(5464 0335/www.bape.com).
Omotesando station (Chiyoda, Ginza,
Hanzomon lines), exit A5.* **Open** *11am-
7pm daily.* **Map** p75 E3 ㉛
Founded by stylist, DJ and entrepre-
neur Nigo in 1993, this pseudo-retro
brand has evolved into the epitome of
Japanese cool. You'll have to hunt for
the entrance; the lack of sign is all part
of maintaining the brand's exclusivity.

Atelier Shinji

*5-6-24 Minami-Aoyama, Minato-ku
(3400 5211/www.ateliershinji.com).
Omotesando station (Chiyoda, Ginza,
Hanzomon lines), exit A5.* **Open** *11am-
8pm Mon-Fri.* **Map** p75 D3 ㉜
This small Aoyama shop, located
behind the Spiral building (p81), sells
the original creations of noted jeweller
Shinji Naoi.

Comme des Garçons

*5-2-1 Minami-Aoyama, Minato-ku
(3406 3951). Omotesando station
(Chiyoda, Ginza, Hanzomon lines),
exit A5.* **Open** *11am-8pm daily.*
Map p75 E3 ㉝
Comme des Garçons' Rei Kawakubo is
one of the pioneers who put Japanese

Spiral p81

designers on the fashion map. The extraordinary exterior of this flagship store beckons the shopper into a maze of psychedelic prints, classically themed suits and smart formal wear. Tax-exemption service available.

Gallery Samurai

Aoyama TIM Bldg 3F, 3-13-20 Minami-Aoyama, Minato-ku (5474 6336/www.nihonto.co.jp). Omotesando station (Chiyoda, Ginza, Hanzomon lines), exits A3, A4. **Open** 11am-7pm daily. **Map** p75 E3 ㊹

A small shop in the heart of Aoyama, crowded with antique swords, guns, armour and helmets, not to mention screens, statues, woodblock prints and less classifiable curios. The staff speak fluent English.

Issey Miyake

3-18-11 Minami-Aoyama, Minato-ku (3423 1407/1408/www.isseymiyake. com). Omotesando station (Chiyoda, Ginza, Hanzomon lines), exit A4. **Open** 11am-8pm daily. **Map** p75 E3 ㊺

Issey Miyake is one of the big three designers, along with Yohji Yamamoto and Rei Kawakubo, who transformed Japanese fashion back in the late 1980s.

In his Tokyo store, you'll find original creations and collaborations between designers and artists that can't be seen anywhere else.

Kampo Boutique Aoyama

3-3-13 Kita-Aoyama, Minato-ku (5775 6932/www.nihondo.co.jp). Omotesando station (Chiyoda, Ginza, Hanzomon lines), exit A4. **Open** 10am-7pm daily. **Map** p75 E2 ㊻

This shop employs the *kampo* method of product development, which uses the principles of traditional Chinese medicine. It sells a wide range of products, including natural cosmetics, health foods and herbal teas.

Loveless

3-17-11 Minami-Aoyama, Minato-ku (3401 2301). Omotesando station (Chiyoda, Ginza, Hanzomon lines), exit A4. **Open** noon-10pm Mon-Sat; noon-8pm Sun. **Map** p75 E3 ㊼

Venture past French luggage-maker Goyard on the ground level, down into the dungeon-like basement floors to see an astounding assortment of wacky fashions, including plenty of upcoming Japanese labels that you won't find anywhere else.

Omotesando Hills

*4-12-10 Jingumae, Shibuya-ku
(3497 0310/www.omotesandohills.com).
Omotesando station (Chiyoda, Ginza,
Hanzomon lines), exit A2.* **Open** *Shops*
11am-9pm Mon-Sat; 11am-8pm Sun.
Restaurants 11am-11pm Mon-Sat;
11am-10pm Sun. **Map** p75 D2 **49**
Another shopping complex from the
people behind Laforet (p78) and
Roppongi Hills (p112), this Tadao
Ando-designed centre fails to inspire
design- or shop-wise. Highlights inside
include a sake boutiqe and a café by
popular Japanese confectioners Toraya.

Undercover

*Unimat Bleu Cinq Point Bldg,
5-3-18 Minami-Aoyama, Minato-ku
(3407 1232). Omotesando station
(Chiyoda, Ginza, Hanzomon lines),
exit A5.* **Open** 11am-8pm daily.
Map p75 E3 **49**
Undercover designer Jun Takahashi
commands a fanatically loyal army of
punk fashion rebels who adore his
edgy clothes. Enter his unsettling
world at this store and experience his
artistic side at the gallery-cum-store
Zamiang in the basement.

Yohji Yamamoto

*5-3-6 Minami-Aoyama, Minato-ku
(3409 6006/www.yohjiyamamoto.co.jp).
Omotesando station (Chiyoda, Ginza,
Hanzomon lines), exit A5.* **Open**
11am-8pm daily. **Map** p75 E3 **50**
Paragon of conceptual fashion Yohji
Yamamoto remains hugely respected
by style commentators worldwide.
This store not only stocks the dark, billowing creations on which his reputation was founded, but also Y-3, his
sportswear collaboration with Adidas.

Nightlife

Blue Note Tokyo

*Raika Bldg, 6-3-16 Minami-Aoyama,
Minato-ku (5485 0088/www.bluenote.
co.jp). Omotesando station (Chiyoda,
Ginza, Hanzomon lines), exit B3.* **Open**
Shows from 7pm & 9.30pm Mon-Sat;
from 6.30pm & 9pm Sun. **Admission**
¥6,000-¥10,000. **Map** p75 E3 **51**

The largest jazz club in Tokyo – with
prices to match – is part of the international Blue Note chain and well
supported by the music industry. Jazz,
Latin, world and soul acts all appear.
Expect short sets, expensive food and
strangers sharing your dining table,
but the quality of international talent
keeps the crowds coming.

Cay

*Spiral Bldg B1F, 5-6-23 Minami-
Aoyama, Minato-ku (3498 5790).
Omotesando station (Chiyoda,
Ginza, Hanzomon lines), exit B1.*
Map p75 D3 **52**
An unremarkable restaurant that regularly turns into a great live venue. Cay
is located in the Spiral building (p81),
a centre for contemporary arts and
design. The music matches the setting,
with new electronica and world music-
influenced and 'fusion' acts.

Mix

*B1F, 3-6-19 Kita-Aoyama, Minato-ku
(3797 1313/www.at-mix.com).
Omotesando station (Chiyoda, Ginza,
Hanzomon lines), exits A1, B4.* **Open**
10pm-5am; days vary. **Admission**
¥2,000-¥2,500. No credit cards. **Map**
p75 D3 **53**
This tiny, narrow club is usually
rammed at the weekends and has been
that way for over a decade. Expect a
mixed, friendly crowd grooving to
sounds that tend towards reggae, dub,
hip hop and dancehall.

Velours

NEW *Almost Blue B1, 6-4-6 Minami-
Aoyama (5778 4777/www.velours.jp).
Omotesando station (Chiyoda, Ginza,
Hanzomon lines), exit B3.* **Open**
10.45pm-4am Wed; varies Fri; 11pm-
4am Sat. **Admission** ¥2,000-¥3,500.
Map p75 E3 **54**
Tokyo's extravagant 1980s get a rerun
at this new club, where crystal chandeliers and antique French furnishings
try to disguise the narrow dimensions.
The swanky setting makes it popular
for unashamedly glitzy events by the
likes of *Dazed & Confused* magazine
and various fashion brands.

TOKYO BY AREA

Kanda Yabu Soba p95

Marunouchi

Marunouchi, meaning 'within the moat or castle walls', is Tokyo proper. It's the home of the **Imperial Palace**, the site of Tokyo's geographical zero marker **Nihonbashi** (see box p97) and the centre of the capital's financial and political activity. More recently it has also become a consumer centre, with numerous high-rise shopping and dining complexes popping up.

For tourists the big draw is still the Imperial Palace, home of the Japanese royals since 1868. Although the main grounds are out of bounds for all but two days a year (Jan 2, Dec 23), the **East Gardens** are well worth a wander, and there are plenty of photo-ops from the outside. Much to the dismay of the Imperial household, you can also now get a good peek from the neighbouring skyscrapers,

although most of the vantage points have been leased as office space.

The other major sight in the area is the notorious **Yasukini Shrine** and its adjacent war museum, the **Yushukan**. As both the national war memorial and home to the souls of 14 Class A war criminals, the shrine has become a focal point for nationalists. Nonetheless, it's an impressive shrine set in spacious grounds that include a Noh theatre and sumo ring.

Locals have been lured here by the revamped **Naka Dori**, lined with big foreign brand boutiques, and a pair of more affordable high-rises, the **Marunouchi Building** and **Shin Marunouchi Building**. As the area abuts the consumer frenzy of Ginza, it's best to approach it as a respite from, rather than an extension of, your spending.

Sights & museums

Bank of Japan

2-1-1 Nihonbashi-Hongokucho, Chuo-ku (English tours 3279 1111/www.boj.or. jp). Mitsukoshimae station (Ginza, Hanzomon lines), exits A8, B1. **Tours** (1hr; book 1wk ahead) 9.45am, 11am, 1.30pm, 3pm Mon-Fri. **Admission** free. **Map** p89 E3 ❶

The Bank of Japan has two buildings, descriptively named Old and New. The New Building is where the banking activities occur, and the Old Building... well, just looks nice. The first Western-style construction by Japanese builders, the Old Building is said to be modelled on London's Bank of England.

Base Gallery

Koura Bldg 1 1F, 1-1-6 Nihonbashi-Kayabacho, Chuo-ku (5623 6655/ www.basegallery.com). Kayabacho station (Hibiya, Tozai lines), exits 7, 8; or Nihonbashi station (Asakusa, Ginza, Tozai lines), exit D2. **Open** 11am-7pm Mon-Sat. **Map** p89 F4 ❷

This well-established space represents blue-chip contemporary Japanese artists, such as painter Ohtake Shinro, and younger names, including photographer Yokozawa Tsukasa.

Bridgestone Museum of Art

1-10-1 Kyobashi, Chuo-ku (3563 0241/ www.bridgestone-museum.gr.jp). Tokyo station (Yamanote, Chuo, Marunouchi, Sobu lines), Yaesu (central) exit. **Open** 10am-8pm Tue-Sat; 10am-6pm Sun. **Admission** ¥800; ¥500-¥600 reductions. **Map** p89 E4 ❸

Ishibashi Shojiro, founder of the giant Bridgestone Corporation, wheeled his private collection into this museum back in 1952. Impressionism, European modernism and Japanese Western-style paintings form the core holdings, but exhibitions can cover genres ranging from Ancient Greek to 20th-century abstraction.

Communications Museum

2-3-1 Otemachi, Chiyoda-ku (3244 6811). Otemachi station (Chiyoda, Hanzomon, Marunouchi, Mita, Tozai lines), exit A5. **Open** 9am-4.30pm Tue-Sun. **Admission** ¥110; ¥50 reductions. **Map** p89 D3 ❹

This massive museum relays the histories of national public broadcasting company NHK, telecom giant NTT and the defunct Post & Telecommunications Ministry. Philatelists can view 280,000 old and new stamps from around the world. Children can race post-office motorbikes in a video game, compare international postboxes and ogle a room-sized mail sorter. On the telecoms floor, ample interactive displays teach visitors how the telephone works.

Currency Museum

1-3-1 Nihonbashi-Hongokucho, Chuo-ku (3277 3037/www.imes.boj.or.jp/cm/ english_htmls/index.htm). Mitsukoshimae station (Ginza, Hanzomon lines), exits A5, B1. **Open** 9.30am-4.30pm Tue-Sun. Closed 5, 6 Mar. **Tours** (1hr) 1.30pm Tue, Thur. **Admission** free. **Map** p89 E3 ❺

Run by the Bank of Japan, this museum traces the long history of local money, from the use of imported Chinese coins in the 12th century to the creation of the yen and the central bank in the second half of the 19th century. There are also occupation-era notes from Indonesia and the Philippines, Siberian leather money and Thai leech coins. Or get the feel for some serious dosh by lifting ¥100 million (about the size of two phone books), safely stored inside a perspex box.

Idemitsu Museum of Arts

Tei Geki Bldg 9F, 3-1-1 Marunouchi, Chiyoda-ku (3213 9404/www.idemitsu. co.jp/museum). Hibiya station (Chiyoda, Hibiya, Mita lines), exit B3. **Open** 10am-5pm Tue-Thur, Sat, Sun; 10am-7pm Fri. **Admission** ¥800; free-¥500 reductions. No credit cards. **Map** p88 C5 ❻

Sazo Idemitsu collected traditional Chinese and Japanese art for more than 70 years. This museum (opened in 1966) features displays drawn from a respected permanent collection of ceramics, calligraphy and painting. Good view of the Imperial Palace too.

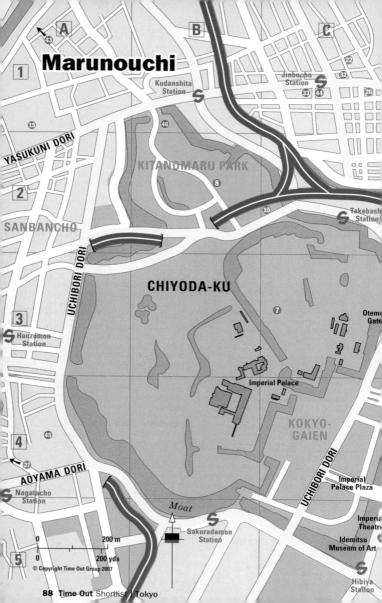

Marunouchi

A
43
1

B

C
22
32

Kudanshita
Station
S

Jinbocho
Station
S
33 44
26

15
YASUKUNI DORI

46

KITANOMARU PARK

8

SANBANCHO

2

10

Takebashi
Station
S

UCHIBORI DORI

CHIYODA-KU

7

Otema
Gate

Hanzomon
Station
S
3

Imperial Palace

4
45

KOKYO-
GAIEN

27
AOYAMA DORI

Nagatacho
Station
S

UCHIBORI DORI

Imperial
Palace Plaza

Moat

Sakuradamon
Station
S

Imperia
Theatre

Idemitsu
Museum of Art

0   200 m
0   200 yds
© Copyright Time Out Group 2007

5

Hibiya
Station
S

D   E   F

Akihabara JR Station

🟦 Akihabara Station

1

🟦 Sights & museums
🟦 Eating & drinking
🟦 Shopping
🟦 Nightlife
🟦 Arts & leisure

23   14

YASUKUNI DORI   19

42

Awajicho Station   🟦

Kanda Station   🟦

KANDA TSHIKICHO

HONGO DORI

Kanda JR Station

UGHIKANDA

CHUO DORI

Kodenmacho Station   🟦   2

CHUO-KU

Otemachi Station   🟦

OTEMACHI

4

Otemachi Station   🟦

1   24   29

Mitsukoshi

🟦   5

🟦 Mitsukoshimae Station

3

35

Tokyo Station

Nihonbashi Station   🟦

13

MARUNOUCHI   37   🟦

NAKA DORI

Tokyo Station   🟦

12

Daimaru

31

Maruzen Bookstore

9

39

Takashimaya

38

Chuo Police Station   🟦   4   2

18   30

HIBIYA DORI

Marunouchi Building

34

✉   Central Post Office

Pokemon Center   36

SOTOBORI DORI

CHUO DORI

Pokemon Center   36

NIHONBASHI

YAESU

SHOWA DORI

Kayabacho Station

TCVB Tourist Office
i

40

25 20   28

Tokyo International Forum

11   17

21   Kyobashi Station   🟦   KYOBASHI

16   3

Bridgestone Museum of Art

Yurakucho Station   🟦

National Film Centre

SHIN OHASHI DORI

Hatchobori Station   🟦

5

Imperial Palace East Gardens (Kokyo Higashi Gyoen)

Chiyoda, Chiyoda-ku. Otemachi station (Chiyoda, Hanzomon, Marunouchi, Mita, Tozai lines), exits C10, C13B. **Open** 9am-4.30pm daily. **Admission** free; token collected at gate to be submitted on leaving. **Map** p88 C3 ❼

The main park of the Imperial Palace is accessible through three ancient gates: Otemon (which is five minutes from Tokyo station), Hirakawamon (close to the Takebashi bridge) and Kita-Hanebashimon (not far from Kitanomaru Park). There are few historical features in the manicured park, except for two old watch-houses, the remains of the old dungeon at the northern end and a wall of hand-carved stones dropping a great height into the water. There's also the small Museum of Imperial Collections.

Japan Science Foundation Science Museum (Kagaku Gijutsukan)

2-1 Kitanomaru Koen, Chiyoda-ku (3212 8544/www.jsf.or.jp). Kudanshita station (Hanzomon, Shinjuku, Tozai lines), exit 2; or Takebashi station (Tozai line), exit 1A. **Open** 9.30am-4.50pm daily. **Admission** ¥600; ¥250-¥400 reductions. No credit cards. **Map** p88 B2 ❽

This museum takes to extremes the maxim 'learning by doing'. The unique five-spoke building, in a corner of Kitanomaru Park, consists of five floors of interactive exhibits. Its drab, dated entrance belies the fun displays inside. Children can learn the rudiments of scientific principles while standing inside a huge soap bubble, lifting a small car using pulleys and generating electricity by shouting. There's not a lot of English used in the museum, but much of the interaction requires no translation.

Kite Museum

Taimeiken 5F, 1-12-10 Nihonbashi, Chuo-ku (3275 2704/www.tako.gr.jp). Nihonbashi station (Asakusa, Ginza, Tozai lines), exit A4, C5. **Open** 11am-

5pm Mon-Sat. **Admission** ¥200; ¥100 reductions. No credit cards. **Map** p89 F4 ❾

A cornucopia of kites, including one made of Indonesian dried leaves, a giant woodblock-print samurai and a huge styrofoam iron. The former owner of the first-floor restaurant (one of Tokyo's earliest forays into Western-style dining) spent a lifetime collecting the 2,000 kites now layering the walls, packing display cases and crowding the ceiling. Don't expect detailed explanations of the exhibits; this is more of a private hobby on public display. The museum is not clearly marked – look for the long white sign on the building.

National Museum of Modern Art

3-1 Kitanomaru Koen, Chiyoda-ku (5777 8600/www.momat.go.jp/english/index.html). Takebashi station (Tozai line), exits 1A, 1B. **Open** *Art Museum* 10am-5pm Tue-Thur, Sat, Sun; 10am-8pm Fri. *Crafts Gallery* 10am-5pm Tue-Sun. **Admission** ¥420; free-¥130 reductions. Free 3 Nov, 1st Sun of mth. No credit cards. **Map** p88 C4 ❿

This is an alternative-history MoMA, one consisting mostly of Japanese art since the turn of the 20th century. Noteworthy features of the permanent collection are portraits by early Japanese modernist Ryusei Kishida and grim wartime paintings by Tsuguharu Fujita. Its location next to the moat and walls of the Imperial Palace makes it a prime stop for viewing springtime cherry blossoms and autumn foliage. Nearby is the Crafts Gallery, an impressive 1910 European-style brick building, once the base for the Imperial Palace guards.

Tokyo International Forum

3-5-1 Marunouchi, Chiyoda-ku (3286 6716/http://paper.cup.com/forum). Yurakucho station (Yamanote line), Tokyo International Forum exit; (Yurakucho line), exit A4B. **Open** 10am-8pm daily. **Map** p89 D5 ⓫

Rafael Vinoly's stunning landmark convention and performance centre is an architectural highlight of the area.

Imperial Palace East Gardens

The halls, including one with a 5,000 capacity, offer superb acoustics. The building also houses a gallery showcasing contemporary Japanese objets d'art, arts and crafts.

Tokyo Station Gallery

Inside Tokyo station, 1-9-1 Marunouchi, Chiyoda-ku (3212 2485/www.ejrcf. or.jp). Tokyo station (Yamanote, Chuo, Marunouchi, Sobu lines). **Open** 10am-7pm Tue-Fri; 10am-6pm Sat, Sun. **Admission** ¥600; free-¥400 reductions. No credit cards. **Map** p89 D4 ⑫

Your JR train ticket helps to support this small museum, run by East Japan Railways and located inside sprawling Tokyo station, near the Marunouchi central entrance. The station's aged brick walls aren't a traditional backdrop for paintings, but they do offer a look into the past. With no permanent collections, the museum brings in shows from around Japan and the rest of the world.

Tokyo Stock Exchange (Tokyo Shoken Torihiki Sho)

2-1 Nihonbashi-Kabutocho, Chuo-ku (3665 1881/www.tse.or.jp). Kayabacho station (Hibiya, Tozai lines), exit 11. **Open** 9am-4.30pm Mon-Fri. **Tours** (English) 1.30pm daily. **Admission** free. **Map** p89 F4 ⑬

Sadly, you won't be able to witness much wailing and gnashing of teeth here, since the Tokyo Stock Exchange (TSE), home to global giants such as Toyota and Sony, abolished its trading floor back in 1999. Nowadays the building is eerily quiet, the former trading floor taken over by a huge glass cylinder with real-time stock prices revolving at the top. To catch what little action is left, visit on a weekday during trading hours (9-11am, 12.30-3pm). The guided tour lasts around 40 minutes and includes a 20-minute video that explains the history and function of the TSE.

Transportation Museum (Kotsu Hakubutsukan)

1-25 Kanda-Sudacho, Chiyoda-ku (3251 8481/www.kouhaku.or.jp). Akihabara station (Yamanote, Hibiya lines), Electric Town exit. **Open** 9.30am-5pm Tue-Sun. **Admission** ¥310; ¥150 reductions. No credit cards. **Map** p89 E1 ⑭

From rickshaws to rockets, this large museum is a compendium of land, sea, air and space transport. It began life as a railway museum in 1921, and that section is where you'll still find the kids. See how Tokyo's JR lines start their day in a massive model railway set-up. Virtually drive a Yamanote-line train through Tokyo in a real conductor car, or change antique switching lights from red to green. The museum has the first train used in Japan – an 1872 steam locomotive – and the latest, an experimental mag-lev system.

Yasukuni Shrine & Yushukan War-Dead Memorial Museum

3-1-1 Kudankita, Chiyoda-ku (3261 8326/www.yasukuni.or.jp). Kudanshita station (Hanzomon, Shinjuku, Tozai lines), exits 1, 3; or Ichigaya station (Chuo, Nanboku, Shinjuku, Sobu, Yurakucho lines), exits A3, A4. **Open** *Grounds 6am-5pm daily. Museum 9am-5pm daily.* **Admission** *Shrine free. Museum ¥800; ¥300-¥500 reductions.* No credit cards. **Map** p88 A1 ⓯

Yasukuni, one of Tokyo's grandest shrines, is also the nation's most controversial landmark. It houses the souls of almost 2.5 million war dead, but 14 in particular have brought the shrine notoriety – the Class A war criminals from World War II. The neighbouring Yushukan war museum stokes the flames with an intriguing take on historic events, arguing, for example, that the Russo-Japanese War (1904-5) inspired Mahatma Gandhi, and suggesting that the Pearl Harbor attack saved the US economy.

Zeit-Foto Salon

Matsumoto Bldg 4F, 1-10-5 Kyobashi, Chuo-ku (3535 7188/www.zeit-foto.com). Tokyo station (Yamanote, Marunouchi lines), Yaesu exit; or Kyobashi station (Ginza line), exit B6. **Open** 10.30am-6.30pm Tue-Fri; 10.30am-5.30pm Sat. Closed 1wk Aug, 2wks Dec-Jan. **Map** p89 E4 ⓰

This space behind the Bridgestone Museum of Art (p87) claims to be the first photography gallery in Japan

(it opened its doors back in 1978). It's certainly one of the strongest, with over 3,000 works in its possession. Expect inspired, reliable and wide-ranging exhibitions by both Japanese and international photographers.

Eating & drinking

Aroyna Tabeta

3-7-11 Marunouchi, Chiyoda-ku (5219 6099/www.tabeta.com/urakucho). Tokyo station (Yamanote, Marunouchi lines), Tokyo Forum exit. **Open** 11am-10.30pm Mon-Sat; 11am-10pm Sun. **¥**. No credit cards. **Thai**. English menu. **Map** p89 D5 ⓱

Nowhere in Tokyo makes Thai street food that's as authentic and cheap as at this funky little diner. Simple set meals (including curries, fried noodles and the house speciality, braised pork) are just ¥630 each: a veritable bargain, especially for this upwardly mobile stretch of the city.

Bar de España Muy

Tokyo Bldg Tokia 2F, 2-3-3 Marunouchi, Chiyoda-ku (5224 6161/http://r.gnavi.co.jp/a634205). Tokyo station (Yamanote, Marunouchi lines), Marunouchi south exit. **Open** 11.30am-2.30pm, 5.30-11pm Mon-Fri; 11.30am-4pm, 5.30-11pm Sat, Sun. **¥¥**. **Tapas**. **Map** p89 D4 ⓲

Chic and contemporary Barcelona-style tapas served in a setting of steel, glass and polished wood. The bar runs half the length of the building, giving brilliant views over the passing trains as you sip cava and nibble *albondigas*, freshly made mini-tortillas or ink-black paella. The small outdoor terrace looks up at the dramatic International Forum (p90).

Botan

1-15 Kanda-Sudacho, Chiyoda-ku (3251 0577). Kanda station (Yamanote line), east exit; (Ginza line), exits 5, 6; Awajicho station (Marunouchi line), exit A3; or Ogawamachi station (Shinjuku line), exit A3. **Open** 11.30am-8pm Mon-Sat. **¥¥¥**. No credit cards. **Sukiyaki**. **Map** p89 E1 ⓳

Marunouchi's makeover

For years, the Marunouchi exit of Tokyo Station was a pretty, if scruffy, gateway to the Imperial Palace. And not much else. The station's red-brick façade – a postwar reconstruction based loosely on the fire-bombed 1914 original – led on to a plaza littered with stubby, anonymous buildings hardly warranting a second look.

Marunouchi's emergence as a playground for upwardly mobile retail junkies has changed all that. A black-steel behemoth called the **Shin Marunouchi Building** (p98) is the most recent addition to the area's thicket of skyscrapers.

Even Japan Railways caught the renovation bug, with plans to restore Tokyo station (the nearest thing Tokyo has to Edwardian elegance) to its prewar glory and adapt the century-old design to modern earthquake regulations. Due for completion in 2011, the renovation is part of a larger project that sees both sides of the station compete in a tug-of-war to attract commuters and the golden goose of Japanese retail – young, fashion-conscious women.

The Yaesu exit's **Daimaru** department store (p96) gave it a magnetic hold on them, but this has been weakened – if not completely broken – by the **Marunouchi Building** (pictured; p96) and its recently added companion the Shin Marunouchi Building on the other side. Its airy interior, glass atrium, international cuisine and upscale supermarket have proved a winning formula.

Mitsubishi Real Estate, the architect of the Marunouchi revival, also provided the **Tokia Building**, which includes a nightclub (p99), Belgian bistro and day-care centre, and the **Oazo** complex (p96), another glass atrium-based temple to Mammon.

All this activity has been warmly received by all but one local. Between 1919 and 1963 it was illegal to construct anything taller than 31 metres in the vicinity of the **Imperial Palace** (p90). Even after that law was repealed, public and imperial pressure prevented any structures from overlooking the palace grounds. The 20-metre camphor trees that sit atop the palace's stone walls were a response to the construction in 2003 of the Marunouchi Building – the first to offer a view of the residence. According to the press, the latest addition has also drawn complaints, on the grounds that restaurants on upper floors of the palace side of the Shin Marunouchi Building represent an invasion of privacy and an Imperial security hazard.

Tokyo station

There's only one thing on Botan's menu, chicken sukiyaki, served in the old style. You'll be well taken care of by matrons dressed in kimonos, who bring glowing charcoal to your table-top grill, set a small iron dish on top of it and then begin cooking: chicken, onion, tofu and vegetables, all simmering in the delicious, rich, sweet house sauce. The classic wooden premises adds to the charm.

Brasserie aux Amis

Shin-Tokyo Bldg 1F, 3-3-1 Marunouchi, Chiyoda-ku (6212 1566/www.aux amis.com/brasserie). Tokyo station (Yamanote, Marunouchi lines), Marunouchi exit; or Yurakucho station (Yamanote, Yurakucho lines), International Forum exit. **Open** 11am-2pm, 6-10.30pm Mon-Fri; 11am-2pm, 5.30-9.30pm Sat, Sun. **¥¥. Brasserie. Map** p89 D5 ⑳

A slice of Paris in Marunouchi, right down to the red banquettes, brass fittings and menu chalked on the large wall mirrors. There's a small bar by the door, for a quick espresso or a glass of *vin ordinaire*, as well as a top-notch wine list to go with the authentically hearty brasserie food.

Dhaba India

2-7-9 Yaesu, Chuo-ku (3272 7160/ www.dhabaindia.com). Kyobashi station (Ginza line), exit 5. **Open** 11.15am-3pm, 5-11pm Mon-Fri; noon-3pm, 5-10pm Sat, Sun. **¥¥. Indian.** English menu. **Map** p89 E5 ㉑

The best Indian food in town. Modest and unpretentious, this is one of the few places where you can find South Indian specialities. Delicious masala dosas, curries and thali meals, served with real basmati rice (evenings only), prepared by ever-friendly staff from the subcontinent.

Ieyasu Hon-jin

1-30 Kanda-Jinbocho, Chiyoda-ku (3291 6228). Jinbocho station (Hanzomon, Mita, Shinjuku lines), exit A7. **Open** 5-10pm Mon-Fri. **¥¥.** No credit cards. **Yakitori. Map** p88 C1 ㉒

This cosy, top-class *yakitori* bar, named after the first of the Tokugawa shoguns, has only a dozen seats, so everyone crowds around the counter. The food is excellent, as is the beer and sake, which amiable owner Taisho dispenses with natural flair, pouring into small cups from a great height. Avoid the 6-8pm after-work rush and don't go in a group of more than three.

Kanda Yabu Soba

2-10 Kanda-Awajicho, Chiyoda-ku (3251 0287). Kanda station (Yamanote, Ginza lines), exits 5, 6; Ogawamachi station (Shinjuku line), exit A3; or Awajicho station (Marunouchi line), exit A3. **Open** 11.30am-8pm daily. **¥**. **Soba**. Map p89 E1 ㉓
Like a living museum dedicated to the traditional art of the buckwheat noodle, Kanda Yabu Soba dishes up excellent soba in a low Japanese house furnished with *shoji* screens, tatami and woodblock prints.

Mandarin Bar

NEW *Mandarin Oriental Hotel 37F, 2-1-1 Nihonbashi-Muromachi, Chuo-ku (3270 8800/www.mandarinoriental. com). Mitsukoshimae station (Ginza line), exit A7.* **Open** 11.30am-midnight daily. **Bar**. Map p89 E3 ㉔
Oozing sophistication, this spacious lounge and counter bar serves inventive cocktails. Plush seating, perfect service and a view that stretches to Mount Fuji help make this a candidate for Tokyo's best hotel bar. See box p175.

Marunouchi Café

Shin Tokyo Bldg 1F, 3-3-1 Marunouchi, Chiyoda-ku (3212 5025/www.marunouchicafe.com). Yurakucho station (Yamanote line), Tokyo International Forum exit; (Yurakucho line), exit A1; or Nijubashimae station (Chiyoda line), exit B7. **Open** 8am-9pm Mon-Fri; 11am-8pm Sat, Sun. **¥**. No credit cards. **Café**. Map p89 D5 ㉕
If the Japanese coffee shop is essentially a place to hang out, this popular innovator could be a glimpse of a new, low-cost future. Connoisseurs may not care for canned coffee dispensed from

vending machines, but it's difficult to argue with the price (¥120). Internet access and magazines are available.

Mironga

1-3 Kanda-Jinbocho, Chiyoda-ku (3295 1716). Jinbocho station (Hanzomon, Mita, Shinjuku lines), exit A7. **Open** 10.30am-10.30pm Mon-Fri; 11.30am-6.30pm Sat, Sun. **¥**. No credit cards. **Café**. Map p88 C1 ㉖
Probably the only place in Tokyo where non-stop (recorded) tango provides seductive old-style accompaniment to the liquid refreshments. Argentina's finest exponents of the dance feature in the impressive array of fading monochromes on the walls, and there's also a selection of printed works on related subjects lining the bookshelves. Of the two rooms, the larger and darker gets the nod for atmosphere. As well as a wide range of coffees, Mironga proffers good import beers and reasonable food.

Shisen Hanten

Zenkoku Ryokan Kaikan 5F-6F, 2-5-5 Hirakawa-cho, Chiyoda-ku (3263 9371/ http://szechwan.jp). Nagatacho station (Hanzomon, Nanboku, Yurakucho lines), exit 5. **Open** 11.30am-2pm, 5-10pm daily. **¥¥¥**. **Chinese**. English menu. Map p88 A4 ㉗
Good Szechuan cuisine, albeit with the spices toned down for Japanese palates, from chef Kenichi Shin, best known for his appearances in the Iron Chef TV cooking shows. His classic dish is *mapo-dofu* (spicy minced meat with tofu), but in summer queues form for his *hiyashi chuka* (chilled Chinese-style noodles and chopped vegetables topped with sesame or vinegar sauce).

Takara

Tokyo International Forum B1 Concourse, 3-5-1 Marunouchi, Chiyoda-ku (5223 9888/www.t-i-forum.co.jp/ general/guide/shops/takara/index.php). Tokyo station (Yamanote, Marunouchi lines), Tokyo Forum exit. **Open** 11.30am-2.30pm, 5-11pm Mon-Fri; 11.30am-3pm, 5-10pm Sat, Sun. **¥¥¥**. **Izakaya**. English menu. Map p89 D5 ㉘

TOKYO BY AREA

Takara offers welcome sanctuary in amongst the echoing concrete of the International Forum's basement. The food is reliable – standard modern *izakaya* fare, bolstered with a few Spanish-style tapas – but the main draw here is the brilliant selection of sake, plus fine microbrewed ales and a better-than-expected wine list. The place also serves good set lunches.

Tapas Molecular Bar

NEW *Mandarin Oriental Hotel 38F, 2-1-1 Nihonbashi-Muromachi, Chuo-ku (3270 8800/www.mandarinoriental. com). Mitsukoshimae station (Ginza, Hanzomon lines), exit A8.* **Open** 6pm, 8pm (reservations only). **¥¥¥¥. Tapas.** English menu. **Map** p89 E3 ㉙

Tokyo's first outpost of molecular gastronomy, high up in the Mandarin Oriental tower. It's no rival to Spain's El Bulli or the UK's Fat Duck in either scale or creativity, but it's still remarkable culinary theatre, watching as your food – 25 courses or more – emerges from syringes or super-chilled distilling retorts. With only seven seats and two sittings per night, reservations need to be made well in advance.

Shopping

American Pharmacy

Marunouchi Bldg B1F, 2-4-1 Marunouchi, Chiyoda-ku (5220 7716/www.tomods.jp). Tokyo station (Yamanote, Chuo lines), Shin Marubiru, south exits; (Marunouchi line), Marunouchi Bldg exit. **Open** 9am-9pm Mon-Fri; 10am-9pm Sat; 10am-8pm Sun. **Map** p89 D4 ㉚

Popular among expats for its imported over-the-counter drugs, cosmetics and snacks, American Pharmacy also stocks English-language magazines.

Daimaru

1-9-1 Marunouchi, Chiyoda-ku (3212 8011/www.daimaru.co.jp/english/tokyo. html). Tokyo station (Yamanote, Chuo lines), Yaesu (central) exit; (Marunouchi line), exits 1, 2. **Open** 10am-9pm Mon-Fri; 10am-8pm Sat, Sun. **Map** p89 E4 ㉛

Far from the most glamourous department store in town, Daimaru has the advantage of a prime location inside Tokyo station. Japanese souvenirs are on the seventh and tenth, and an art museum on the 12th opens sporadically.

Ebisu-Do Gallery

Kamesawa Bldg 2F, 1-12 Kanda-Jinbocho, Chiyoda-ku (3219 7651/ www.ebisu-do.com). Jinbocho station (Hanzomon, Mita, Shinjuku lines), exit A5. **Open** 11am-6.30pm Mon-Sat. **Map** p88 C1 ㉜

Ebisu-do sells original *ukiyo-e* prints (from around ¥20,000) and reproductions (from ¥3,000) by masters such as Hiroshige, Hokusai and Harunobu.

Hara Shobo

2-3 Kanda-Jinbocho, Chiyoda-ku (5212 7801/www.harashobo.com). Jinbocho station (Hanzomon, Mita, Shinjuku lines), exit A6. **Open** 10am-6pm Tue-Sat. **Map** p88 C1 ㉝

Hara Shobo sells all kinds of woodblock prints, both old and new. The company issues a catalogue, *Edo Geijitsu* ('Edo Art'), twice a year. The staff here speak good English.

Marunouchi Building

2-4-1 Marunouchi, Chiyoda-ku (5218 5100/www.marubiru.jp/index2.html). Tokyo station (Yamanote, Chuo lines), Shin Marubiru exit; (Marunouchi line), exit 5. **Open** *Shops* 11am-9pm Mon-Sat; 11am-8pm Sun. *Restaurants* 11am-11pm Mon-Sat; 11am-10pm Sun. **Map** p89 D4 ㉞

Essentially an office tower, 'Marubiru' (as it is affectionately known) devotes its first four floors and basement to a 'Shopping Zone', while the fifth, sixth, 35th and 36th belong to the 'Restaurant Zone'. The basement food hall focuses on big-name gourmet products.

Oazo

1-6-4 Marunouchi, Chiyoda-ku (5218 5100/www.oazo.jp). Tokyo station (Yamanote, Chuo lines), Marunouchi north exit; (Marunouchi line), exits 10, 12, 14. **Open** *Shops* 11am-9pm daily. *Restaurants* 11am-11pm daily. **Map** p89 D3/4 ㉟

Highway from hell

The road that obscures an icon.

Nihonbashi, or 'Bridge of Japan', is a national icon that has been popping up in Japanese art and literature for centuries. It dates back to 1603, when shogun Tokugawa Ieyasu built a wooden crossing that marked the starting point of the city's five key trading routes, including the pilgrimage to Kyoto. The original wood is long gone, replaced with a stone version in 1911, but the bridge is still considered the capital's nucleus. When road signs give distances to Tokyo, they are referring specifically to these Renaissance-style arches.

The bridge also once offered a view of that other great emblem of Japan: Mount Fuji. But in the mid 1960s, with over a quarter of a million people migrating to the capital each year and the city gearing up to host the Olympic Games, a rush to improve the city's infrastructure saw overhead expressways pop up across Tokyo, including one that ran directly above the much-loved landmark.

It must have seemed a good idea at the time, but these days the overpass obscuring this designated 'cultural asset' is stirring up a serious debate. Local business leaders began campaigning for removal of the unsightly expressway, and the issue reached the cabinet in 2005, with then-prime minister Junichiro Koizumi endorsing a plan to move the thoroughfare underground at an estimated cost of between ¥500 billion and ¥1 trillion.

Tokyo governor Shintaro Ishihara opposes the plan, arguing it would be a waste of public money. In typically candid style he suggested that if people cared so much about this little bridge they should shift it to another river. Unsentimental as it may be, his stance grows more and more persuasive as central Tokyo's skyline rises ever higher, and scenic views grow rarer.

To see the classic bridge and its overhead companion, travel on the Ginza line to Mitsukoshimae station and take exit B6.

Oazo p96

This gleaming glass complex of shops, restaurants and offices opposite Tokyo station is affiliated to the nearby Marunouchi Building. Pride of place goes to Maruzen's multi-storey flagship bookstore (with a decent-sized English-language section). You can also find the Japan Aerospace Exploration Agency's showroom here.

Pokemon Center

3-2-5 Nihonbashi, Chuo-ku (5200 0707/www.pokemoncenter-online.com). Nihonbashi station (Asakusa line), exit D3; (Ginza, Tozai lines), exits B1, B2; or Tokyo station (Yamanote, Chuo, Marunouchi lines), Yaesu (north) exit. **Open** 10am-7pm daily. **Map** p89 E4 ⊛
'Pocket Monster' may have lost ground to Yu-Gi-Oh! and a variety of other games, but Pikachu's furry yellow paw still has an iron grip on Japanese pop culture. Come and see the monster-masters' central Tokyo stronghold.

Shin Marunouchi Building

NEW *1-5-1 Marunouchi, Chiyoda-ku (5218 5100/www.shinmaru.jp). Tokyo station (Yamanote, Chuo lines), Maru-nouchi Central exit; (Marunouchi line), adjoins station.* **Open** *Shops* 11am-9pm Mon-Sat; 11am-8pm Sun. *Restaurants* 11am-11pm Mon-Sat; 11am-10pm Sun. **Map** p89 D4 ⊛
No real suprises in the latest shopping/restaurant/office tower, but there are seven floors of fashion, food and cosmetics to peruse in a swank setting. Trendy hat-makers CA4LA have an outlet on the first floor, while the basement includes a 'milk boutique' and Point et Ligne, the city's most expensive bakery, selling loaves in a setting that feels as though it should have a DJ playing impeccable French house in the corner.

Takashimaya

2-4-1 Nihonbashi, Chuo-ku (3211 4111/ www.takashimaya.co.jp). Nihonbashi station (Asakusa line), exit D3; (Ginza, Tozai lines), exits B1, B2. **Open** 10am-8pm daily. **Map** p89 E4 ⊛
There's plenty of fashion and furniture on the upper floors, but the best place to browse is the basement, where a stellar gourmet grocery selection awaits.

Yamamoto Yama

2-5-2 Nihonbashi, Chuo-ku (3281 0010/ www.yamamotoyama.co.jp). Nihonbashi station (Asakusa line), exit D3; (Ginza,

Tozai lines), exit B4. **Open** 9.30am-7pm daily. **Map** p89 E4 ㊴
A branch of a citywide chain, this shop sells a wide selection of Japanese and Chinese teas and implements for *sado*, the tea ceremony.

Nightlife

Cotton Club

NEW *Tokyo Bldg Tokia 2F, 2-7-3 Marunouchi, Chiyoda-ku (3215 1555/ www.cottonclubjapan.co.jp). Tokyo station (Yamanote, Chuo, Sobu lines), Marunouchi South exit; (Marunouchi line), exit 4.* **Open** *Shows* 5.30pm, 8.30pm Mon-Sat; 4pm, 6.30pm Sun. **Map** p89 D5 ㊵
This sister venue of the Blue Note (p85) opened in late 2005 and operates in much the same way: pay ¥8,000-¥10,000 to enter, order your pricey dinner, then sit back for just under an hour of Tito Jackson or Sheena Easton. The artists span the soul/funk/disco/R&B spectrum, though the emphasis seems to be on international has-beens.

Tokyo TUC

Tokyo Uniform Center, Honsha Biru B1F, 2-16-5 Iwamotocho, Chiyoda-ku (3866 8393/www.tokyouniform.com/ tokyotuc). Akihabara station (Yamanote, Hibiya lines), Showa Dori exit; or Kanda station (Yamanote, Ginza lines), north exit. **Open** *Shows* from 7.45pm Fri; from 7pm Sat. **Map** p89 F1 ㊶
An excellent venue that regularly operates as a jazz club. Expect to hear a superb selection of musicians from Japan and overseas.

Arts & leisure

Casals Hall

1-6 Kanda-Surugadai, Chiyoda-ku (3294 1229/www.nu-casalshall.com). Ochanomizu station (Chuo, Marunouchi, Sobu lines), Ochanomizubashi exit. No credit cards. **Map** p89 D1 ㊷
This beautiful hall in the heart of Tokyo's university and bookshop district was designed exclusively for chamber music and small ensembles, and is recognised for its great acoustics.

Institut Franco-Japonais

15 Ichigaya-Funagawaramachi, Shinjuku-ku (5206 2500/www.ifj tokyo.or.jp/services/cinema.php). Iidabashi station (Chuo, Sobu lines), west exit; (Oedo Nanboku, Tozai, Yurakucho lines), exit B3. **Map** p88 A1 ㊸
A pearl of the Japanese cinema scene, this French culture centre shows contemporary French films at weekends, often with English subtitles.

Iwanami Hall

Iwanami Jinbocho Bldg 10F, 2-1 Kanda-Jinbocho, Chiyoda-ku (3262 5252/www.iwanami-hall.com). Jinbocho station (Hanzomon, Mita, Shinjuku lines), exit A6. **Map** p88 C1 ㊹
This highbrow cinema has been screening international works of social realism since the 1970s. The focus is on female directors and political work.

National Theatre

4-1 Hayabusa-cho, Chiyoda-ku (3230 3000/www.ntj.jac.go.jp/english/index. html). Nagatacho station (Hanzomon, Nanboku, Yurakucho lines), exit 4. **Map** p88 A4 ㊺
Kabuki is staged seven months a year in the National Theatre's Large Hall, while *bunraku* puppet theatre is staged in the Small Hall four months a year. English language programmes and audio guides are available.

Nippon Budokan

2-3 Kitanomaru-koen, Chiyoda-ku (3216 5100/www.nipponbudokan. or.jp). Kudanshita station (Hanzomon, Shinjuku, Tozai lines), exit 2. **Map** p88 B1 ㊻
The classic Tokyo live venue (think *Dylan at the Budokan*). Unfortunately, this reputation allows a horrible space to continue hosting major rock shows. Built for martial-arts competitions at the 1964 Olympics, it's still used for sports events. The acoustics are poor, the vibe sombre, and the huge, ever-present Japanese flag hanging from the centre of the hall does not inspire a rock 'n' roll atmosphere. And up in the balcony, you might as well be outside.

TOKYO BY AREA

Roppongi Hills p112

Roppongi

The traditional heart of Tokyo's hedonism has half a century of revelry to its name. Its main drag is packed with establishments that satisfy the visceral needs of the expat party crowd. Think tequila shots, deafening music and fast-track mating rituals. But Roppongi also has a new, more wholesome side as home to the city's two grandest consumer complexes and the stunning new **National Art Center, Tokyo**. Back in 2003 **Roppongi Hills** opened to great fanfare, and its popularity has yet to wane. Official figures claim 100,000 visitors each weekday, rising to 300,000 at the weekend. **Tokyo Midtown** followed in 2007, just a stone's throw from its predecessor, with a remarkably similar template of luxury hotel, upscale dining, mainstream fashion and major art museum. Midtown also boasts Tokyo's tallest tower, but Roppongi Hills' Mori Tower has a spectacular observation deck, complete with the city's best art museum in the middle.

Whether the combined might of these upscale mini cities puts the squeeze on the sleaze remains to be seen, but for now the two sides of Roppongi's co-exist harmoniously.

Sights & museums

21_21 Design Sight

NEW *9-7-6 Akasaka, Minato-ku (3475 2121/www.2121designsight.jp). Roppongi Station (Hibiya, Oedo lines), exit 8.* **Open** 11am-8pm Mon, Wed-Sun. **Admission** ¥1,000; free-¥800 reductions. **Map** p101 B1 ❶
An impressive new design centre from Tadao Ando and Issey Miyake. See box p103.

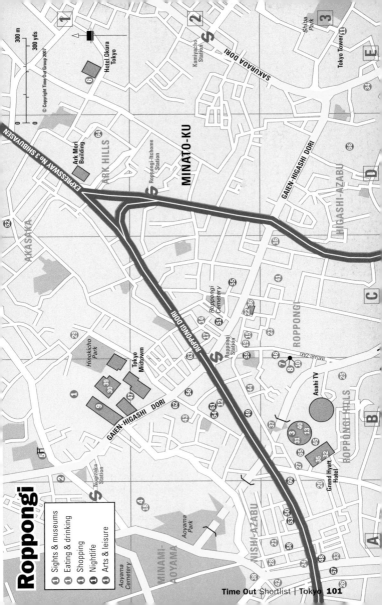

Roppongi

- ① Sights & museums
- ① Eating & drinking
- ① Shopping
- ① Nightlife
- ① Arts & leisure

MINAMI-AOYAMA

Aoyama Cemetery

Aoyama Park

AKASAKA

ARK HILLS

Hinokicho Park

Tokyo Midtown

ROPPONGI DORI

GAIEN-HIGASHI DORI

EXPRESSWAY NO 3 SHIBUYASEN

Ark Mori Building

Hotel Okura Tokyo

MINATO-KU

Roppongi-Itchome Station

Kamiyacho Station

SAKURADA DORI

Shiba Park

Tokyo Tower

GAIEN-HIGASHI DORI

HIGASHI-AZABU

Roppongi Cemetery

Roppongi Station

ROPPONGI

ROPPONGI HILLS

Asahi TV

Grand Hyatt Hotel

NISHI-AZABU

Nogizaka Station

© Copyright Time Out Group 2007

300 m
300 yds

Gallery Ma

Toto Nogizaka Building 3F, 1-24-3 Minami-Aoyama, Minato-ku (3402 1010/www.toto.co.jp/gallerma). Nogizaka station (Chiyoda line), exit 3. **Open** 11am-6pm Tue-Thur, Sat; 11am-7pm Fri. Closed 3wks Dec-Jan. **Map** p101 B1 ❷

Sponsored by toilet titan Toto, Gallery Ma hosts some of the city's best modern and contemporary architecture shows. There's a small bookshop on site too.

Mori Art Museum & Tokyo City View

Mori Tower 52F-53F, 6-10-1 Roppongi, Minato-ku (6406 6100/www.mori.art. museum/html/eng/index.html). Roppongi station (Hibiya, Oedo lines), exit 1. **Open** 10am-10pm Mon, Wed, Thur; 10am-5pm Tue; 10am-midnight Fri-Sun. **Admission** ¥1,500. **Map** p101 B3 ❸

World-class exhibitions, emphasising contemporary culture, are just one reason to head to the top of Mori Tower. The lofty landmark also offers spectacular views, a stylish bar (Mado Lounge, p108), a café and a shop. Exhibitions are deliberately varied and always imaginative.

National Art Center, Tokyo

NEW *7-22-2 Roppongi, Minato-ku (6812 9900/www.nact.jp). Nogizaka station (Chiyoda line), exit 6.* **Open** 10am-6pm Mon, Wed, Thur, Sat, Sun; 10am-8pm Fri. **Admission** varies. **Map** p101 A2 ❹

Tokyo's largest art museum opened in early 2007 and it has the potential to become a major player on the city's art scene – if they can fill the 14,000sq m (150,000sq ft) with consistent quality. The opening exhibition offered an imaginative look at consumerism in art, but also showed teething troubles, with some curiously handmade signage and befuddled staff.

Nogi Jinja

8-11-27 Akasaka, Minato-ku (3478 3001/house enquiries 3583 4151/ www.nogijinja.or.jp). Nogizaka station (Chiyoda line), exit 1; or Roppongi station (Hibiya, Oedo lines), exit 7. **Open** *Walkway* 8.30am-5pm daily.

House 9.30am-5pm 12, 13 Sept. **Admission** free. **Map** p101 B1 ❺

When Emperor Meiji died, on 13 September 1912, General Nogi Maresuke and his wife proved their loyalty by joining him in death. The house in which they committed suicide is adjacent to the memorial Nogi Shrine. It's open only two days a year, on the eve and anniversary of their deaths, but on other days you can peek in through the windows and catch a glimpse of Nogi's bloodstained shirt.

Okura Shukokan Museum of Fine Art

Hotel Okura, 2-10-4 Toranomon, Minato-ku (3583 0781/www.okura. com/tokyo/info/shukokan.html). Roppongi-Itchome station (Nanboku line), exits 2, 3. **Open** 10am-4.30pm Tue-Sun. **Admission** ¥800; ¥400- ¥500 reductions. No credit cards. **Map** p101 E1 ❻

This two-storey Chinese-style building sits in front of the retro-modern Hotel Okura (p172), one of Tokyo's finest. Inside there's a small mix of Asian antiquities: paintings, calligraphy, Buddhist sculpture, textiles, ceramics, swords, archaeological artefacts, lacquerware and metalwork. The exhibitions change five or six times a year.

Ota Fine Arts

Complex 1F, 6-8-14 Roppongi, Minato-ku (5786 2344/www.jade.dti.ne.jp/~aft/ home.html). Roppongi station (Hibiya, Oedo lines), exits 3, 5. **Open** 11am-7pm Tue-Sat. **Map** p101 B3 ❼

Some of Japan's best-known contemporary artists – such as Kusama Yayoi, Ozawa Tsuyoshi and others who deal with the politics of identity – show at this well-established gallery.

roentgenwerke

Complex 3F, 6-8-14 Roppongi, Minato-ku (3475 0166/http://roentgenwerke. com). Roppongi station (Hibiya, Oedo lines), exits 3, 5. **Open** 11am-7pm Tue-Sat. **Map** p101 B3 ❽

Roentgen (German for 'X-ray') was first the largest and then the smallest gallery in Tokyo. Now the place is of a happy

21_21 Design Sight

Ando and Miyake's new design museum.

Japan is well known for its designs and designers, from Asics shoes to Aibot dogs, Isamu Noguchi to Nigo, but until March 2007 it had no modern design museum.

Built on land that previously was home to Japan's Defence Agency, **21_21 Design Sight** (p100) is a fine museum and an inspiring addition to inner-city Tokyo. The centre has no permanent collection. Instead, it gives visitors the chance to see impressive new designs from established names and a rare opportunity to discover emerging international designers. Many visitors will be drawn by the Tadao Ando building, an architectural tour de force set in picturesque grounds in the new Midtown complex (p112).

Viewed from the outside, Ando's building looks small and simple. But its oddly shaped steel roof – painstakingly sanded and painted to look like a long sheet of folded steel – hides a two-storey structure housing an Italian restaurant run by chef and television personality Takamasa Uetake, a pair of generous exhibition halls and workshop space.

21_21 Design Sight's main backer is renowned fashion designer Issey Miyake. And it was from Miyake's clothing designs that Ando took his inspiration – folding and twisting everything in the building, big and small, from the angular glass-panelled courtyard down to the serpentine fire-extinguisher stands.

From day one, the centre's directors (Miyake, Muji designer Naoto Fukasawa and graphic artist Taku Satoh) have worked with young designers from around the world, inviting them to Japan to look at objects in a different way, then displaying their creations. The temporary exhibitions tend to be thematic – chocolate, water and *raguko* (a 17th-century form of comedic storytelling) were some of the subjects in the museum's first year of operation.

21_21 Design Sight offers visitors a chance to witness the beginnings of the next Japanese design revolution – or just respite from the consumer frenzy that fills the rest of Midtown.
■ www.2121designsight.jp/index-e.html

medium-small size, holding exhibitions of conceptual work, mostly by Japanese artists, such as Yanobe Kenji.

Suntory Museum of Art

NEW *Tokyo Midtown Gardenside 9-7-4, Minato-ku (3479 8600/www. suntory.com/culture-sports/sma/index. html). Roppongi Station (Oedo, Hibiya lines).* **Open** *10am-8pm Wed-Sat; 10am-6pm Mon, Sun.* **Admission** *varies.* **Map** p101 B1 **⑨**

The Suntory has relocated to the Midtown development in Roppongi, and received a makeover in the process. Described as a 'living room for the city', the new venue is actually very restrained, but that's as it should be for one of the most distinguished private collections of Japanese art and antiquities. Not huge, it's big enough for all but the serious connoisseur. Excellent English-language earphone guides.

Taro Nasu Gallery

Complex 2F, 6-8-14 Roppongi, Minato-ku (5411 7510/www.taronasugallery. com). Roppongi station (Hibiya, Oedo lines), exits 3, 5. **Open** *11am-7pm Tue-Sat.* **Map** p101 B3 **⑩**

Works by young and emerging Japanese and international artists – the likes of Matsue Taiji – are displayed here, under Taro Nasu's unusually thin fluorescent strip lighting.

Tokyo Tower

4-2-8 Shiba Koen, Minato-ku (3433 5111/5112/www.tokyotower.co.jp). Kamiyacho station (Hibiya line), exit 1; Onarimon station (Mita line), exit A1; or Akabanebashi station (Oedo line), Akabanebashi exit. **Open** *Tower 9am-10pm daily. Other attractions 10am-9pm daily.* **Admission** *Main Observatory ¥820; ¥310-¥460 reductions. Special Observatory ¥600; ¥350-¥400 reductions. Waxwork Museum ¥870; ¥460 reductions. Trick Art Gallery ¥400; ¥300 reductions. Mysterious Walking Zone ¥410; ¥300 reductions. Combined ticket ¥1,900; ¥950-¥1,100 reductions. No credit cards.* **Map** p101 E3 **⑪**

The resemblance to the Eiffel Tower is deliberate, as is the 13m (43ft) superior height. Back in 1958, when it was built, it must have been impressive. But its days as the observation deck of choice are long gone. The attractions inside,

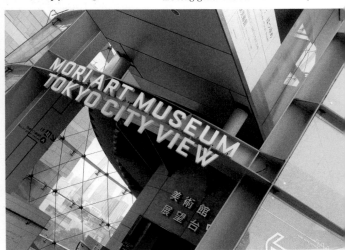

including a wax museum and trick art gallery, only date the tower further. It is, however, Tokyo's most striking attraction when viewed from any other observation deck.

Eating & drinking

Agave

Clover Building B1F, 7-15-10 Roppongi (3497 0229/www.lead-off-japan.co.jp/ tempo/agave/index.html). Roppongi station (Hibiya, Oedo lines), exit 4B. **Open** 6.30pm-2am Mon-Thur; 6.30pm-4am Fri, Sat. **Bar**. **Map** p101 B2 ⑫

Agave is a perfect replica of an upmarket Mexican cantina in all ways but two: few cantinas stock 400 varieties of tequila and mescal, and no joint in Mexico would charge so much for them. With single measures costing up to an impressive ¥9,400, this is the only place in Roppongi where customers don't hurl their cactus juice straight down their throats.

L'Atelier de Joël Robuchon

Roppongi Hills Hillside 2F, 6-10-1 Roppongi, Minato-ku (5772 7500/

Mori Art Museum p102

www.robuchon.com). Roppongi station (Hibiya, Oedo lines), exit 1. **Open** 11.30am-2pm, 6-10pm daily. **¥¥¥¥**. **French**. **Map** p101 B3 ⑬

Robuchon now has his 'casual' (a relative term, in this case) counter-style Atelier restaurants on three continents, and the Tokyo operation befits upmarket Roppongi Hills. Sit at the plush counter, ordering one or two dishes at a time as if it were a sushi counter or a tapas bar (the Spanish influence is also strong in the cuisine). Set dinners start from ¥8,400. Reservations are accepted for the first sitting at 6pm; after that, it's first come, first served.

Bangkok

Woo Building 2F, 3-8-8 Roppongi, Minato-ku (3408 7353). Roppongi station (Hibiya, Oedo lines), exit 1. **Open** 11.30am-2pm Mon-Fri; 5-11pm Mon-Sat; 11.30am-9pm Sun. Closed 3rd Sun of mth. **¥¥**. No credit cards. **Thai**. English menu. **Map** p101 C2 ⑭

This funky second-floor diner is well worth tracking down, since it produces good Thai street food without fuss or delay. Among the highlights are *tom kha kai* soup served in traditional clay pots, and the minced-meat *larb* 'salads', which are spiked with chillies, lemongrass, mint and onion.

Bauhaus

Reine Roppongi Building 2F, 5-3-4 Roppongi (3403 0092/www.e-bauhaus. jp). Roppongi station (Hibiya, Oedo lines), exit 3. **Open** 8pm-1am Mon-Sat. **Bar**. **Map** p101 C2 ⑮

One of those 'only in Japan' experiences, this is a music venue that has featured the same band for over 20 years. Nowhere else in the world can you listen to flawless covers of the Rolling Stones, Pink Floyd or Madonna performed by men and women who can't speak three words of English, and then have them serve you food and drink between sets. It's pricey, though, with a ¥2,700 music charge.

Bernd's Bar

Pure 2F, 5-18-1 Roppongi, Minato-ku (5563 9232/www.berndsbar.com).

Roppongi station (Hibiya, Oedo lines), exit 3. **Open** 5-11pm Mon-Sat. **Bar**. **Map** p101 C3 ⑯

Bernd's is a little corner of Germany, with fresh pretzels on the tables, and Bitburger and Erdinger on tap for washing down your Wiener schnitzel. Try to get a window table for the view of Roppongi's nightlife. If you happen to meet owner Bernd Haag, you'll find he can chat with you in English, German and Spanish, as well as Japanese. The place often stays open until it's empty.

Bincho

Marina Building 2F, 3-10-5 Roppongi, Minato-ku (5474 0755). Roppongi station (Hibiya, Oedo lines), exit 5. **Open** 5.30-11.30pm Mon-Sat; 5.30-11pm Sun. **¥¥¥**. **Yakitori**. English menu. **Map** p101 C2 ⑰

Settle back in Bincho's dark, romantic and typically Japanese-style interior and enjoy the heady aroma of premium yakitori chicken and seasonal vegetables – grilled over top-quality Bincho charcoal, of course. The yakitori is complemented with a large array of side dishes, as well as sake sourced from all over the country.

Brasserie Paul Bocuse Le Musée

NEW *7-22-2 Roppongi, National Art Center 3F, Minato-ku. (5770 8161/ www.nact.jp/restaurant). Roppongi Station (Hibiya, Oedo Lines), exit 8.* **Open** 11am-10pm Mon, Wed-Sun. **¥¥**. **French**. **Map** p101 A2 ⑱

Perched dramatically atop a grey concrete cone inside the glass and steel curves of the new National Art Museum, this brasserie tries hard to please. Unfortunately the food falls far short of the standards set by Chef Bocuse in Lyon. The menu offers little of note, and the bread is frozen and shipped from France. Lucky the setting is so dramatic.

Cavern Club

Saito Building 1F, 5-3-2 Roppongi (3405 5207/www.kentos-group.co.jp/ cavern). Roppongi station (Hibiya, Oedo lines), exit 3. **Open** 6pm-2.30am Mon-Sat; 6pm-midnight Sun. **Bar**. **Map** p101 C2 ⑲

Tokyo's famous Beatles imitators play here most nights – look for the Silver Beats on the schedule. Some say they sound better live than the originals. In low light, if you're drunk and wearing dark-enough glasses, you might even convince yourself you're back in 1960s Liverpool. The music fee is ¥1,500.

China Café Eight

3-2-13 Nishi Azabu, Minato-ku (5414 5708/www.cceight.com). Roppongi station (Hibiya, Oedo lines), exit 3. **Open** 24hrs daily. **¥¥**. **Chinese**. English menu. **Map** p101 A3 ㉔
The staff can be surly and the seating cramped, but you won't find cheaper Peking duck in town. The suggestive decor has novelty value and the location – right across from the sumptuous Grand Hyatt – makes it feel even more surreal, especially in the wee hours, when it fills up with clubbers.

Coriander

B1F, 1-10-6 Nishi-Azabu, Minato-ku (3475 5720/www.simc-jp.com/ coriander). Roppongi station (Hibiya, Oedo lines), exit 2. **Open** 11.30am-2pm Mon-Fri; 6-11pm Mon-Sat. **¥¥**. **Thai**. English menu. **Map** p101 A3 ㉑
A cosy basement restaurant that markets itself as 'new Thai', Coriander serves tasty dishes that are lighter on the chillies than its more authentic cousins and often contain unusual ingredients, as with the carrot *tom yam* soup. The decor is pleasant, heavy on the cushions, greenery and incense, and service is keen if not always efficient.

Erawan

Roi Building 13F, 5-5-1 Roppongi, Minato-ku (3404 5741/www.gnavi. co.jp/gn/en/g038502h.htm). Roppongi station (Hibiya, Oedo lines), exit 3. **Open** 5.30-11.30pm Mon-Fri; 5-10.30pm Sat, Sun. **¥¥¥**. **Thai**. English menu. **Map** p101 C2 ㉒
The teak-wood interior and tropical artefacts make Erawan one of the classiest Thai restaurants in town. The chefs don't stint on the spices, and the Thai waitresses serve it all up with customary grace. A great choice for something a bit different.

Fukuzushi

5-7-8 Roppongi, Minato-ku (3402 4116/www.roppongifukuzushi.com). Roppongi station (Hibiya, Oedo lines), *exit 3.* **Open** 11.30am-2pm, 5.30-11pm Mon-Sat; 5.30-10pm Sun. **¥¥¥**. **Sushi**. English menu. **Map** p101 C3 ㉓
Tokyo has more exclusive (and even pricier) sushi shops than Fukuzushi, but few are as welcoming or accessible. Superlative seafood in an elegant yet casual setting that feels miles away from the gritty hubbub of Roppongi.

Gonpachi

1-13-11 Nishi-Azabu, Minato-ku (5771 0170/www.global-dining.com). Roppongi station (Hibiya, Oedo lines), exit 1. **Open** 11.30am-5am daily. **¥¥**. **Traditional Japanese**. English menu. **Map** p101 A3 ㉔
Dominating Nishi-Azabu crossing like a feudal era castle, Gonpachi was supposedly an inspiration for the film *Kill Bill*. Sit at rustic wooden tables and dine on simple country-style Japanese fare. There's a faint whiff of Disney about it, with waiters dressed in folksy *happi* coats and traditional festival music playing over the speakers. Perhaps that's why then-Prime Minister Junichiro Koizumi brought George W Bush here. The separate third-floor sushi restaurant is more sophisticated, in both atmosphere and food.

Hainan Jeefan Shokudo

6-11-16 Roppongi, Minato-ku (5474 3200/www.route9g.com). Azabu-Juban station (Nanboku, Oedo lines), exit 7. **Open** 11.30am-2pm, 6-11pm Mon-Sat. **¥¥**. **Singaporean**. **Map** p101 B3 ㉕
The lunchtime speciality at this friendly little Singapore-style diner is Hainanstyle soft-simmered chicken served with rice. At dinner, the place also knocks out an extensive range of Singapore-style street-stall staples, including curries, stir-fries and spicy *laksa lemak* noodles. The small outdoor terrace is popular in summer.

Harmonie

4-2-15 Nishi-Azabu, Minato-ku (5466 6655). Hiroo station (Hibiya line), exit 1; or Roppongi station (Hibiya, Oedo lines), exit 1. **Open** noon-3pm, 6pm-2am Mon-Sat. **¥¥¥**. **French**. English menu. **Map** p101 A3 ㉖

Chef Jitsuhiro Yamada was a pioneer in matching casual bistro food with top wine (he has an astounding cellar of Burgundies). His winter menu features *gibiers* (boar, venison and wild fowl), much of which he hunts himself. The cosy, wood-clad second-floor dining room is entirely no-smoking, but you can head to his intimate stand-up bar downstairs for your Cohiba and rare Armagnac.

Heartland

West Walk Roppongi Hills, 6-10-1 Roppongi, Minato-ku (5772 7600/ www.heartland.jp). Roppongi station (Hibiya line), exit A1; (Oedo line), exit 3. **Open** 11am-5am daily. **Bar.** **Map** p101 B3 ㉗

A recent addition to the busy Roppongi drinking stable, Heartland is a chrome and glass, standing-room-only DJ bar that serves the eponymous Heartland beer. It's also a meat market, albeit for rather upmarket meat. There's an open-air courtyard to enjoy during warm weather.

High Tide

1-10-14 Nishi-Azabu, Minato-ku (5785 3684/www.bar-hightide.com). Roppongi station (Hibiya, Oedo lines), exit 2. **Open** 6pm-5am Mon-Sat; 6pm-3am Sun. **Bar.** **Map** p101 A3 ㉘

What sets High Tide apart from the other diminutive, dimly-lit bars in the area is the semi-private room, where customers lounge on the floor cushions, prop their drinks on a polished slice of tree trunk and make the most of the ultra low-key service. It's a place for dates, not mates.

Hinokiya

6-19-45 Akasaka, Minato-ku (6808 6815/www.pjgroup.jp/hinokiya). Akasaka station (Chiyoda line), exit 6; or Roppongi station (Hibiya line), exit 6; (Oedo line), exit 7. **Open** 6-11pm Mon-Sat. **¥¥¥. Grill.** English menu. **Map** p101 C1 ㉙

Hidden away behind the brand-new Midtown complex, Hinokiya offers an upmarket version of a *robata-yaki* grill. Pick out whichever ingredients you

fancy – seafood, meat, vegetables or tofu – and the kitchen staff cook them over charcoal in front of you, passing it to you across the counter on long wooden paddles. It's theatrical, fun and remarkably tasty.

Kafka

NEW *Tokyo Midtown 3F, 9-7-4 Akasaka, Minato-ku, (5413 7700/ www.kafka-d.jp). Roppongi Station (Hibiya, Oedo lines), exit 8.* **Open** 11am-midnight daily. **¥¥¥¥. Soba.** **Map** p101 B1 ㉚

This supremely stylish Japanese restaurant is a dark, softly lit refuge from the crowds coursing through Midtown. Sit at the black ceramic counter for a four-course soba lunch of pristinely fresh, seasonal ingredients selected from across Japan. A glass of champagne is a surprisingly natural companion for this top-quality soba. Dinner is a progression of *kaiseki*-style dishes.

Mado Lounge

Mori Tower 52F, 6-10-1 Roppongi, Minato-ku (6406 6652/www.tokyocity view.com/en/index.html). Roppongi station (Hibiya line), exit 1C; (Oedo line), exit 3. **Open** 10am-11pm Mon-Thur, Sun; 10am-midnight Fri, Sat. **Bar.** **Map** p101 B3 ㉛

Part of the Tokyo City View observation deck in Roppongi Hills, Mado Lounge opened in 2006, supplementing the great view with booze and quality local DJs. The elevator that takes you up to the 52nd floor costs ¥1,500, but the fee also gets you entrance to the Mori Art Museum (p102), which resides in the centre.

Maduro

Grand Hyatt Tokyo 4F, 6-10-3 Roppongi, Minato-ku (4333 1234/ freephone 0120 588 288/www.grand hyatttokyo.com). Roppongi station (Hibiya line), exit 1C; (Oedo line), exit 3. **Open** 6pm-2am Mon-Thur, Sun; 6pm-3am Fri, Sat. **Bar.** **Map** p101 B3 ㉜

The luxurious bar of the five-star Grand Hyatt Tokyo hotel, Maduro is the place to go once that business deal

Agave p105

has been safely sealed. The jet-set clientele don't object to the ¥1,575 seating charge; they come for the spacious lounge setting and the superior menu of drinks. If you know your Speysides from your Islays and a bottle of Krug from a bottle of cava, this could be your kind of venue.

Maimon

3-17-29 Nishi-Azabu, Minato-ku (3408 2600/www.maimon.jp). Roppongi station (Hibiya, Oedo lines), exit 1. **Open** 6pm-4am Mon-Thur; 6pm-5am Fri, Sat; 6pm-midnight Sun. **¥¥¥. Oyster bar**. English menu. **Map** p101 A3 ③③
This immensely stylish oyster bar (which is run by the same company that is behind New York's oh-so-hot Megu) offers an astounding 40 varieties of the mollusc, served either raw in the shell or cooked in numerous ways. Alternatives include yakitori and other charcoal-grilled delicacies (beef tongue, pork, shellfish and more). Maimon also offers a great range of sake and shochu.

Nodaiwa

1-5-4 Higashi-Azabu, Minato-ku (3583 7852/www.geocities.co.jp/Milkyway/ 8859/nodaiwa). Akabanebashi station (Oedo line), Akabanebashi exit; or Kamiyacho station (Hibiya line), exit 1. **Open** 11am-1.30pm, 5-8pm Mon-Sat. **¥¥. Eel**. English menu. **Map** p101 E3 ③④
Housed in a converted *kura* storehouse transported from the mountains, Nodaiwa is the most refined *unagi* shop in the city. It only uses eels that have been caught in the wild, and the difference is noticeable in the texture, especially if you try the *shirayaki* (grilled without any added sauce and eaten with a dip of shoyu and wasabi).

Oak Door

Grand Hyatt Hotel 6F, 6-10-3 Roppongi, Minato-ku (4333 8784/ www.grandhyatttokyo.com/cuisine/ oakdoor.htm). Roppongi station (Hibiya, Oedo lines), exit 1. **Open** 11.30am-4pm (last orders 2.30pm), 6-11.30pm (last orders 10.30pm) daily. **¥¥¥. Steak**. English menu. **Map** p101 B3 ③⑤

Pecha Kucha

The designer show and tell.

Six minutes 40 seconds – that's all the time each presenter gets to talk about their passions at Tokyo's biggest and best show-and-tell event, **20x20 Pecha Kucha**.

Brainchild of expat architects Mark Dytham and Astrid Klein, Pecha Kucha – a Japanese onomatopoeia for 'chit chat' – invites 14 people to present their creative work to an enthusiastic, art-and-design-savvy crowd on the last Wednesday of every month.

The event – which starts at precisely 20.20 – has spawned replicas in more than 50 cities, cities as far afield as Hamburg, Harvard and Hobart.

Hosted in chic Super-deluxe bar (p115), Pecha Kucha presenters are permitted to show just 20 images for 20 seconds each – a good way to ensure no one strays into drawn-out theoretical discussions. The work ranges from creative doodles to holiday snaps to prototypes of major new products, and has attracted award-winning architects Toyo Ito and Jun Aoki, as well as leading London illustrators Zara Wood and Ron Jonzo, industrial designer Ron

Arad, and one of the brains behind Sony computers, Dr Ivan Poupyrev.

Being the original Pecha Kucha, the Tokyo version doesn't try to impress as do some of its offspring. Instead it offers an ego-free environment where the crowd is as much a part of the night as the people holding the mic.

The dress code is casual and the audience multicultural; all you need do is show up early (the club regularly fills up on Pecha Kucha nights, pulling up to 400 people), and grab some wine or the bar's must-try microbrew Tokyo Ale. Then find a space on the modular seating next to someone who looks interesting – Pecha Kucha nights have justly earned a reputation as a meeting place for creatives: you might find yourself next to a magazine editor, design firm boss or international filmmaker.

The relaxed atmosphere means show-and-tellers feel free to share half-finished projects, thoughts and concepts, and to listen to any feedback. To find the creative pulse of Tokyo, Pecha Kucha should be your first stop.
■ www.Pecha-Kucha.org

A huge selection of premium steaks (each *wagyu* steer individually identified), cooked to order in wood-burning ovens, and a gleaming cellar of New World wines: no wonder Oak Door is so popular with the expense-account expat community.

Paddy Foley's Irish Pub

Roi Building B1F, 5-5-1 Roppongi, Minato-ku (3423 2250/www.paddy foleystokyo.com). Roppongi station (Hibiya, Oedo lines), exit 3. **Open** 5pm-1am daily. **Bar. Map** p101 C2 **36**

One of Tokyo's first Irish pubs, Paddy Foley's still offers the best craic, despite increasing competition. Guinness, naturally, is the house speciality, and the food is good. It can get as crowded as a London pub at weekends, something the locals (who always sit down to drink) regard with mild bemusement.

Pintokona

Hollywood Plaza B2F, 6-4-1 Roppongi, Minato-ku (5771 1133). Roppongi station (Hibiya, Oedo lines), exit 1. **Open** 11am-11pm daily. **¥¥. Sushi. Map** p101 B3 **37**

This is a conveyor-belt sushi bar with a difference. Here, you can either help yourself to whatever's going past, or peruse the menu, sing out your order and wait for it to be prepared and delivered straight to you. Quality and freshness are definitely superior, but then so are the prices.

Porterhouse Steaks

1-15-4 Nishi-Azabu, Minato-ku (5771 5788/www.chanto.com/restauranto/porterhouse/index.html). Nogizaka station (Chiyoda line), exit 5. **Open** 6pm-midnight Mon-Sat; 5-9.30pm Sun. **¥¥¥¥. Steak**. English menu. **Map** p101 A2 **38**

Taking over from the now-defunct Ken's Chanto Dining, Porterhouse Steaks is a temple devoted to the pleasures of premium beef, grilled perfectly and served in style. Top of the line is the eponymous porterhouse – a 21oz offering for just ¥11,000. A must for fans of red meat.

Roti

NEW *Tokyo Midtown, 9-7-4 Akasaka, Minato-ku (5413 3655/www.rotico. com). Roppongi station (Hibiya, Oedo lines), exit 1.* **Open** 11am-midnight daily. **¥¥¥. American**. English menu. **Map** p101 B1 **39**

The new Midtown branch of this much-loved 'modern American brasserie' has a more upmarket feel than the original spot, but still serves the speciality rotisserie chicken and offers a wide selection of New World wines. Families still favour the older location, which is in the same district (Piramide Bldg 1F, 6-6-9 Roppongi, Minato-ku, 5785 3672), but this one has more romance.

Roy's

West Walk 5F, 6-10-1 Roppongi, Minato-ku (5413 9571/www.soho-s. co.jp/roys/index_fs.html). Roppongi station (Hibiya, Oedo lines), exit 1. **Open** 11am-4pm, 5.30-11.30pm daily. **¥¥¥. Fusion**. English menu. **Map** p101 B3 **40**

Hawaii-based Roy Yamaguchi's Euro-Asian-Pacific cuisine is fusion food at its best, incorporating Japanese and other Asian flavours into dishes such as seared shrimp with spicy miso butter sauce or Mediterranean-style seafood frittata with pickled ginger and spicy sprouts. The evening views are fabulous.

Shunju

House 530 B1, 5-16-47 Roppongi, Minato-ku (3583 2611/www.shunju. com/ja/restaurants/toriizaka). Roppongi station (Hibiya, Oedo lines), exit 3. **Open** 6-11.30pm daily. **¥¥¥. Izakaya**. English menu. **Map** p101 C3 **41**

Shunju is a typical modern *izakaya*, the nearest Japanese equivalent to a British pub. This one is a sophisticated blend of the modern and the traditional, of farmhouse and urban, of Japanese and imported. You'll find pleasing food with many creative touches, a stylish design sense and a young (but not too young) and casual crowd. Shunju can get smoky and noisy, but it never gets boisterous or out of hand.

These

2F, 2-13-19 Nishi-Azabu, Minato-ku (5466 7331/www.these-jp.com). Roppongi station (Hibiya, Oedo lines), exit 1. **Open** *7pm-4am daily.* **Bar. Map** p101 A3 ㊷

As much library as bar, These ('tay-zay') exudes the feel of a British gentlemen's club, with superior service. The bar has shelves and shelves of magazines and books, both foreign and Japanese, for browsing while indulging in one of the long list of whiskies. Harry Potter fans should watch out for the secret room.

Tokyo Sports Café

Fusion Building 2F, 7-13-8 Roppongi, Minato-ku (5411 8939/www.tokyo-sportscafe.com). Roppongi station (Hibiya, Oedo lines), exits 2, 4. **Open** *6pm-5am Mon-Sat.* **Bar. Map** p101 B2 ㊸

One of the longest-established, largest sports bars in Tokyo, this place screens all major sporting events from around the world, with space to show two at once. It offers an extensive range of beers – domestic and imported – and cocktails. Happy hour lasts from 6pm to 8pm daily, and closing time varies depending on when matches finish.

Vietnamese Cyclo

Piramide Building 1F, 6-6-9 Roppongi, Minato-ku (3478 4964/http://r.gnavi.co.jp/g222004). Roppongi station (Hibiya, Oedo lines), exit 3. **Open** *11.30am-3pm, 5-9.30pm Mon-Sat; noon-9.30pm Sun.* **¥¥. Vietnamese.** *English menu.* **Map** p101 B2 ㊹

There's more style than content to this Saigon eaterie, down to the cyclo trishaw parked at the door. Vietnamese flavours have been toned down for Japanese tastes, but the *goi cuon* spring rolls are still undeniably tasty.

Shopping

Roppongi Hills

6-10 Roppongi, Minato-ku (6406 6000/ www.roppongihills.com). Roppongi station (Hibiya line), exit 1C; (Oedo line), exit 3. **Map** p101 B3 ㊺

Opening back in 2003, Roppongi's mammoth shopping and entertainment development had received more than 49 million visitors by the end of its first year of operation. It's a quite colossal complex that houses 200 shops and restaurants, the Grand Hyatt hotel, many private apartment buildings, a multiplex cinema, a TV studio and the imposing Mori Tower. It's also fiendishly difficult to navigate and, shop-wise, geared almost exclusively to twenty-something ladies.

Roppongi Pharmacy

6-8-8 Roppongi, Minato-ku (3403 8879). Roppongi station (Hibiya, Oedo lines), exit 3. **Open** *10am-1am daily. Closed 2nd Sun of mth. No credit cards.* **Map** p101 C3 ㊻

You won't find Western medicines here, but their Eastern equivalents and all the other drug-store standards can be found at this late-night pharmacy.

Tokyo Midtown

NEW *6-10 Roppongi, Minato-ku (6406 6000/www.roppongihills.com). Roppongi station (Hibiya, Oedo lines), exit 8.* **Map** p101 B1/2 ㊼

Occupying almost 20 acres, this sparkling new consumer megaplex has most of the key ingredients of its local rival, Roppongi Hills, but eschews the navigation nightmares in favour of a simple layout and stylish interior. The shopping encompasses fashion, design and gourmet groceries and includes a dazzling branch of trendy fashion emporium Restir.

Nightlife

328 (San Ni Pa)

B1F, 3-24-20 Nishi-Azabu, Minato-ku (3401 4968/www.3-2-8.jp). Roppongi station (Hibiya, Oedo lines), exit 1. **Open** *from 8pm daily.* **Admission** *¥2,000 (incl 2 drinks) Mon-Thur, Sun; ¥2,500 (incl 2 drinks) Fri, Sat. No credit cards.* **Map** p101 A3 ㊽

You'll spot the large neon sign that indicates 328 from the Nishi-Azabu crossing. A real veteran of the club scene, it opened way back in 1979.

Gonpachi p107

Expect a mix of genres, from soul to dance classics, and an older crowd. On Saturday the focus turns to rare groove, and 328 gets packed (it's small), so arrive early. It usually stays open past midnight on weekends.

Alfie

Hama Roppongi Building 5F, 6-2-35 Roppongi, Minato-ku (3479 2037/ http://homepage1.nifty.com/live/alfie). Roppongi station (Hibiya, Oedo lines), exit 1. **Open** *Shows 8pm-4am daily; jam sessions after midnight.* **Admission** ¥3,500. **Map** p101 B2 ④⑨

A jazz oasis in drunken Roppongi, Alfie has a sleek interior and an upscale audience paying upscale prices to hear international musicians as well as top-flight local bands.

Alife

1-7-2 Nishi-Azabu, Minato-ku (5785 2531/www.e-alife.net). Roppongi station (Hibiya, Oedo lines), exit 2. **Open** *from 9pm Thur-Sat.* **Admission** ¥2,000-¥3,500. No credit cards. **Map** p101 A3 ⑤⓪

This big club is fairly well appointed, with a spacious party lounge on the second floor, a stylish café on the ground floor and a large dance area downstairs in the basement. It has a hedonistic atmosphere and is a haven for hard-core clubbers. Guest DJs play trance or house on a Sunday morning.

Bar Matrix

Mizobuchi Building B1F, 3-13-6 Roppongi, Minato-ku (3405 1066). Roppongi station (Hibiya, Oedo lines), exit 3. **Open** 6pm-4am daily. **Admission** free. **Map** p101 C2 ⑤①

Named after the Keanu Reeves movie, this Roppongi bar/club has a futuristic, metallic interior and a cyber feel. It could be considered emblematic of Tokyo, or at least of what travellers expect Tokyo to be. The music is a mishmash of everything, but tends towards hip hop and R&B.

B Flat

Akasaka Sakae Building B1F, 6-6-4 Akasaka, Minato-ku (5563 2563/www. bflat.jp). Akasaka station (Chiyoda line), exit 5A. **Open** *Shows from 7.30pm daily.* **Admission** ¥2,500-¥7,000. **Map** p101 D1 ⑤②

A large operation that also serves decent food (sandwiches, pizza and Japanese dishes). The groups are often the best in the city, and bands from the US and Europe perform a couple of times a month.

Bullet's

Kasumi Building B1F, 1-7-11 Nishi-Azabu, Minato-ku (3401 4844/www.bul-lets.com). Roppongi station (Hibiya, Oedo lines), exit 2. **Open** 10pm-5am Fri; 11pm-5am Sat. **Admission** ¥2,000 Fri; ¥1,500 Sat. No credit cards. **Map** p101 A3 ⑤

If nothing else, this is the cosiest venue in Tokyo. Half the place is carpeted, and guests are asked to remove their shoes. There are also sofas and mattresses to lounge on while you listen to an often experimental line-up of DJs.

Core

TSK CCC Building B1F-B2F, 7-15-30 Roppongi, Minato-ku (3470 5944/www.clubcore.net). Roppongi station (Hibiya line), exit 4B; (Oedo line), exit 7. **Open** from 10pm Wed-Sun. **Admission** usually ¥2,500 (incl 1 drink). No credit cards. **Map** p101 B2 ⑤

Yet another club apparently too shy to hang a sign. This one is a mid-size venue with a very varied line-up, although house and techno dominate. It's classier than most of Roppongi's night-time options, but that's faint praise. The bar snacks are impressive (for a club) and drinks start at ¥600.

Gas Panic

2F-3F, 3-15-24 Roppongi, Minato-ku (3405 0633/www.gaspanic.co.jp). Roppongi station (Hibiya, Oedo lines), exit 3. **Open** 6pm-5am daily. No credit cards. **Map** p101 C2 ⑤

Gas Panic is a Roppongi institution, where young people go to grope other young people. The music is so loud that your mating ritual needs to be physical rather than verbal. To give an idea of what it's like, note that you must be holding a drink at all times, and drinking water is not in evidence. Drinks are ¥400 all night on Thursdays.

Lovenet

Hotel Ibis, 7-14-4 Roppongi, Minato-ku (5771 5511/www.lovenet-jp.com). Roppongi station (Roppongi station (Hibiya, Oedo lines), exit 4A. **Open** 6pm-5am Mon-Sat; 6pm-11pm Sun. **Map** p101 B2 ⑤

An antidote to the garish tack of most karaoke joints, Lovenet offers a range of sumptuous themed rooms, ranging in size from the cosy 4-person 'Kiss Room' to a 100-capacity Banquet Suite. Dining options vary from à la carte pizza and pasta to an ¥8,000 set menu.

Muse

4-1-1 Nishi-Azabu, Minato-ku (5467 1188/www.muse-web.com). Roppongi station (Hibiya, Oedo lines), exit 1. **Open** from 7pm Mon-Thur, Sun; 7pm-5am Fri, Sat. **Admission** ¥2,000 (incl 2 drinks) Mon-Thur, Sun; ¥3,000 (incl 2 drinks) Fri, Sat. No credit cards. **Map** p101 A3 ⑤

This three-level club features a stellar bar, cave-like areas, and billiards and ping-pong tables in the basement. So it's a shame that it's just a massive meat market. Note their ambiguous 'not too casual' dress code.

Space Lab Yellow

Cesaurus Nishi-Azabu Building B1F-B2F, 1-10-11 Nishi-Azabu, Minato-ku (3479 0690/www.club-yellow.com). Roppongi station (Hibiya, Oedo lines), exit 2. **Open** 10pm-5am; days vary. **Admission** ¥3,000-¥4,000. No credit cards. **Map** p101 A3 ⑤

Better known as simply 'Yellow', this is the original hip venue in Japan; everyone from 808 State to Laurent Garnier and Timo Maas have played here. It faces stiffer competition than it used to, and from more conveniently located venues, but Yellow still draws the megastars, and then tests how many people it can squeeze in.

STB139

6-7-11 Roppongi, Minato-ku (5474 1395/http://stb139.co.jp). Roppongi station (Hibiya, Oedo lines), exit 3. **Open** Shows from 8pm Mon-Sat. **Admission** from ¥5,000. **Map** p101 C2 ⑤

Combine wining and dining with world-class jazz. The only competition to Blue Note Tokyo (p85), STB139 does some things better: the layout is much friendlier and the atmosphere a bit more relaxed. There's more variety in the music too, which veers towards soul, Latin, R&B and classics rather than just plain jazz.

Super-deluxe

B1F, 3-1-25 Nishi-Azabu, Minato-ku (5412 0515/www.super-deluxe.com). Roppongi station (Hibiya, Oedo lines), exit 1B. **Open** 6pm-2am Mon-Sat. **Map** p101 A/B3 **60**

Picked up by *Time* magazine as Asia's best spot for 'avant-garde idling', Super-deluxe is the brainchild of a pair of architects who envisaged the spot as 'a bar, a gallery, a kitchen, a jazz club, a cinema, a library, a school…' and so on. More like an artists' salon than a bar, Super-deluxe offers something different every night, from slide shows to mock hostess nights. It's also home to Tokyo Ale – the city's finest microbrew.

Vanilla

TSK Building, 7-15-30 Roppongi, Minato-ku (3401 6200/www.club vanilla.com). Roppongi station (Hibiya, Oedo lines), exits 4A, 4B. **Open** 7pm-5am Thur-Sat. **Admission** usually ¥3,000-¥3,500 (incl 1 drink). No credit cards. **Map** p101 B2 **61**

Probably the most underused space in Tokyo. Vanilla is a vast club that can accommodate over 5,000 people, yet it never attracts a name big enough to lure such a crowd. Hence most of the best rooms are usually closed and punters are herded to the huge dancefloor for a night of the cheesiest house.

Y2K

Aban Building B1F, 7-13-2 Roppongi, Minato-ku (5775 3676/www.explosion works.net/y2k). Roppongi station (Hibiya line), exit 4A; (Oedo line), exit 7. **Map** p101 B2 **62**

Opened in the heart of Roppongi in 1999 with a mission to bring live music to clubbers, this 450-capacity venue hosts smaller, local, rock-minded bands.

Arts & leisure

Haiyu-za

4-9-2 Roppongi, Minato-ku (3470 2880/ www.haiyuzagekijou.co.jp). Roppongi

station (Oedo line), exit 6; (Hibiya line), exit 4A. **Map** p101 C2 **63**

Roppongi's venerable, 300-seater, fleapit film venue opens irregularly, but when it does, its speciality is avant-garde films from all continents. A Tokyo treasure that is worth a visit, if you can catch it open.

Suntory Hall

1-13-1 Akasaka, Minato-ku (3505 1001/www.suntory.co.jp/suntory hall/english). Roppongi-Itchome station (Nanboku line), exit 3. **Map** p101 D1 **64**

Used mainly for orchestral concerts and recitals, this two-space venue was described by legendary conductor Herbert von Karajan as 'truly a jewel box of sound'. The huge, Austrian-made pipe organ is the most striking visual feature of the 2,000-seater Large Hall, giving it an almost church-like appearance. The Small Hall seats 430.

Toho Cinemas Roppongi Hills

6-10-2 Roppongi, Minato-ku (5775 6090/www.tohocinemas.co.jp/roppongi/ index.html). Roppongi station (Hibiya line), exit 1C; (Oedo line), exit 3. **Map** p101 B3 **65**

This nine-screen multiplex in Roppongi Hills is one of the most comfy cinemas. It offers all-night screenings on a Thursday, Friday and Saturday, as well as on the day that precedes a national holiday. Couples can book two-seater 'love seats' for ¥3,000.

Tokyo International Players

Performances at Tokyo American Club, 2-1-2 Azabudai, Minato-ku (3224 3670/www.tokyoamerican club.org). Kamiyacho station (Hibiya line), exit 2; or Azabu-Juban station (Nanboku, Oedo lines), exit 6. No credit cards. **Map** p101 D3 **66**

A keen group of amateur and professional actors, TIP (information 090 6009 4171, www.tokyoplayers.org) usually stages productions at the long-running Tokyo American Club.

Center Gai

Shibuya

Shibuya is the bright, brash centre of Tokyo's teen culture. The area's innumerable shops, cafés, clubs, bars and restaurants are geared towards Tokyo's youngsters, making it fast, fun and affordable. Daytime is all about shopping, with music and fashion dominating the stores, but when darkness falls and the neon is switched on, myriad clubs, bars, cinemas, live venues and less salubrious establishments keep the area throbbing till dawn.

The JR station's Hachiko exit is the gateway to most of the area's attractions. Straight ahead is the world's busiest pedestrian crossing and diagonally opposite is the narrow, pedestrianised street known as **Center Gai**, which offers a rather dull shopping or

dining experience, but a wonderful people-watching opportunity. This is the catwalk for some of Tokyo's most garish trendsetters, who mill around in the latest bright fashions. The likely source of their threads is **109**, a nearby ten-storey cylindrical collection of boutiques. The store's most committed ambassadors are known as *gyaru* – an approximation of the English 'gal'. They have become the icons of Shibuya, but the youth culture bubbling around these streets extends to the hip hop crowds, clubbers and trendy, design-savvy youths. The one demographic missing from Shibuya is grown-ups, who tend to steer clear of the cacophony.

Despite the area's long-standing reputation as an after-hours school-yard, some hefty investment has been made in an attempt to push

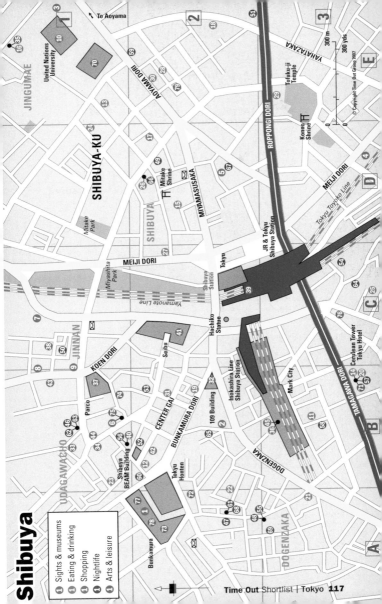

Shibuya

- ● Sights & museums
- ● Eating & drinking
- ● Shopping
- ● Nightlife
- ● Arts & leisure

To Aoyama

JINGUMAE

United Nations University

SHIBUYA-KU

Mitake Park

AOYAMA DORI

SHIBUYA

Mitake Shrine

MIYAMASUSAKA

MEIJI DORI

Miyashita Park

Yamanote Line

Shibuya Station

JR & Tokyu Shibuya Station

ROPPONGI DORI

YAHATAZAKA

Tofuku-ji Temple

Konno Shrine

MEIJI DORI

Tokyu Toyoko Line

© Copyright Time Out Group 2007

300 m
300 yds

E

D

C

B

A

JINNAN

KOEN DORI

Seibu

Parco

UDAGAWACHO

CENTER GAI

BUNKAMURA DORI

Shibuya BEAM Building

Tokyu Honten

Bunkamura

DOGENZAKA

TAMAGAWA DORI

Cerulean Tower Tokyu Hotel

Hachiko Statue

Inokashira Line Shibuya Station

Mark City

Tokyu

Open mic nights

Tokyo's thriving arts scene features world-class galleries, musicians, DJs and plenty more. It's also home to a bubbling underbelly of hipster misfits, part-time poets and derelict raconteurs. Ebisu's expat haunt **What the Dickens** (Roob 6 Bldg 4F, 1-13-3 Ebisu-Nishi, Shibuya-ku, 3780 2099) has been giving poets and writers an open mic for over a decade, but now there are mics opening up in venues across the city. Here comedians, DJs, musicians and performance artists get to test the crowds.

Shibuya's **Pink Cow** (p123) hosts Artsy Bugsy (2nd Sun of month), which offers splashes of music, comedy and live painting, and Flo-Union (3rd Sun of month), for multimedia work by amateur auteurs and video artists. A couple of blocks away, **CoZmo's Café** (p121) opens its floor each Thursday for an assortment of dancers, MCs and musicians. It also stages a pure poetry open mic of mainly expat performers every other month. Elsewhere in Shibuya, the **Ruby Room** (p131) offers fledgling musicians its tiny stage on Wednesdays, as does Roppongi's **Rock Factory** (5-16-52 Roppongi, Minato-ku, 5545 4242, www.rock-factory. net) each Monday.

For anyone not deterred by the language barrier, **Ben's Café** (1-29-21 Takadanobaba, Shinjuku-ku, 3202 2445, www.benscafe. com/en) in Takadanobaba hosts a poetry jam, predominantly in Japanese, on the third and fourth Sunday of each month.

Shibuya's image upmarket. First, a trio of train operators joined forces to tack **Mark City** on to the side of the existing station. Then came the grand **Cerulean Tower Tokyu Hotel**, with its many attractions. And work is underway on a Tadao Ando-designed extension to the station, scheduled to open in 2012, which looks set to persuade the more mature city residents to spend more time here.

Sights & museums

Bunkamura The Museum

Bunkamura B1, 2-24-1 Dogenzaka, Shibuya-ku (3477 9111/www. bunkamura.co.jp). Shibuya station (Yamanote, Ginza lines), Hachiko exit; (Hanzomon line), exit 3A. **Open** 10am-7pm Mon-Thur, Sun; 10am-9pm Fri, Sat. **Admission** usually ¥1,000. **Map** p117 A2 ❶
One of the best museums in Tokyo is run by the Tokyu department-store chain. Bunkamura hosts international art blockbusters featuring subjects and artists ranging from Tintin to Picasso. Elsewhere in this major shopping and cultural centre are boutiques, an art-house cinema, two theatre/music spaces, an art bookshop and restaurants.

Eyeglass Museum

Iris Optical 6F-7F, 2-29-18 Dogenzaka, Shibuya-ku (3496 3315). Shibuya station (Yamanote, Ginza lines), Hachiko exit; (Hanzomon line), exits 1, 3A. **Open** 11am-5pm Tue-Sun. **Admission** free. **Map** p117 B2 ❷
Not the flashiest of Tokyo's museums, this slightly dilapidated spot above an optician's is nevertheless an interesting diversion from a shopping trip in Shibuya. Glasses galore sit quietly, with very few annotations, for the viewing pleasure of spectacle fanatics. A 19th-century eyeglass workshop specially imported from France is complemented by a chipped mannequin.

Galeria Building

5-51-3 Jingumae, Shibuya-ku. Omotesando station (Chiyoda,

Ginza, Hanzomon lines), exit B2.
Open 11am-7pm Tue-Sun; hours
can vary. **Map** p117 E1 **❸**
This building houses three galleries:
Promo-Arte (3400 1995, www.promo-
arte.com), which is Tokyo's main Latin
American art space; Art-U Room (5467
3938, www.mmjp.or.jp/art-u/index.
html), specialising in contemporary
Asian art; and Gallery Gan (5574 8178,
www.presskit.co.jp), which represents
mainly Japanese artists.

Gallerie Le Déco

*Le Déco Bldg, 3-16-3 Shibuya,
Shibuya-ku (5485 5188/http://
home.att.ne.jp/gamma/ledeco).
Shibuya station (Yamanote line),
east exit; (Ginza line), Toyoko exit;
(Hanzomon line), exit 9.* **Open**
11am-7pm Tue-Sun. Closed 2wks
Dec-Jan. **Map** p117 D3 **❹**
Regular exhibitions of work by young
Japanese artists working in a range of
media fill the six floors of this rental
space. There's also a café and lounge
area on the ground floor.

Nanzuka Underground

*Shibuya Ibis Bldg B1F, 2-17-3 Shibuya,
Shibuya-ku (3400 0075/www.nug.jp).
Shibuya station (Yamanote line),
east exit; (Ginza line), Toyoko exit;
(Hanzomon line), exit 12.* **Open**
1-8pm Wed-Sun. **Map** p117 D2 **❺**
Nanzuka presents new-generation art
with a hip, urban edge. Illustrations,
futuristic fashion and vintage record
sleeves have all adorned the walls of
this gallery, located appropriately in
Tokyo's yoof centre of Shibuya.

Parco Museum of Art & Beyond

*Parco Part 3 7F, 15-1 Udagawacho,
Shibuya-ku (3464 5111/www.parco-
art.com). Shibuya station (Yamanote,
Ginza lines), Hachiko exit; (Hanzomon
line), exits 3A, 6, 7.* **Open** 10am-8.30pm
during exhibitions. **Admission** ¥500;
¥400 reductions. **Map** p117 B1 **❻**
The Parco Museum's programming policy makes a perfect fit with the Shibuya
demographic. There are regularly
changing shows on pop-culture themes,
plus work by only the trendiest

photographers and designers from
Japan and overseas. Past exhibitions
have featured photos by the dog-loving
William Wegman and images of endur-
ing pop icon Che Guevara.

TEPCO Electric Energy Museum (Denryoku-kan)

*1-12-10 Jinnan, Shibuya-ku (3477 1191/
www5.mediagalaxy.co.jp/Denryokukan).
Shibuya station (Yamanote, Ginza lines),
Hachiko exit; (Hanzomon line), exits 6, 7.*
Open 10am-6pm Mon, Tue, Thur-Sun.
Admission free. **Map** p117 C1 **❼**
'Let's make friends with electricity' is
the slogan of this energy giant's six-
storey homage to the joy of electrons
and protons. Adults might tire quickly
of the corporate message, but it's a
great place to keep the kids busy.
Teaching your offspring to play with
electricity might not seem the sagest of
lessons, but the innovative games and
multimedia activities will keep them
genuinely entertained.

Tobacco & Salt Museum

*1-16-8 Jinnan, Shibuya-ku (3476
2041/www.jti.co.jp/Culture/museum).
Shibuya station (Yamanote, Ginza
lines), Hachiko exit; (Hanzomon line),
exits 6, 7.* **Open** 10am-6pm Tue-Sun.
Admission ¥100; ¥50 reductions.
No credit cards. **Map** p117 B/C1 **❽**
The tenuous rationale for this pairing
of themes is that both were once nation-
alised commodities. Tobacco gets the
most exposure, with two floors devoted
to the history, manufacture and culture
of the killer leaf. Sodium-based exhibits
occupy the third floor, but the top floor
is often the best, with a frequently
changing exhibition that has, in the
past, ranged from tequila production to
19th-century prostitutes' wigs. If you're
inspired to spark up, the gift shop sells
a range of cigarettes.

Tokyo Wonder Site

*1-19-8 Jinnan, Shibuya-ku (3463 0603/
www.tokyo-ws.org/english/shibuya/index.
html). Shibuya station (Yamanote, Ginza
lines), Hachiko exit; (Hanzomon line),
exit 7.* **Open** 11am-7pm Tue-Sun.
Map p117 B/C1 **❾**

The most significant and convenient of a trio of government-funded sites that aim to nurture young creatives. There's a gallery space, regular seminars, a café and an art market.

United Nations University Centre

United Nations University Bldg, 5-53-70 Jingumae, Shibuya-ku (3499 2811/library 5467 1359/ www.unu.edu/ctr.html). Omotesando station (Chiyoda, Ginza, Hanzomon lines), exit B2. **Open** 10am-1pm, 2-5.30pm Mon-Fri. **Admission** free. **Map** p117 E1 ⑩

The UNU Centre houses a permanent UN staff, hosts international conferences on global problems and offers classes. On the eighth floor is a good library for exploring human-rights issues and global concerns. The galleries on the first and second floors are also worth checking out.

Eating & drinking

Ankara

Social Dogenzaka B1F, 1-14-9 Dogenzaka, Shibuya-ku (3780 1366/ www.ankara.jp). Shibuya station (Yamanote, Ginza lines), Hachiko exit; (Hanzomon line), exit 1. **Open** 5-11.30pm Mon-Sat; 5-10pm Sun. **¥¥**. **Turkish**. English menu. **Map** p117 B3 ⑪

Tucked away in the backstreets, this cheerful little Turkish restaurant serves up an array of delicious meze and other Turkish delicacies.

Bar Tube

Kusuhara Bldg 3F, 33-13 Udagawacho, Shibuya-ku (5458 6226). Shibuya station (Yamanote, Ginza lines), Hachiko exit; (Hanzomon line), exits 6, 7. **Open** 9pm-midnight Mon-Sat. **Bar**. **Map** p117 B2 ⑫

YouTube viewing is the gimmick at this limited hours bar. See box p79.

Beacon

NEW *1-2-5 Shibuya, Shibuya-ku (6418 0077/www.tyharborbrewing. co.jp/home/restaurants/beacon_e.html). Omotesando station (Chiyoda, Ginza,* Hanzomon lines), exit B2. **Open** 11.30am-3pm; 6-10pm daily. **¥¥¥¥**. **Steak**. English menu. **Map** p117 E1 ⑬

Beacon describes itself as an 'urban chop-house', which means prime steaks from grain-fed Aussie Angus cattle, free-range chicken, Loch Fyne salmon and more, all grilled expertly over charcoal. The cellar is stocked with New World wines and the adjoining bar pours killer cocktails. Just the place for celebrating or entertaining.

Bello Visto

Cerulean Tower Tokyu Hotel 40F, 26-1 Sakuragaoka-cho, Shibuya-ku (3476 3000/www.ceruleantower-hotel.com). Shibuya station (Yamanote, Ginza, Hanzomon lines), south exit. **Open** 4pm-midnight Mon-Fri; 3pm-midnight Sat, Sun. **Bar**. **Map** p117 B3 ⑭

There are more luxurious hotel bars in town, but the enormous glass windows of the 40th-floor Bello Visto make this a spot worth checking out. The menu focuses on wine, with a frankly terrifying list of expensive tipples from all over the world. Booking is advisable to ensure you get a seat by the window.

Chandelier Bar/Red Bar

1-12-24 Shibuya, Shibuya-ku. Shibuya station (Yamanote, Ginza, Hanzomon lines), east exit. **Open** 8pm-5am Mon-Thur, Sun; 8pm-11am Fri, Sat. **Bar**. **Map** p117 D2 ⑮

Once the pick of Tokyo's late-night/ early morning bars, this spot has lost some of its popularity due to snooty staff and the fickleness of Tokyo's trendies. But it's still the best place to hit in Shibuya when everywhere else shuts. The tiny, dual-named bar is, of course, red and stuffed with chandeliers.

Las Chicas

5-47-6 Jingumae, Shibuya-ku (3407 6865/www.vision.co.jp/lc/index.html). Omotesando station (Chiyoda, Ginza, Hanzomon lines), exit B2. **Open** 11am-11pm Mon-Thur, Sun; 11am-11.30pm Fri, Sat. **¥¥**. **International**. English menu. **Map** p117 E1 ⑯

This complex is a long-time fixture on the expat social scene, comprising a restaurant, bar, café, DJ lounge and exhibition space. The cuisine, which shows strong Aussie influences, includes decent seafood and grills, and the patio is perfect for chilling with a crisp Aussie chardonnay. Due to reopen after refurbishment in February 2008.

CoZmo's Café

1-6-3 Shibuya, Shibuya-ku (3407 5166/www.cozmoscafe.com). Shibuya station (Yamanote, Ginza, Hanzomon lines). **Open** 6pm-midnight Mon-Wed; 6pm-2am Thur-Sat. **Bar**. **Map** p117 D2 ⑰

CoZmo's is an airy venue on a Shibuya backstreet run by an American expat. The menu specialises in inventive cocktails (chocolate martini, anyone?), but makes you pay for them with a hefty ¥1,000 charge that would be more appropriate in a Ginza lounge bar. Still, the atmosphere is warm and the open mic nights worth a look (see box p118).

Don Ciccio

2-3-6 Shibuya, Shibuya-ku (3498 1828). Shibuya station (Yamanote, Ginza lines), east exit; (Hanzomon line), exit 11. **Open** 6pm-midnight Mon-Sat. **¥¥¥**. **Italian**. **Map** p117 E2 ⑱

Friendly and casual, this new mid-market trattoria specialises in the *vini* and *cucina* of Sicily. The pastas and hearty main dishes (both seafood and meat) are excellent, though desserts are not so special. There may be cheaper Italian places in town, but few can match the quality of the ingredients or the enthusiasm of the staff here.

Insomnia Lounge

Ikuma Bldg B1F, 26-5 Udagawacho, Shibuya-ku (3476 2735/www.gnavi.co. jp/miwa). Shibuya station (Yamanote, Ginza, Hanzomon lines), Hachiko exit. **Open** 6pm-5am daily. **Bar**. **Map** p117 B2 ⑲

Hachiko p116

Beacon p120

This womb-like basement bar is covered from floor to ceiling in soft red fabric. For the ultimate queasy experience, try sitting at the bar and gazing into the mirrored lights above it. There's an extensive food and cocktail menu, and a cover charge of ¥525. Remove your shoes when you enter.

Kanetanaka-so

Cerulean Tower Tokyu Hotel 2F, 26-1 Sakuragaoka-cho, Shibuya-ku (3476 3420/www.kanetanaka.co.jp/so/index. html). Shibuya station (Yamanote, Ginza lines), west exit; (Hanzomon line), exit 8. **Open** 11.30am-3pm, 5.30-11pm daily. **¥¥¥¥**. **Kaiseki**. Map p117 B3 ⑳

Kanetanaka is one of Tokyo's most exclusive *ryotei* (traditional restaurants), but this sleek, chic offshoot in the Cerulean Tower Hotel is thoroughly modern and accessible. Instead of the familiar tatami mats and washi paper screens, it's furnished with tables and chairs, and blinds of silvery metal. The multi-course *kaiseki* meals give Japan's traditional haute cuisine an inventive, contemporary slant.

Legato

E Space Tower 15F, 3-6 Maruyama-cho, Shibuya-ku (5784 2121/www. legato-tokyo.jp). Shibuya station (Yamanote, Ginza lines), Hachiko exit; (Hanzomon line), exit 1. **Open** 11.30am-2pm, 5.30-10.30pm daily. **¥¥¥**. **Fusion**. English menu. Map p117 A3 ㉑

Legato occupies the top floor of a tower at the top of Dogenzaka hill, and its food is as theatrical as the lavish decor that surrounds you. The menu mixes influences from Asia and the West, in accordance with Tokyo's current vogue, featuring Vietnamese spring rolls and Chinese noodles alongside lamb chops and pizza. There's also a bar/lounge open until 4am on Friday and Saturday nights.

Lion

2-19-13 Dogenzaka, Shibuya-ku (3461 6858/http://lion.main.jp). Shibuya station (Yamanote, Ginza, Hanzomon lines), Hachiko exit. **Open** 11am-10.30pm daily. **¥**. No credit cards. **Café**. Map p117 A/B2 ㉒

There's an air of reverence at this sleepy shrine to classical music. A pamphlet listing stereophonic offerings is laid out before the customer, seating is in pew-style rows facing an enormous pair of speakers, and conversation is discouraged. If you must talk, do so in a whisper. The imposing grey building is an unexpected period piece amid Dogenzaka's gaudy love hotels.

Negiya Heikichi

36-18 Udagawa, Shibuya-ku (3780 1505/www.kiwa-group.co.jp/restaurant/a100118.html). Shibuya station (Yamanote, Ginza lines), Hachiko exit; (Hanzomon line), exits 6, 7. **Open** 11.30am-2.30pm, 5-11pm Mon-Sat; 11.30am-2.30pm, 5-10.30pm Sun. **¥¥**. **Leek**. English menu. **Map** p117 B1 ㉓
A welcome retreat from Shibuya's brash Center Gai, Heikichi has a rustic, retro feel. The menu is typical of a modern *izakaya*, with one major difference – just about everything features leeks. Unless you're a big fan of the vegetable, then the ¥4,000 set dinner may be overkill. But don't miss the *negi-no-kuroyaki* (charcoal-charred leek).

Pink Cow

Villa Moderna B1F, 1-3-18 Shibuya, Shibuya-ku (3406 5597/www.thepinkcow.com). Shibuya station (Yamanote, Ginza, Hanzomon lines), east exit. **Open** 5pm-late Tue-Thur, Sun; 5pm-3am Fri, Sat. **¥**. **International**. English menu. **Map** p117 D1 ㉔
With an interior that's either garish or funky, depending on your taste, the Pink Cow is not the low-key venue its backstreet location would suggest. It's popular with artistic expats, and the regular events are as quirky and diverse as a knitting salon and a short-film festival. The Friday and Saturday buffet is a reasonable ¥2,500. See also box p118.

Plate of Pie.Pop

15-17 Sakuragaoka-cho, Shibuya-ku (5459 4100/www.dualwave.co.jp/shop/pop/index.html). Shibuya station (Yamanote line), south exit; (Ginza, Hanzomon lines), Hachiko exit 5. **Open** 24hrs daily. **Bar**. **Map** p117 C3 ㉕
A terrific no-frills, all-night drinking spot. See box p175.

Respekt Café

NEW *2F, 1-11-1 Shibuya, Shibuya-ku (6418 8144/www.cafecompany.co.jp). Shibuya station (Yamanote, Ginza, Hanzomon lines), east exit.* **Open** 11.30am-2am Mon-Thur; 11.30am-5am Fri, Sat; 11.30am-midnight Sun. **¥**. **Café**. English menu. **Map** p117 D2 ㉖
Though the name might suggest aspiring b-boys and skate punks, Respekt is actually the new favourite of Shibuya's DJ and design crowd. It's the creation of Café Company, who have been opening trendy but casual cafés across town with all the hooks to lure the young crowd: designer seating, an affordable menu of fusion dishes, jazzy house music and internet access.

Satei Hato

1-15-19 Shibuya, Shibuya-ku (3400 9088). Shibuya station (Yamanote line), east exit; (Ginza line), Toyoko exit; (Hanzomon line), exit 9. **Open** 11am-11.30pm daily. **¥**. No credit cards. **Café**. **Map** p117 C2 ㉗

TOKYO BY AREA

Step through the marble-tiled entrance and into a top-grade traditional coffee shop. A huge collection of china cups stands behind the counter, while sweeping arrangements of seasonal blooms add colour to a dark wood interior that recalls an earlier age. The most expensive coffee on the menu is Blue Mountain at ¥1,000.

Sushi Ouchi

2-8-4 Shibuya, Shibuya-ku (3407 3543). Shibuya station (Yamanote, Ginza lines), east exit; (Hanzomon line), exit 11. **Open** noon-1.30pm, 5-11.30pm daily. **¥¥¥**. No credit cards. **Sushi**. Map p117 E2 ㉘

Owner-chef Hisashi Ouchi ensures all his seafood is wild, adds no sugar or MSG to his rice, uses only free-range eggs and shuns all artificial additives. This is no mere gimmick. Ouchi's sushi is wonderful, and so are the premises, a plain but comfortable room with wooden beams and antique furniture.

Tantra

Ichimainoe Bldg B1F, 3-5-5 Shibuya, Shibuya-ku (5485 8414). Shibuya station (Yamanote, Ginza, Hanzomon lines), east, new south exits. **Open** 8pm-5am daily. **Bar**. Map p117 E3 ㉙

Blink and you'll miss the entrance – the only sign is a small, dimly lit 'T' above a nondescript stairwell. But heave open the imposing metal door and you'll find yourself in what resembles a secret, subterranean drinking club, decorated with stone pillars, veiled alcoves, flickering candles and statues depicting scenes from the Kama Sutra. On your first visit you'll feel you've gatecrashed a private party, but have courage and don't be put off by the ice-cool staff.

Underground Mr Zoogunzoo

Aoyama City Bldg B1, 2-9-11 Shibuya, Shibuya-ku (3400 1496/www.unitedf. com/zoogunzoo). Shibuya station (Yamanote, Ginza lines), east exit; (Hanzomon line), exit 11. **Open** *Bar* 6pm-2am Mon-Sat. *Restaurant* 6pm-11pm Mon-Sat. **¥¥¥**. **Wine bar**. English menu. Map p117 E2 ㉚

This cosy basement wine bar boasts decor every bit as eccentric as its name. There's a great cellar, focusing exclusively on Antipodean wines, with half a dozen always available by the glass. The lights stay dimmed, the welcome is friendly and hectic Tokyo always feels a long way away.

Uogashi Nippon-ichi

25-6 Udagawacho, Shibuya-ku (5728 5451/www.uogashi.jp). Shibuya station (Yamanote, Ginza lines), Hachiko exit; (Hanzomon line), exits 6, 7. **Open** 11am-11pm daily. **¥**. No credit cards. **Sushi**. Map p117 B2 ㉛

Sushi, not sake, is the draw, and it's surprisingly good given rock-bottom prices. There are branches of this sushi chain in many parts of the city, but this one makes a welcome change from the fast-food joints along Center Gai.

Shopping

109

2-29-1 Dogenzaka, Shibuya-ku (3477 5111/www.shibuya109.jp). Shibuya station (Yamanote, Ginza lines), Hachiko exit; (Hanzomon line), exit 3A. **Open** 10am-9pm daily. Map p117 B2 ㉜

This landmark Shibuya store is the domain of the *gyaru* – the fashion-obsessed teenage girls who don't just follow trends but start them. Take a stroll around to see them in action and indulge in some amateur anthropology. Nearby 109-2 sells more of the same to pre-teens.

Cisco

11-1 Udagawa-cho, Shibuya-ku (3462 0366/www.cisco-records.co.jp). Shibuya station (Yamanote, Ginza lines), Hachiko exit; (Hanzomon line), exits 3, 6. **Open** noon-10pm Mon-Sat; 11am-9pm Sun. Map p117 B1 ㉝

Cisco is at the cutting edge of dance music. Its Shibuya branch comprises five buildings close to one another, divided according to sub-genre. This is the place to come to see well-known DJs holding earnest discussions with shop owners across the in-store turntables.

Dance Music Record

36-2 Udagawa-cho, Shibuya-ku (3477 1556/www.dmr.co.jp). Shibuya station (Yamanote, Ginza lines), Hachiko exit; (Hanzomon line), exits 3, 6. **Open** noon-10pm daily. **Map** p117 B1 ㉞
Dance Music Record is the name and dance-music records are the game. The first floor is a vast space with a comprehensive collection of hip hop, club jazz and R&B. Upstairs there's a great selection of the latest house on vinyl.

Intelligent Idiot

5-47-6 Jingumae, Shibuya-ku (5467 5866/www.vision.co.jp). Omotesando station (Chiyoda, Ginza, Hanzomon lines), exit B2. **Open** 2-8pm Mon, Wed-Fri; 12.30-7.30pm Sat, Sun. No credit cards. **Map** p117 E1 ㉟
Part of the eclectic Vision Network empire and located above the Las Chicas café (p120), this shop sells new books in English at discount prices. It is also a showroom for furniture company Kyozon.

Mark City

1-12-1 Dogenzaka, Shibuya-ku (3780 6503/www.s-markcity.co.jp). Shibuya station (Yamanote, Ginza lines), Hachiko exit; (Hanzomon line), exits 5, 8. **Open** *Shops* 10am-9pm daily. *Restaurants* 11am-11pm daily. **Map** p117 B3 ㊱
Shibuya's version of the multi-purpose mall is a relatively modest affair, housing a handful of boutiques and lifestyle stores in a building adjoining Shibuya station. Restaurants and cafés are on the third and fourth floors, women's clothing is on the second, accessories and cosmetics are on the first.

Parco

15-1 Udagawacho, Shibuya-ku (3464 5111/www.parco.co.jp). Shibuya station (Yamanote, Ginza lines), Hachiko exit; (Hanzomon line), exits 6, 7. **Open** 10am-9pm daily. **Map** p117 B1 ㊲
This mid-range clothing store occupies several buildings in Shibuya. Part 1 houses a theatre and an art bookshop, Part 2 specialises in fashion, and Part 3 has an exhibition space that hosts frequent shows by artists and designers

Buzzwords

Japan's love of novelty extends to its language, with the lexicon growing at a staggering pace. As with all good fashions, the hottest new language comes from Shibuya's flamboyant and fickle *gyaru* ('gals'). Their inventions playfully mix foreign influences and abbreviations, and take a liberal approach to grammatical constraints.

In a recent annual poll of 'buzzwords', submitted by the public and voted on by professional writers and editors, the top ten words included *erokawaii*, the latest compliment for local girls. A portmanteau of *eroi* (from the English 'erotic') and *kawaii* ('cute'), the term originated as an adjective for teen idol Kumi Koda, whose pouty poses and taste for raunchy outfits meant that 'cute' alone didn't seem right. The masculine equivalent is *erokakkoi* ('erotic cool'), used for centre guys, the biker/cowboy/hair-metal-singer hybrids who hang out on Shibuya's Center Gai.

Eroi, a long-standing import, has been joined recently by some inventive verbs, including *misru* (to make a mistake), *toraburu* (to get into trouble) and *stabaru* (to Starbuck).

Another top-ten term from 2006 shows how false friends are made of familiar phrases. *Metabo* abbreviates the English term 'metabolic syndrome', but rather than referring to a complex medical condition, *metabo* here means 'fat gut'. The Japanese are voracious importers of foreign words, but not necessarily their meanings.

TOKYO BY AREA

109 p124

from Japan and abroad. Another branch is home to the top-quality concert venue Club Quattro (p129).

RagTag

1-17-7 Jinnan, Shibuya-ku (3476 6848/www.ragtag.jp). Shibuya station (Yamanote, Ginza lines), Hachiko exit; (Hanzomon line), exit 6. **Open** noon-9pm daily. **Map** p117 C1 ⑱
The Shibuya branch of this designer recycle shop is an excellent browsing ground for those in search of designer labels at heavily discounted prices.

ranKing ranQueen

West Bldg 2F, Tokyu Department Toyoko branch, 2-24-1 Shibuya, Shibuya-ku (3770 5480/www.ranking-ranqueen.net). Shibuya station (Yamanote, Ginza lines), Hachiko exit; (Hanzomon line), exits 3, 3A. **Open** 10am-11.30pm daily. **Map** p117 C2 ⑲
The Japanese are obsessed with making lists and charts of what's popular, which they call 'rankings' – hence the puns in this shop's name. At ranKing ranQueen, a citywide chain with a branch inside Shibuya JR station, you'll find the top ten products for CDs, cosmetics, dieting aids, magazines and so on. It's an intriguing insight into the mind of the Japanese consumer.

Recofan

Shibuya Beam 4F, 31-2 Udagawa-cho, Shibuya-ku (3463 0090/www.recofan. co.jp). Shibuya station (Yamanote, Ginza lines), Hachiko exit; (Hanzomon line), exit 3A. **Open** 11.30am-9pm daily. **Map** p117 B1 ⑳
Recofan is a music chain selling new releases at bargain basement rates. This enormous Shibuya branch also has an extensive selection of second-hand vinyl and CDs covering all genres. Regular shoppers receive a loyalty card for even bigger discounts.

Seibu

21-1 Udagawa-cho, Shibuya-ku (3462 0111/www.seibu.co.jp). Shibuya station (Yamanote, Ginza lines), Hachiko exit; (Hanzomon line), exits 6, 7. **Open** 10am-8pm Mon-Wed, Sun; 10am-9pm Thur-Sat. **Map** p117 C2 ㊶

The Shibuya branch of this department store chain is split into two buildings, Annexes A and B, which are opposite each other. Annex A sells mainly womenswear, while Annex B has menswear, children's clothes and accessories. Seibu also runs retailers Loft and Movida, both of which are within easy walking distance of the store. Aimed at a young crowd, Loft sells interior decorations and various knick-knacks, while Movida houses top-end fashion store Via Bus Stop.

Technique

33-14 Udagawacho, Shibuya-ku (3464 7690/www.technique.co.jp). Shibuya station (Yamanote, Ginza lines), Hachiko exit; (Hanzomon line), exits 3, 6. **Open** 1-11pm daily. **Map** p117 B2 ㊷
Technique is the purveyor of all strands of dance-music vinyl – from progressive house to nu-jazz. Several listening decks and knowledgeable staff make this the store of choice for many local DJs.

Three Minutes Happiness

3-5 Udagawa-cho, Shibuya-ku (5459 1851). Shibuya station (Yamanote, Ginza lines), Hachiko exit; (Hanzomon line), exits 6, 7. **Open** 11am-9pm daily. **Map** p117 B1 ㊸
Think of this as a high-class 100-yen shop, selling a large and eclectic mix of original household goods, most costing less than ¥1,000. It's owned by the Comme Ça fashion chain.

Tokyu Hands

12-18 Udagawa-cho, Shibuya-ku (5489 5111/www.tokyu-hands.co.jp). Shibuya station (Yamanote, Ginza lines), Hachiko exit; (Hanzomon line), exits 6, 7. **Open** 10am-8.30pm daily. **Map** p117 B1 ㊹
From stationery to toilet-seat covers, this is the largest household goods store in Tokyo, packed with knick-knacks for the home. Particularly interesting is the party supplies section, which gives a unique glimpse into the Japanese sense of humour.

Zoff

Mark City 4F, 1-12-5 Dogenzaka, Shibuya-ku (5428 3961/www.zoff.co.jp). Shibuya station (Yamanote, Ginza lines), Hachiko exit; (Hanzomon line), exits 5, 8. **Open** 10am-9pm daily. **Map** p117 B3 45

Zoff is a funky little chain of eyewear stores. This branch is convenient, despite being hidden away in the Mark City complex (p125).

Nightlife

Ball

Kuretake Bldg 4F, 4-8 Udagawacho, Shibuya-ku (3476 6533/www.club-ball.com). Shibuya station (Yamanote, Ginza lines), Hachiko exit; (Hanzomon line), exits 3, 6. **Open** 10pm-5am Mon-Sat; varies Sun. **Admission** ¥2,000. No credit cards. **Map** p117 B1 46

There's a great view across Shibuya to be had from this little venue during the night, but sadly that is the place's best feature, notwithstanding the moderately priced bar (drinks from ¥600). The sound system simply isn't up to scratch – and given that the choice of music is house, this is a very serious shortcoming indeed. The tiny dance-floor is another drawback.

Club Asia

1-8 Maruyamacho, Shibuya-ku (5458 2551/www.clubasia.co.jp). Shibuya station (Yamanote, Ginza lines), Hachiko exit; (Hanzomon line), exit 3A. **Open** usually from 11pm. **Admission** ¥2,000-¥3,500. No credit cards. **Map** p117 A2 47

Club Asia offers three bars and two dancefloors, with a high ceiling that looks spectacular but doesn't always do the sound any favours. It is increasingly being used as a live venue rather than a club, and is a favourite space with private-party organisers, so be sure to check the schedule.

Club Atom

Dr Jeekahn's Bldg 4F-6F, 2-4 Maruyamacho, Shibuya-ku (5428 5195/www.clubatom.com). Shibuya station (Yamanote, Ginza lines), Hachiko exit; (Hanzomon line), exit 3A. **Open** 9pm-5am Thur-Sat. **Admission** ¥3,000. No credit cards. **Map** p117 A3 48

There are two reasonably open dance-floors at this roomy venue. The one on the fifth floor focuses on mainstream trance or house music, while the cave-like fourth floor offers R&B and hip hop. The place is wildly popular with heavily made-up, super-tanned Shibuya 'gals' and, as such, is more interesting from a sociological perspective than a musical one.

Club Bar Family

Shimizu Bldg B1F, 1-10-2 Shibuya, Shibuya-ku (3400 9182). Shibuya station (Yamanote line), Miyamasuaka (east) exit; (Ginza line), Inokashira, Tamagawa exits; (Hanzomon line), exit 11. **Open** 10.30pm-4am Mon-Thur; 10.30pm-5am Fri, Sat. **Admission** ¥2,000. No credit cards. **Map** p117 D2 49

A tiny space that pours out a stream of heavy bass sounds, Family features ground-level hip hop at its best. It's the perfect venue if you like thundering rap beats and it's rare to see a non-Japanese face here, which can make for a warm reception for any visitor who does venture inside. Drinks are a good deal at around ¥600.

Club Camelot

NEW *1-18-2 Shibuya, Shibuya-ku (5728 5613/www.clubcamelot.jp). Shibuya station (Yamanote, Ginza lines), west exit; (Hanzomon line), exit 12.* **Open** 7pm-5am Thur-Sat. **Admission** ¥2,500-¥3,000. **Map** p117 C1 50

While Camelot wants to court the well-heeled and more mature trendsetters, its dress code is never enforced, and the weekend crowd varies from scruffy young Shibuya kids to dressed-up businesspeople. The smaller of the two floors holds 300 and specialises in hip hop, R&B and reggae. Downstairs, 700 people can gather on the marble floor or lounge on the white leather sofas. Try 'Ultimate Saturday' for a mix of house and hip hop.

Club Hachi

Aoyama Bldg 1F-4F, 4-5-9 Shibuya,
Shibuya-ku (5766 4887). Shibuya
station (Yamanote line), Miyamasuraka
(east) exit; (Ginza line), Inogashira,
Tamagawa exits; (Hanzomon line),
exit 11. **Open** 10pm-5am Mon-Sat;
5-11pm Sun. **Admission** ¥2,000
Mon-Thur, Sun; ¥2,500 Fri, Sat.
No credit cards. **Map** p117 E2 ⑤①

It's dingy, but that's part of the charm.
Hachi occupies the whole of a run-
down, four-storey building on
Roppongi Dori. The first floor contains
a yakitori bar, the second a DJ bar, the
third a dark dancefloor, and the top
floor is a lounge bar. Events here vary
massively in genre and quality. Hachi
was once the regular haunt of globally
fêted DJ Ken Ishii.

Club Quattro

Parco 4F, 32-13 Udagawa-cho,
Shibuya-ku (3477 8750/www.
club-quattro.com). Shibuya station
(Yamanote, Ginza, Hanzomon lines),
Hachiko exit. **Open** 11am-9pm daily.
Map p117 B2 ⑤②

Despite the name, Club Quattro is a live
venue rather than nightclub. There are
some view-restricting pillars on the
main floor, but this is nonetheless one
of the most appealing music venues in
town, attracting artists who could play
larger venues.

La Fabrique

Zero Gate B1F, 16-9 Udagawacho,
Shibuya-ku (5428 5100/www.la
fabrique.jp). Shibuya station (Yamanote,
Ginza lines), Hachiko exit; (Hanzomon
line), exit 6. **Open** 11am-2am Mon-
Thur; 11am-5am Fri, Sat. **Admission**
¥3,000-¥4,000. No credit cards. **Map**
p117 B2 ⑤③

This branch of a Parisian dining club
offers French dining during daylight
hours and dancing by night. The
weekend events, which draw quality
local acts and the odd visiting star, kick
off at around 11pm. Downtempo
sounds are usually played during the
week; but for the weekend's revels the
music speeds up to include a mix of
house music and disco.

Gig-antic

Sound Forum Bldg 2F, 3-20-15
Shibuya, Shibuya-ku (5466 9339/
www.gig-antic.co.jp). Shibuya station
(Yamanote, Ginza, Hanzomon lines),
Miyamasuraka (east) exit. **Map**
p117 C3 ⑤④

Ironically, Gig-antic is a small venue.
It's *the* place to see hardcore and punk
bands from around Japan. Because of
its size and the dedicated hordes of
friends the bands bring with them,
events can sell out.

Harlem

Dr Jeekahn's Bldg 2F-3F, 2-4
Maruyamacho, Shibuya-ku (3461
8806/www.harlem.co.jp). Shibuya
station (Yamanote, Ginza lines),
Hachiko exit; (Hanzomon line),
exit 3A. **Open** 10pm-5am Tue-Sat.
Admission ¥2,000 Tue-Thur;
¥3,000 Fri, Sat. No credit cards.
Map p117 A3 ⑤⑤

Located in the same building as Club
Atom (p128), Harlem has been the
mecca of hip-hop culture in Japan since
the mid 1990s. If you want to see
b-boys and fly girls shakin' it, as well
as some of Japan's up-and-coming
MCs, this is the spot. DJ Hasebe and
other well-known Japanese spinners
often play here.

J-pop Café

Beam Bldg.7F, 31-2 Udagawacho,
Shibuya-ku (5456 5767/www.j-pop
cafe.com). Shibuya station (Yamanote,
Ginza lines), Hachiko exit; (Hanzomon
line), exits 6, 7. **Open** 5pm-midnight
Mon-Fri; noon-midnight Sat, Sun.
Map p117 B1 ⑤⑥

The dining club concept is applied to
the syrupy sounds of J-pop in this
spacious hall, which sometimes hosts
surprisingly big names. Many of your
fellow diners will be spending their
pocket money, so the prices are rock
bottom and the shows start early.
Gaudy good fun.

JZ Brat

Cerulean Tower Tokyu Hotel 2F,
26-1 Sakuragaoka-cho, Shibuya-
ku (5728 0168/www.jzbrat.com).
Shibuya station (Yamanote, Ginza,

Hanzomon lines), south exit. **Open**
Shows from 7.30pm daily. **Map**
p117 B3 ➎

This smart jazz club, housed inside the
sprawling Cerulean Tower hotel, is
expensive but worth it. The booking
policy is consistently good, with occasional overseas players performing.
The space is large, so you can move
and chat while the music plays. Plus
point: the bar is open until 4am on
Fridays and Saturdays.

La.mama Shibuya

*Premier Dogenzaka B1F, 1-15-3
Dogenzaka, Shibuya-ku (3464 0801/
www.lamama.net). Shibuya station
(Yamanote, Ginza, Hanzomon lines),
south exit.* **Map** p117 B3 ➎

La.mama is a punky little basement
venue that's been presenting bands at
the start of (one hopes) successful
careers for more than 20 years. Plenty
of J-pop and commercial rock on the
schedule here.

Loop

*B1F, 2-1-13 Shibuya, Shibuya-ku
(3797 9933/www.club-loop.com).
Shibuya station (Yamanote line),
Miyamasusaka (east) exit; (Ginza
line), Inokashira, Tamagawa exits;
(Hanzomon line), exit 11; or
Omotesando station (Chiyoda,
Ginza, Hanzomon lines), exit B1.*
Open 10pm-5am daily. **Admission**
¥2,000 Mon-Thur; ¥2,500 Fri-Sun.
No credit cards. **Map** p117 E2 ➎

Between Shibuya and Omotesando
stations, Loop has a stylish, bare-
concrete interior and is an ideal hide-
out for dance-music aficionados. The
dancefloor has moody lighting, an
excellent sound system (the music is
mainly deep house, tech house and
techno) and a friendly vibe. For local
talent, check out 'Smoker' (Wednesday)
and 'In the Mix' (Saturday).

Module

*M&I Bldg B1F-B2F, 34-6
Udagawacho, Shibuya-ku (3464
8432/www.clubmodule.com). Shibuya
station (Yamanote, Ginza lines),
Hachiko exit; (Hanzomon line),
exits 3, 6.* **Open** from 10pm

Mon-Sat. **Admission** ¥2,000
Mon-Thur; ¥2,500 Fri, Sat. No
credit cards. **Map** p117 B2 ➏

There's a relaxing split-level bar on the
first basement floor, and a very different pitch-black dancefloor below. The
sound system is loud enough to cause
the foundations to shudder and a
glitter ball is the only source of light.
Module pulls a much better selection of
DJs and a more knowledgeable crowd
than many of its peers. Being owned by
Yellow (p114) helps.

Neo

*TLC Bldg 5F, 2-21-7 Dogenzaka,
Shibuya-ku (5459 7230/www.club
asia.co.jp). Shibuya station (Yamanote,
Ginza lines), Hachiko exit; (Hanzomon
line), exit 3A.* **Open** 11pm-5am; days
vary. **Admission** ¥3,000-¥3,500.
No credit cards. **Map** p117 A2 ➏

Neo's location among Shibuya's
biggest clubs (Womb, Vuenos, Club
Asia) means it's often overlooked by
clubbers, but it can offer a more chilled-
out experience. The venue has no music
policy – so you could be listening to
dancehall, reggae or progressive house.

Club Camelot p128

Organ Bar

Kuretake Bldg 3F, 4-9 Udagawacho, Shibuya-ku (5489 5460/www.organ-b.net). Shibuya station (Yamanote, Ginza lines), Hachiko exit; (Hanzomon line), exit 6. **Open** 9pm-5am daily. **Admission** ¥2,000 Mon-Sat; ¥1,000 Sun. No credit cards. **Map** p117 B1 ⑫
Another small joint in the same building as Ball (p128). What the tiny dancefloor lacks in space, it makes up for in atmosphere. The focus is on soul, jazz and bossa nova, which attracts a slightly older crowd. All drinks cost ¥700.

Rockwest

Tosen Udagawacho Bldg 7F, 4-7 Udagawacho, Shibuya-ku (5459 7988). Shibuya station (Yamanote, Ginza lines), Hachiko exit; (Hanzomon line), exit 6. **Open** 10pm-5am daily. **Admission** ¥2,000-¥2,500. No credit cards. **Map** p117 B1 ⑬
Formerly a happy hardcore venue, Rockwest now moves to a slower beat, with hip hop and soul dominating the schedule. Plus points are the air-con, good sound system, relatively roomy dancefloor and re-entry system.

Room

Daihachi Tohto Bldg B1F, 15-19 Sakuragaoka, Shibuya-ku (3461 7167/ www.theroom.jp). Shibuya station (Yamanote line), south exit; (Ginza line), central exit; (Hanzomon line), exit 8. **Open** 10pm-5am Mon-Sat. **Admission** ¥1,000-¥2,000 Mon-Thur; ¥2,500 Fri, Sat. No credit cards. **Map** p117 C3 ⑭
The Room is well hidden, so you'll have to keep an eye out for the red light that pokes out from the basement. Owned by members of Kyoto Jazz Massive, it's a small venue with a preference for house, jazz, crossover or breakbeats. Top DJs sometimes come here to try out new sets on their nights off, much to the delight of the clientele.

Ruby Room

Kasumi Bldg 4F, 2-25-17 Dogenzaka, Shibuya-ku (3780 3022/www.rubyroom tokyo.com). Shibuya station (Yamanote, Ginza lines), Hachiko exit; (Hanzomon line), exit 3A. **Open** 7pm-5am daily. **Admission** free Mon-Thur, Sun; ¥1,500 Fri, Sat. No credit cards. **Map** p117 B2 ⑮

TOKYO BY AREA

A little box of a venue that punches well above its size. Ruby Room holds around 150 people, yet has drawn acts including Basement Jaxx, Hernan Cattaneo and Belle & Sebastian to play impromptu sets. It remains a hugely popular spot for expats and club-conscious Tokyoites, despite a bizarre renovation in 2006 that saw a huge chunk of the floor space given over to a semi-private booth that resembles a toilet. See also box p118.

Seco Bar

NEW *B1, 1-11-1 Shibuya, Shibuya-ku (6418 8144/www.secobar.jp). Shibuya station (Yamanote, Ginza, Hanzomon lines), east exit.* **Open** 6pm-4am Mon-Sat; 6pm-midnight Sun. **Admission** ¥2,000-¥2,500. No credit cards. **Map** p117 D2 **66**

Seco Bar was one of Shibuya's hottest hangouts until it underwent a temporary closure back in 2004. Re-opening in 2007 in this new location, which has a darker and more industrial look, the venue is still finding its feet, but the atmosphere is fun, the sound decent and we're expecting good things. The music programming steers towards house and techno.

Shibuya Nuts

B2, 2-17-3 Shibuya, Shibuya-ku (5466 8814/www.clubnuts.net). Shibuya station (Yamanote, Ginza lines), west exit; (Hanzomon line), exit 8. **Open** 11pm-5am Tue-Sun. **Admission** ¥2,000-¥3,000. No credit cards. **Map** p117 D2 **67**

Hip hop and reggae dominate here, making it a genuine, and much friendlier, rival to the larger Harlem (p129) on the opposite side of Shibuya, Shibuya Nuts sometimes pulls in remarkably big international names. Sunday's 'Raga Nuts' is a Tokyo phenomenon – a rammed Sunday night, with locals bouncing off the walls to Japanese and Jamaican MCs.

Vuenos Bar Tokyo

1F-B1F, 2-21-7 Dogenzaka, Shibuya-ku (5458 5963/www.clubasia.co.jp). Shibuya station (Yamanote, Ginza

lines), Hachiko exit; (Hanzomon line), exit 3A. **Open** 11pm-5am; days vary. **Admission** ¥2,500-¥3,000. No credit cards. **Map** p117 A2 **68**

Across from and owned by Club Asia (p128), Vuenos opened in 1998 with a mission to spread the word about Latin, soul and dance music. On many levels it succeeded, though, at weekends, the line-up skews to hip hop, R&B and reggae. Vuenos attracts a younger crowd and is very popular, so be prepared to queue to get in, especially later in the evening.

Womb

2-16 Maruyamacho, Shibuya-ku (5459 0039/www.womb.co.jp). Shibuya station (Yamanote, Ginza lines), Hachiko exit; (Hanzomon line), exit 3A. **Open** usually 10pm-5am Thur-Sat. **Admission** ¥2,000-¥4,000. No credit cards. **Map** p117 A3 **69**

For serious clubbers, Womb is quite simply the best venue in town. It offers a vast dancefloor, great lighting, a super-bass sound system and what claims to be 'Asia's largest mirror ball'. House, techno and drum 'n' bass are the usual sounds here. Womb's schedule is packed with foreign names, but DJ Aki (drum 'n' bass) is one local hero who plays here.

Arts & leisure

Aoyama Round Theatre

5-53-1 Jingumae, Shibuya-ku (3797 5678/box office 3797 1400/www. aoyama.org). Omotesando station (Chiyoda, Ginza, Hanzomon lines), exit B2. No credit cards. **Map** p117 E1 **70**

As its name suggests, this is a theatre that can be used in the round – one of very few in Tokyo. It attracts leading contemporary performers.

Cerulean Tower Noh Theatre

Cerulean Tower Tokyu Hotel B2F, 26-1 Sakuragaoka-cho, Shibuya-ku (5728 0168/www.ceruleantower.com). Shibuya station (Yamanote, Ginza, Hanzomon lines), south exit. **Map** p117 B3 **71**

Housed in the basement of the Cerulean Tower hotel (p172), this is the city's newest venue for traditional Japanese theatre. It hosts both professional and amateur *Noh* and *kyogen* performances – without English translation.

Ciné Amuse

Fontis Bldg 4F, 2-23-12 Dogenzaka, Shibuya-ku (3496 2888/www.cine amuse.co.jp). Shibuya station (Yamanote, Ginza lines), Hachiko exit; (Hanzomon line), exit 3A. **Map** p117 A2 🟣

Eclectic programming sees international releases such as *Borat* play alongside Japanese classics.

Le Cinema

Bunkamura 6F, 2-24-1 Dogenzaka, Shibuya-ku (3477 9264/www. bunkamura.co.jp). Shibuya station (Yamanote, Ginza lines), Hachiko exit; (Hanzomon line), exit 3A. **Map** p117 A2 🟣

This two-screener in the giant Bunkamura arts complex offers predominantly French fare. It's also the principal venue for the Tokyo International Film Festival (p36) each year from late October.

Cinema Rise

13-17 Udagawacho, Shibuya-ku (3464 0051/www.cinemarise.com). Shibuya station (Yamanote, Ginza lines), Hachiko exit; (Hanzomon line), exit 6. **Map** p117 B1 🟣

A champion of independent cinema, this is where Tokyoites watched *Buena Vista Social Club* and *The Corporation*. Foreign students (who must show ID) pay only ¥1,000.

Ciné Quinto

Parco Part 3 8F, 14-5 Udagawa-cho, Shibuya-ku (3477 5905/www.parco-city.co.jp/cine_quinto). Shibuya station (Yamanote, Ginza lines), Hachiko exit; (Hanzomon line), exit 6. **Map** p117 B1 🟣

Quinto often screens new British films, and offers bizarre film-based discounts. For example, when Hong Kong film *The Eye* was on, anyone carrying a photo of a ghost got a discount of

¥800. Different rules are stipulated for each film. Keep your ticket stub to enter for just ¥1,000 on your next visit.

Euro Space

Q-AX Bldg, 1-5 Maruyama-cho, Shibuya-ku (3461 0211/www. eurospace.co.jp). Shibuya station (Yamanote,Ginza lines), Hachiko exit; (Hanzomon line), exit 5. **Map** p117 C3 🟣

An art-house specialist, Euro Space has now been around for two decades, playing a selection of independent films from Europe and Asia. It moved to a new location in January 2006.

Orchard Hall

Bunkamura, 2-24-1 Dogenzaka, Shibuya-ku (3477 9999/www. bunkamura.co.jp). Shibuya station (Yamanote, Ginza, Hanzomon lines), Hachiko exit. **Map** p117 A2 🟣

This is the largest shoebox-shaped hall in Japan, designed to produce the best possible acoustics – though some complain it's rather echoey. Classical, opera and ballet are the norm, but works in other genres are also staged.

Theatre Cocoon

Bunkamura, 2-24-1 Dogenzaka, Shibuya-ku (3477 9999/www. bunkamura.co.jp). Shibuya station (Yamanote, Ginza lines), Hachiko exit; (Hanzomon line), exit 3A. **Map** p117 A2 🟣

The medium-sized venue in the giant Bunkamura arts centre is used mainly for musicals, ballet, concerts and opera, but has also staged performances of modern kabuki.

Theatre Image Forum

2-10-2 Shibuya, Shibuya-ku (5766 0114/www.imageforum.co.jp). Shibuya station (Yamanote, Ginza lines), east exit; (Hanzomon line), exit 12. **Map** p117 E2 🟣

The TIF is one of the leading supporters of avant-garde film-making in Japan. Founded in 1977, the group has helped keep the experimental scene alive with film festivals, seminars and this screen in Shibuya which plays both Japanese and foreign films.

歌舞伎町一番街

Kabuki-cho

Shinjuku

Shinjuku is the neon-lit Tokyo you've seen in the movies. It's the largest sub-centre and easily the most cosmopolitan area, with luxurious department stores, sleazy strip clubs, smoky jazz bars and gay porn shops all just a few blocks from each other. The area is divided into two distinct east and west sections by the JR Yamanote and Chuo train lines. The clean-cut west is home to the city government, corporate skyscrapers and the luxurious **Park Hyatt Tokyo** (p174), while the cacophonous east offers everything from big-brand shopping to neon-lit sex parlours.

It is also a major transportation hub. In fact, Shinjuku station is the busiest in the world. Those photos you've seen of commuters being pushed on to crowded trains by uniformed guards in rush hour? Shinjuku station, every morning of the week, from 7.30am onwards. Get up early and take a camera, but don't expect there to be much room on the platform. And with over 50 exits, miles of tunnels and several different levels, it's also the station you're most likely to get lost in – which means it's essential to know which exit you need.

Compared to the gastronomic wonderlands of Ginza, Roppongi or Aoyama, Shinjuku falls a little short in terms of top-class dining options. But there are plenty of cheap and cheerful restaurants and *izakaya,* and it boasts two of the best drinking areas of the capital: the San-chome district, which is packed with friendly, affordable music-oriented bars, and Golden Gai, a tiny patch of land on the

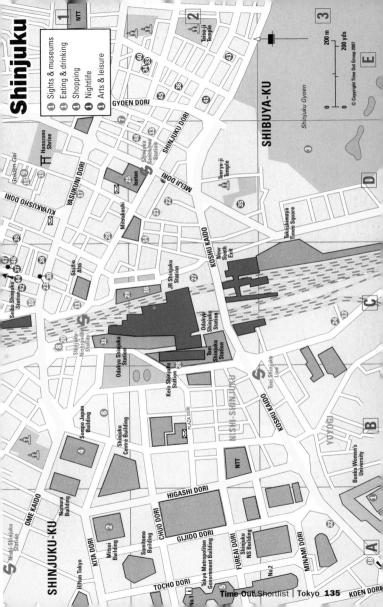

Shinjuku

Key:
- 🔵 Sights & museums
- 🟣 Eating & drinking
- 🟠 Shopping
- 🔴 Nightlife
- 🟢 Arts & leisure

SHINJUKU-KU

SHIBUYA-KU

Shinjuku Gyoen

Hanazono Shrine

Golden-Gai

Isetan

Mitsukoshi

Studio Alta

JR Shinjuku Station

Odakyu Shinjuku Station

Toei Shinjuku Station

Keio Shinjuku Station

Shinjuku-Nishiguchi Station

Seibu Shinjuku Station

Nishi-Shinjuku Station

Hilton Tokyo

Nomura Building

Sompo Japan Building

Shinjuku Centre Building

Mitsui Building

Sumitomo Building

Tokyo Metropolitan Government Building

Shinjuku NS Building

Bunka Women's University

Taiso-ji Temple

Tenryu-ji Temple

Takashimaya Times Square

New South Exit

Shinjuku Sanchome Station

Toei Shinjuku Line

NTT

YASUKUNI DORI

KUYAKUSHO DORI

GYOEN DORI

SHINJUKU DORI

MEIJI DORI

KOSHU KAIDO

OME KAIDO

NISHI-SHINJUKU

HIGASHI DORI

CHUO DORI

GIJIDO DORI

KITA DORI

TOCHO DORI

FUREAI DORI

MINAMI DORI

KOEN DORI

PLAZA DORI

YOYOGI

No.1

No.2

0   200 m
0   200 yds

© Copyright Time Out Group 2007

A   B   C   D   E

1   2   3

View from Tokyo Metropolitan Government Building No.1

edge of the red-light action. Over 250 of Tokyo's tiniest drinking establishments are squeezed into Golden Gai's character-laden alleys, but the reception for new faces ranges from convivial (as in the four bars we've listed) to downright hostile (expect cold shoulders and outrageous bills).

A few blocks from Golden Gai is the capital's gay scene – eerily quiet by day, pounding with energy each night. We've listed a few highlights under Nightlife (p144).

Sights & museums

Bunka Gakuen Costume Museum

3-22-7 Yoyogi, Shibuya-ku (3299 2387/ www.bunka.ac.jp/museum/hakubutsu. htm). Shinjuku station (Yamanote, Chuo, Sobu lines), south exit; (Oedo, Shinjuku lines), exit 6. **Open** 10am-4.30pm Mon-Sat. **Admission** ¥500; ¥200-¥300 reductions. No credit cards. **Map** p135 A3 ❶

This small collection includes examples of historical Japanese clothing, such as an Edo-era fire-fighting coat and a brightly coloured, 12-layer *karaginumo* outfit. Kamakura-period scrolls illustrate the types of dress worn by different classes of people. The displays change four or five times a year.

epSITE

Shinjuku Mitsui Bldg 1F, 2-1-1 Nishi-Shinjuku, Shinjuku-ku (3345 9881/ http://epsite.epson.co.jp). Nishi-Shinjuku station (Marunouchi line), exit 1. **Open** 10.30am-6pm daily. Closed 1wk Aug, 1wk Dec-Jan. **Map** p135 A1 ❷

Epson uses its latest digital technology to create the enormous, impressively detailed photo prints displayed in this, its showcase gallery.

Shinjuku Gyoen

11 Naito-cho, Shinjuku-ku (3350 0151/www.shinjukugyoen.go.jp). Shinjuku-Gyoenmae station (Marunouchi line), exit 1. **Open** *Park* 9am-4.30pm Tue-Sun; daily during cherry blossom (early Apr)

The views from this 42nd-floor museum are spectacular. Perhaps to compete, the insurance company that owns it purchased Van Gogh's 1889 *Sunflowers* in 1987 for the then record-breaking price of over ¥5 billion. There is now some concern over its authenticity, but this symbol of Japan's go-go Bubble years hangs alongside Cézanne's *Pommes et Serviette* in a dim glass box. The museum's core work is by Japanese artists, specifically Togo Seiji (1897-1978), who donated 200 of his own pieces.

Tokyo Metropolitan Government Building No.1

2-8-1 Nishi-Shinjuku, Shinjuku-ku (5321 1111/observatory 5320 7890/ www.yokoso.metro.tokyo.jp). Tochomae station (Oedo line), exit 4. **Open** *North Observatory 9.30am-11pm Tue-Sun. South Observatory 9.30am-5pm Mon, Wed-Sun.* **Admission** free. **Map** p135 A2 ❺

Two of the best views over Tokyo have the added bonus of being free (unlike the Mori Tower's City View, p102). Each of the TMG twin towers (243m/ 797ft tall) has an observation deck on the 45th floor, affording a 360° panorama interrupted only by the other tower – on a clear day you can see Mount Fuji. The south observatory is the best by day; after dark, the view from the north deck is better.

Toto Super Space

L-Tower Bldg 26F-27F, 1-6-1 Nishi-Shinjuku (3345 1010). Shinjuku station (Yamanote, Chuo, Sobu lines), west exit; (Marunouchi line), exits A16, A17; (Shinjuku line), exit 3; or Shinjuku-Nishiguchi station (Oedo line), exit D1. **Open** 10am-6pm daily. Closed 1st & 3rd Wed of mth. **Admission** free. **Map** p135 B1 ❻

It may be a dubious honour, but Japan leads the world in toilet technology. This showroom has something to intrigue the most jaded loo user. As well as the now-standard bidet toilets, Toto makes baths that automatically fill

& chrysanthemum (early Nov) seasons. *Greenhouse 11am-3pm Tue-Sun.* **Admission** ¥200; ¥50 reductions. No credit cards. **Map** p135 D3 ❸

Shinjuku Gyoen opened as an imperial garden in 1906, during Japan's push for Westernisation, and was the first place in the country where many non-indigenous species were planted. The fascination with the West is evident in the garden's layout: there are both English- and French-style sections, as well as a traditional Japanese garden.

Sompo Japan Museum

Sompo Japan Bldg 42F, 1-26-1 Nishi-Shinjuku, Shinjuku-ku (3349 3081/ www.sompo-japan.co.jp/museum). Shinjuku station (Yamanote, Chuo, Sobu lines), west exit; (Marunouchi line), exits A16, A17; (Shinjuku line), exit 3; or Shinjuku-Nishiguchi station (Oedo line), exit D1. **Open** 10am-6pm Tue-Sun. **Admission** ¥500; free-¥300 reductions; additional charge for special exhibitions. No credit cards. **Map** p135 B1 ❹ themselves and can be switched on via the internet. And for the truly health-conscious, there's a toilet that analyses what's deposited in there. No, really.

Eating & drinking

African Bar Esogie

3F Muraki Bldg, 3-11-2 Shinjuku, Shinjuku-ku (3353 3334/www4.point. ne.jp/~esogie). Shinjuku-Sanchome station (Marunouchi, Shinjuku lines), exit C3. **Open** 6pm-midnight Mon, Tue, Thur; 6pm-4am Fri, Sat; 6-11pm Sun. No credit cards. **Bar**. Map p135 E1 ❼
The San-chome district is crammed with tiny bars, most of them musically themed, and Esogie is arguably the pick of the bunch. Nigerian owner Lucky might just be the friendliest bartender in town, and his djembe performances make it easy to forget you're in a narrow black bar with minimal furnishings. There's also a reasonable range of authentic African dishes.

Albatross

1-2-11 Nishi-Shinjuku, Shinjuku-ku (3342 5758). Shinjuku station (Yamanote, Shinjuku lines), west exit; (Marunouchi, Oedo lines), exit B16. **Open** 5pm-2am daily. No credit cards. **Bar**. Map p135 C1 ❽
Tucked into the tiny, time-worn *yaki-tori* stalls of Omoide Yokocho, by Shinjuku station, Albatross is a tiny three-storey salon that seats, in total, around 30 people. Upper-floor customers place their orders and receive their drinks through a hole in the floor, an operation that becomes increasingly perilous as the night progresses and senses diminish. The crowd is a genuinely eclectic mix of suits, artists, expats and students.

Albatross G

NEW *2F 5th Avenue, 1-1 Kabuki-cho, Shinjuku-ku (3202 3699/www.alba-s. com). Shinjuku station (Yamanote, Chuo lines), east exit; (Marunouchi line), exits B6, B7; (Oedo, Shinjuku lines), exit 1.* **Open** 8pm-5am Mon-Sat. No credit cards. **Bar**. Map p135 D1 ❾
Not all bars in the nostalgic drinking area of Golden Gai welcome foreign faces, but Albatross G, sister bar of the ever-popular Albatross (see above), is one that does. The interior features a cute upper-tier lounge which we suspect was designed as a storage space. The ¥300 seating charge is about the cheapest in the area.

Ban Thai

Dai-ichi Metro Bldg 3F, 1-23-14 Kabuki-cho, Shinjuku-ku (3207 0068/www.ban-thai.jp). Shinjuku station (Yamanote line), east exit; (Marunouchi line), exits B12, B13; (Oedo, Shinjuku lines), exit 1. **Open** 11.30am-3pm, 5pm-midnight Mon-Fri; 11.30am-midnight Sat, Sun. **¥¥**. **Thai**. English menu. Map p135 C1 ❿
After two decades in this convenient location, Ban Thai has become a Tokyo fixture. It remains very reliable, with especially good curries.

Bon

Torüchi Bldg B1, 3-23-1 Shinjuku, Shinjuku-ku (3341 0179). Shinjuku station (Yamanote, Chuo, Sobu lines), east exit; (Marunouchi line), exit A5; (Oedo, Shinjuku lines), exit 1. **Open** 12.30-11.30pm daily. No credit cards. **Café**. Map p135 C1 ⓫
The search for true coffee excellence is pursued with surprising vigour at this pricey but popular Shinjuku basement. The cheapest choice from the menu will set you back a cool ¥1,000, but at least the cups will be bone china – selected from an enormous collection. Special tasting events are held periodically for connoisseurs.

China Grill – Xenlon

Odakyu Hotel Century Southern Tower 19F, 2-2-1 Yoyogi, Shibuya-ku (3374 2080/www.xenlon.com/Shinjuku.index. html). Shinjuku station (Yamanote line), south exit; (Marunouchi, Oedo lines), exit A1; (Shinjuku line), exit 6. **Open** 11.30am-11pm daily. **¥¥¥**. **Chinese**. English menu. Map p135 C3 ⓬
Impeccable service and impressive views of the neon skyline make this stylish Chinese restaurant well worth

the splurge. The Cantonese menu, which nods towards Western rather than Japanese influences, includes excellent dim sum at lunchtime.

Clubhouse Tokyo

Marunaka Bldg 3F, 3-7-3 Shinjuku, Shinjuku-ku (3359 7785/www.clubhouse-tokyo.com). Shinjuku-Sanchome station (Marunouchi, Shinjuku lines), exits C3, C4. **Open** 5pm-midnight Mon-Fri; 3pm-late Sat, Sun. No credit cards. **Bar**. Map p135 D2 ⑬
Clubhouse is the only specialist sports bar in Shinjuku and can get phenomenally crowded on big game nights. Premiership football is screened, but the true passion here is rugby. There are British and Irish beers on tap.

Dubliners

Shinjuku Lion Hall 2F, 3-28-9 Shinjuku, Shinjuku-ku (3352 6606/ www.gnavi.co.jp/lion/05.html). Shinjuku station (Yamanote line), east exit; (Marunouchi, Oedo, Shinjuku lines), exit A8. **Open** noon-1am Mon-Sat; noon-11pm Sun. **Bar**. Map p135 D2 ⑭
The oldest and scruffiest of the growing chain of Irish pubs owned by Sapporo, one of Japan's largest brewers and also its Guinness importer. Draught Guinness and cider (little

known in Japan) accompany standard domestic beers, while the menu offers semi-authentic fish and chips.

La Jetée

1-1-8 Kabuki-cho, Shinjuku-ku (3208 9645). Shinjuku station (Yamanote, Chuo lines), east exit; (Marunouchi line), exits B6, B7; (Oedo, Shinjuku lines), exit 1. **Open** from 7pm Mon-Sat. No credit cards. **Bar**. Map p135 D1 ⑮
A tiny Golden Gai institution, owned by a film fanatic (the place gets its name from the Chris Marker classic) who speaks fluent French but little English. Popular with French expats and creative types, it's also a favourite haunt of visiting film-makers, from Wim Wenders to Quentin Tarantino.

Kitchen Shunju

Lumine Est 8F, 3-38-1 Shinjuku, Shinjuku-ku (5369 0377/www.shunju. com/ja/restaurants/shinjuku). Shinjuku station (Yamanote, Marunouchi, Oedo, Shinjuku lines), east exit. **Open** 11am-3pm, 5-11.30pm daily. **¥¥**. **Modern Japanese**. English menu. Map p135 C2 ⑯
The Shunju ethos – light, creative, modern Japanese food served in a stylish, casual setting – dovetails perfectly with the decor of its stylishly revamped mini

Albatross G

Shinjuku Dori

mall home. Sit at the long open kitchen where you can watch the chefs at work, or just relax in one of the cosy private alcoves. Lumine Est (p142) is located above the station's east exit.

New Dug

B1, 3-15-12 Shinjuku, Shinjuku-ku (3341 9339/www.dug.co.jp). Shinjuku station (Yamanote, Chuo, Sobu lines), east exit; (Marunouchi line), exit B10; (Oedo, Shinjuku lines), exit 1. **Open** *Restaurant* noon-2am Mon-Sat; noon-midnight Sun. *Bar* 6.30pm-2am Mon-Sat; 6.30pm-midnight Sun. **¥. Café.** **Map** p135 D1 ⓱

Way back in the 1960s and early '70s, Shinjuku was sprinkled with jazz coffee shops. Celebrated names of that bygone era included Dug, an establishment whose present-day incarnation is a cramped brick-lined basement on Yasukuni Dori. Everything about the place speaks serious jazz credentials, with carefully crafted authenticity and assorted memorabilia. A basement bar annexe below the nearby KFC is used for live performances.

New York Grill

Park Hyatt Tokyo 52F, 3-7-1-2 Nishi-Shinjuku, Shinjuku-ku (5323 3458/www.parkhyatttokyo.com). Shinjuku station (Yamanote line), west exit; (Marunouchi line), exit A13; (Oedo, Shinjuku lines), exit 6. **Open** 11.30am-2.30pm, 5.30-10.30pm daily. **¥¥¥¥.** **Steak/seafood.** English menu. **Map** p135 A3 ⓲

The seafood and meat dishes – prepared in modern New World style – are consistently excellent, service is polished and the well-thought-out selection of North American wines unrivalled in Japan. Spectacular views are the icing on the cake. Sunday brunch is an expat institution, as are evening cocktails in the adjoining New York Bar.

Shot Bar Shadow

1-1-8 Kabuki-cho, Shinjuku-ku (3209 9530). Shinjuku station (Yamanote, Chuo lines), east exit; (Marunouchi line), exits B6, B7; (Oedo, Shinjuku lines), exit 1. **Open** 5pm-midnight Mon-Fri; 6pm-midnight Sat. No credit cards. **Bar.** **Map** p135 D1 ⓳

The master of this tiny Golden Gai bar speaks Arabic, German, Russian and French, thanks to his time in the Foreign Legion. For you to become a member (which means you're allowed in after midnight), he must be able to remember your name, which is not as easy a feat as it might sound. A friendly, fun place where six is a crowd.

Tajimaya

1-1-6 Nishi-Shinjuku, Shinjuku-ku (3342 0881/www.shinjuku.or.jp/tajimaya). Shinjuku station (Yamanote, Chuo, Sobu lines), west exit; (Marunouchi line) exit A17; (Oedo, Shinjuku lines), exit 3. **Open** 10am-11pm daily. **¥**. No credit cards. **Café**. Map p135 C1 ⑳

Caught between the early post-war grunge of its immediate neighbours and the skyscraper bustle of the rest of west Shinjuku, Tajimaya responds with abundant bone china, coffees from all over the world, non-fetishist use of classical music, and milk in the best copperware. Scones on the menu provide further evidence of advanced sensibilities, but the deeply yellowed walls and battered wood suggest a struggle to keep up appearances.

Tsunahachi

3-31-8 Shinjuku, Shinjuku-ku (3352 1012/www.tsunahachi.co.jp). Shinjuku station (Yamanote line), east exit; (Marunouchi line), exit A6; (Oedo, Shinjuku lines), exit 1; or Shinjuku-Sanchome station (Marunouchi, Shinjuku lines), exits A1-A5. **Open** 11am-10.30pm daily. **¥¥**. **Tempura**. English menu. Map p135 D2 ㉑

Who says tempura has to be expensive? Surviving amid the gleaming modern buildings of Shinjuku, Tsunahachi's battered wooden premises are a throwback to the early post-war era – as are the prices charged here. The whole place is filled with the whiff of cooking oil, but the food is perfectly good enough for everyday fare.

Shopping

Disk Union

3-31-4 Shinjuku, Shinjuku-ku (3352 2691/www.diskunion.co.jp/top.html). Shinjuku station (Yamanote, Chuo lines), east, central exits; (Marunouchi line), exit A6; (Oedo, Shinjuku lines), exit 1. **Open** 11am-9pm Mon-Sat; 11am-8pm Sun. Map p135 D2 ㉒

Disk Union is a citywide chain of small, specialist music stores. The Shinjuku main store is a tall, narrow building with each floor devoted to a different genre, including world music, jazz, soundtracks and electronica. Staffed by experts, and offering new and used CDs and vinyl, this chain is a top choice for collectors. Branches nearby specialise in reggae, funk, punk and even that much-maligned genre, progressive rock.

Don Quixote

1-16-5 Kabuki-cho, Shinjuku-ku (5291 9211/www.donki.com). Shinjuku station (Yamanote, Chuo lines), east exit; (Marunouchi line), exits B12, B13; (Oedo, Shinjuku lines), exit 1. **Open** 24hrs daily. No credit cards. Map p135 C1 ㉓

Pile 'em high, sell 'em cheap taken to the extreme. The aisles and shelves are deliberately cluttered, disorganized and disorientating. But you'll find everything from snacks to washing machines, if you look hard enough. There are branches in Shinbashi, Okubo and Roppongi, among other locations.

Franc Franc

Shinjuku Southern Terrace, 2-2-1 Yoyogi, Shibuya-ku (5333 7701/www.francfranc.com). Shinjuku station (Yamanote, Chuo, Marunouchi lines), south exit; (Oedo, Shinjuku lines), exit A1. **Open** 11am-10pm daily. Map p135 C3 ㉔

A popular and reasonably priced interiors shop, with a wide range of candles, incense, lamps, bathroom goods and furniture. It also has its own brand of compilation CDs, catering to the massive market for bossa nova music. Branches throughout the city.

Isetan

3-14-1 Shinjuku, Shinjuku-ku (3352 1111/www.isetan.co.jp/iclub). Shinjuku-Sanchome station (Marunouchi, Shinjuku lines), exits B3, B4, B5 or Shinjuku station (Yamanote, Chuo lines), east exit; (Oedo line), exit 1. **Open** 10am-8pm daily. Map p135 D1/2 ㉕

Tokyo's trendiest and friendliest department store is spread out over eight buildings situated very close to each other. In the main building's basement you'll find a superb range of gourmet foods, as well as BPQC – an eclectic selection of concession shops selling cosmetics, perfumes, CDs and household goods. Isetan's Clover clothing comes in larger sizes than the standard Japanese range.

Keio

1-1-4 Nishi-Shinjuku, Shinjuku-ku (3342 2111/www.keionet.com). Shinjuku station (Yamanote line), west exit; (Marunouchi line), exits A12-A14; (Oedo, Shinjuku lines), exit 3. **Open** 10am-8pm daily. **Map** p135 C2 ㉖

This department store stocks womenswear and accessories on the first four floors; menswear on the fifth; kimonos, jewellery and furniture on the sixth; children's clothes and sporting goods on the seventh; and office supplies on the eighth. The store also offers a range of clothing in Westerner-friendly larger sizes called Lilac.

Kihachi Patisserie

Flags Bldg 3F, 3-37-1 Shinjuku, Shinjuku-ku (5366 6384/www. kihachi.co.jp). Shinjuku station (Yamanote, Chuo lines), east-south exit; (Marunouchi line), exits A7, A8; (Oedo, Shinjuku lines), exit 1. **Open** 11am-9pm daily. **Map** p135 C2 ㉗

This popular store makes and sells highly original cakes. They are often a fusion of Western and Japanese elements, using ingredients such as green tea or chestnuts. Look for branches throughout the capital.

Kinokuniya Bookstore

3-17-7 Shinjuku, Shinjuku-ku (3354 0131/www.kinokuniya.co.jp). Shinjuku station (Yamanote, Chuo lines), east exit; (Marunouchi line), exits B7, B8; (Oedo, Shinjuku lines), exit 1. **Open** 10am-9pm daily. **Map** p135 D1 ㉘

The best-known branch of this bookshop chain is on Shinjuku Dori, but the branch behind the nearby Takashimaya (which is on the south side of Shinjuku station) is bigger. Kinokuniya could well have Tokyo's largest selection of new foreign-language books, with English, French and German titles. The stock ranges from new fiction all the way to specialist academic titles.

Lumine Est

3-38-1 Shinjuku, Shinjuku-ku (5269 1111/www.lumine.ne.jp/est/index.html). Shinjuku station (Yamanote, Chuo, Marunouchi lines), east exit; (Oedo, Shinjuku lines), exit 1. **Open** 10.30am-9.30pm daily. **Map** p135 C1 ㉙

Situated above the east exit of Shinjuku station, Lumine Est is chiefly notable for the Shunkan gourmet restaurant area, created by celebrated designer Takashi Sugimoto, on the seventh and eighth floors. The lower floors are laid out in a series of corridors that are fun for people-watching.

No.1 Travel

Don Quixote Bldg 7F, 1-16-5 Kabuki-cho, Shinjuku-ku (3200 8871/www. no1-travel.com). Shinjuku station (Yamanote, Chuo lines), east exit; (Marunouchi line), exit B13; or Shinjuku-Nishiguchi station (Oedo line), exit D1. **Open** 10am-6.30pm Mon-Fri; 11am-4.30pm Sat. **Map** p135 C1 ㉚

No.1 has been in business for 20 years and specialises in last-minute, discounted tickets. The staff speak a number of European and Asian languages.

Odakyu

1-1-3 Nishi-Shinjuku, Shinjuku-ku (3342 1111/www.odakyu-dept.co.jp). Shinjuku station (Yamanote, Chuo lines), west exit; (Marunouchi line), exits A12-A14; (Oedo, Shinjuku lines), exit 3. **Open** 10am-8pm daily. **Map** p135 C1 ㉛

This department store is split into two buildings connected by an elevated walkway and underground passageways. The main building has women's clothing on the first five floors, kimonos on the sixth, and furniture on the eighth, while the annex offers menswear, sportswear, four floors of the electronics retailer Bic Camera, and a basement food hall that includes the Troisgros delicatessen and a range of organic groceries.

Revamping religion

On the face of it things look rosy. Official figures count 95 million Buddhists in Japan, and over 100 million Shinto followers – from a population of just 120 million. But since the faiths are theologically incompatible, with most people switching between the two depending on the ceremony (and borrowing Christianity for weddings), the challenge for the devout is clear.

To bring fresh relevance to their religion, some Tokyo Buddhists are playing with the presentation in inventive and enticing ways.

Eating Zen temple cuisine *shojin ryori* usually entails advance reservations, lengthy sittings and gut-wrenching bills. Not in Daikanyama, though, where Buddhist monk Tenkai Miki (pictured) serves it in bento lunch boxes from his scooter (beside Daikanyama station, weekdays from noon). The location is telling: Daikanyama is populated by young, fashion-obsessed women who would normally be dining in designer cafés. Miki draws them with his healthy organic meal and its beautiful bamboo-sheath box.

Ryunosuke Koiko belongs to the same Jodo Shinshu sect as Miki and, under similar motivation, opened **Iede Café** (4-16-6 Setagaya, Setagaya-ku, 3706 1116, http://iede.cc) in suburban Setagaya Ward in early 2006. 'Temples used to be places for tuning your spirit, but they don't really do that any more', he explains. 'I wanted to create that kind of space again.' Iede certainly has the tranquillity of a temple, but none of the pomp. The decor is art-gallery barren white, but toys and games add an affable vibe, and Iede serves the only *shojin ryori* in the city that comes with smiley face decorations and a menu drawn in crayon.

In the backstreet drinking locale of Yotsuya San-chome, **Vowz Bar** (6 Arakicho, Shinjuku-ku, 3353 1032) stretches religious dogma to breaking point. Buddhism might frown on alcohol consumption, but the former boxer who set up this delightful drinking den takes a more liberal view. Buddhism is more than a novelty theme: the Amidala butsudan (altar) that dominates the tiny bar draws local priests who turn up to chant, before taking a stool at the bar (but never indulge in a drink). The bar snacks are, again, Zen vegetarian fare. Among the many religious artefacts is the framed calligraphic message 'happiness is transitory', which can make all too much sense after a heavy night at Vowz.

Arty Farty

Yamaya

*3-2-7 Nishi-Shinjuku, Shinjuku-ku
(3342 0601/www.yamaya.jp). Shinjuku
station (Yamanote, Chuo lines), south
exit; (Marunouchi line), exits A16,
A17; (Oedo, Shinjuku lines), exit 6.*
Open 10am-10pm daily. **Map**
p135 A3 ㉜

A medium-sized foreign-food and booze
specialist with one unique feature for
Tokyo: it's cheap. It has a vast selection
of imported wines priced from a bud-
get-beating ¥280, along with inexpen-
sive cheeses and snacks. For ¥500
you can also get large orders delivered
to anywhere within the 23 wards of
central Tokyo.

Nightlife

Advocates Bar

*7th Tenka Bldg B1F, 2-18-1
Shinjuku, Shinjuku-ku (3358
8638). Shinjuku-Sanchome station
(Marunouchi, Shinjuku lines), exits
C7, C8.* **Open** 8pm-4am daily. No
credit cards. **Map** p135 E2 ㉝

This small, smoky, basement gay bar
has a separate entrance around the
corner from its sister club, Advocates
Café (below). Weekend DJ nights are
hit and miss; follow the crowd in from
Advocates Café. There is sometimes a
cover charge.

Advocates Café

*7th Tenka Bldg 1F, 2-18-1 Shinjuku,
Shinjuku-ku (3358 3988). Shinjuku-
Sanchome station (Marunouchi,
Shinjuku lines), exits C7, C8.* **Open**
6pm-4am Mon-Sat; 6pm-1am Sun.
Map p135 E2 ㉞

A highlight of Tokyo's gay scene, with
its zebra-striped walls and mirrored
disco balls, this is not your average
pavement café. It's not even your average Tokyo gay bar. Open to all sexes
and sexualities, it's a good place to find
out where the crowds are heading later
(on a weekend it could easily be the DJs
next door to the Advocates Bar, listed
above). The Sunday night 'beer blast'
(6-9pm) offers all the beer you can
drink for ¥1,000.

Antiknock

*Ray Flat Shinjuku B1F, 4-3-15
Shinjuku, Shinjuku-ku (3350 5670/
www.music.ne.jp/~antiknock). Shinjuku
station (Yamanote, Marunouchi lines),
new south exit; (Oedo, Shinjuku lines),
exits 1, 2.* **Map** p135 D2 ㉟

A small club near Takashimaya Times
Square, where Tokyo's colourful punks
gather. It aims to present 'original'
music, but, more importantly, the
music has to rock. Need to vent your
frustration with the Shinjuku-station
hordes? Pop down here.

Arty Farty

Dai 33 Kyutei Bldg 2F, 2-11-6 Shinjuku, Shinjuku-ku (3356 5388/www.arty-farty.net). Shinjuku-Sanchome station (Marunouchi, Shinjuku lines), exits C7, C8. **Open** *7pm-midnight Mon; 7pm-5am Tue-Fri; 5pm-5am Sat, Sun.* **Admission** *¥800 Mon-Thur; ¥900-¥1,000 Fri-Sun.* **Map** p135 E2 ㊱

This friendly gay bar hosts DJs on weekends and is very popular among foreigners. The mint beer served here is, however, an acquired taste. Women are allowed 'with their gay friends' on Fridays and Sundays.

Club Complex Code

Shinjuku Toho Kaikan 4F, 1-19-2 Kabuki-cho, Shinjuku-ku (3209 0702/ www.clubcomplexcode.com). Shinjuku station (Yamanote, Chuo, Sobu lines), east exit; (Marunouchi line) exit B12; (Oedo, Shinjuku lines), exit 1. **Open** *from 7pm daily.* **Admission** *¥3,000-¥3,500. No credit cards.* **Map** p135 C1 ㊲

With three dancefloors, one of which takes a whopping 1,000 people, Club Complex Code is in theory quite a venue. But it enjoys nothing like the stellar reputation of other megaclubs in town and is starting to scrape the creative barrel with 'cyber trance' nights. Still, it's always worth taking a peek at its schedule.

Garam

Dai-Roku Polestar Bldg 7A, 1-16-6 Kabuki-cho, Shinjuku-ku (3205 8668). Shinjuku station (Yamanote, Chuo, Sobu lines), east exit; (Marunouchi line), exit B12; (Oedo, Shinjuku lines), exit 1. **Open** *9pm-6am daily.* **Admission** *¥1,000-¥1,500. No credit cards.* **Map** p135 C1 ㊳

This is a swinging, foreign-owned Jamaican dancehall and reggae club that could double as a walk-in closet. Still, the staff are very friendly, and Garam's become something of an institution, with Japanese MCs, sharp DJs and pounding vibes.

Izm

J2 Bldg B1F-B2F, 1-7-1 Kabuki-cho, Shinjuku-ku (3200 9914/www.clubizm.

net). Shinjuku station (Yamanote, Chuo, Sobu lines), east exit; (Marunouchi line), exit B12; (Oedo, Shinjuku lines), exit 1. **Open** *10pm-5am daily.* **Admission** *¥2,000-¥2,500. No credit cards.* **Map** p135 D1 ㊴

Sitting incongruously in the seediest part of Kabuki-cho, this small venue attracts a teenage clientele for their regular diet of hip hop, with a touch of R&B and reggae.

Kusuo

Sunflower Bldg 3F, 2-17-1 Shinjuku, Shinjuku-ku (3354 5050/www5.ocn. ne.jp/~kusuo). Shinjuku-Sanchome station (Marunouchi, Shinjuku lines), exits C7, C8. **Open** *8pm-4am Mon-Fri, Sun; 8pm-5am Sat. No credit cards.* **Map** p135 E2 ㊵

A karaoke cathedral and one of the biggest gay bars in Tokyo, Kusuo not only has plenty of room to dance but, in the afternoons, sometimes offers tango or square-dancing lessons. What the venue lacks in refined decoration – the walls and ceiling are painted sloppily in black – it makes up for in breathing room and the exuberant, foreigner-friendly staff members. Women are officially welcome, though their first drink will cost ¥1,500, compared to ¥1,000 for men.

Open

2-5-15 Shinjuku, Shinjuku-ku (3226 8855/http://club-open.hp. infoseek.co.jp). Shinjuku-Gyoenmae station (Marunouchi line), Shinjuku Gate exit. **Open** *5pm-5am Mon-Sat.* **Admission** *¥1,000-¥1,500. No credit cards.* **Map** p135 E2 ㊶

Open is the proud inheritor of the roots reggae tradition in Japan. It was set up by the staff of 69 – the country's very first reggae bar/club – when it closed down about a decade ago. It's now Tokyo's best spot for Jamaican sounds.

Oto

2F, 1-17-5 Kabuki-cho, Shinjuku-ku (5273 8264/www.club-oto.com). Shinjuku station (Yamanote, Chuo, Sobu lines), east exit; (Marunouchi line), exit B12; (Oedo, Shinjuku lines), exit 1. **Open** *10pm-5am*

daily. **Admission** ¥2,000-¥2,500.
No credit cards. **Map** p135 C1 ㊷

Oto (meaning 'sound' in Japanese) lives
up to its name, with a PA that would
do a much larger place credit. This
long, thin venue isn't the cosiest place
in town, but if you're there to dance, it's
great. The sounds span the dancier end
of the club-music spectrum.

Rags Room Acid
*Kowa Bldg B1F, 2-3-12 Shinjuku,
Shinjuku-ku (3352 3338/www.acid.jp).
Shinjuku-Gyoenmae station (Marunouchi
line), Shinjuku Gate exit.* **Open** from
10pm; days vary. **Admission**
¥2,000-¥2,500. No credit cards.
Map p135 E2 ㊸

Finding the entrance to Rags Room
Acid (formerly Club Acid) is a challenge in itself – a small sign on
Shinjuku Dori provides the only hint of
its existence. The best method is to
follow your ears, but you might hear
anything booming out of here, from
ska to rock, hip hop to Latin, R&B to
techno to drum 'n' bass.

Shinjuku Loft
*Tatehana Bldg B2F, 1-12-9 Kabuki-
cho, Shinjuku-ku (5272 0382/www.loft-
prj.co.jp). Shinjuku station (Yamanote
line), east exit; (Marunouchi line), exit
B12; (Oedo, Shinjuku lines), exit 1.*
Map p135 C1 ㊹

Loft has been around for more than 25
years and is a dedicated promoter.
Inside are two areas: one is the main
space for gigs, the other a bar with a
small stage. Expect loud music of
any genre here. At times, Loft offers
more than just evening gigs, with all-
night events featuring DJs alongside
the musicians.

Shinjuku Pit Inn
*Accord Shinjuku B1F, 2-12-4 Shinjuku,
Shinjuku-ku (3354 2024/www.pit-
inn.com). Shinjuku-Sanchome station
(Marunouchi, Shinjuku lines), exit C5.*
Open *Shows* from 7.30pm daily.
Admission ¥3,000-¥5,000.
Map p135 E2 ㊺

All chairs here face the stage, in reverence to the most respected jazz groups
in town, who offer their latest to the

adoring crowd. It's not a place for lin-
gering or lounging – the atmosphere is
too hallowed for that – but the music is
always first class. An irregular afternoon slot at 2.30pm offers the stage to
newly emerging bands.

Arts & leisure

Koma Gekijo
*1-19-1 Kabuki-cho, Shinjuku-ku (3200
2213/www.koma-sta.co.jp). Shinjuku
station (Yamanote, Shinjuku lines),
east exit; (Marunouchi, Oedo lines),
exit B7.* **Map** p135 C1 ㊻

This well-known theatre in Tokyo's
red-light district has long been the host
of the kind of variety shows that lure
the pension crowd and bemuse tourists.
The quirky old-time entertainment on
offer involves plenty of singing, dancing, comedy and period costume.

Shinjuku Loft Plus One
*Tatehana Bldg B2F, 1-14-7 Kabuki-
cho, Shinjuku-ku (3205 6864/www.loft-
prj.co.jp). Shinjuku station (Yamanote
line), east exit; (Marunouchi line), exit
B12; (Oedo, Shinjuku lines), exit 1.*
Map p135 C1 ㊼

One of the city's quirkiest venues, Loft
Plus One is a dingy basement specialising in live talk events. This can mean
heavy political discussions or 'seminars' from porn stars. It's known as the
one place in town in which people
speak freely: the place's unofficial
mantra is 'what's said in Loft Plus One,
stays in Loft Plus One'. Needless to say,
it helps if you understand the language
– unless you're attending one of the
adult industry events.

Suehiro-tei
*3-6-12 Shinjuku, Shinjuku-ku (3351
2974/www.suehirotei.com). Shinjuku-
Sanchome station (Marunouchi,
Shinjuku lines), exits B2, C4.* No
credit cards. **Map** p135 D2 ㊽

A charming old theatre standing its
ground amid the drinking dens of
Shinjuku-Sanchome, Suehiro-tei hosts
performances of Japan's traditional
rakugo comedy. Performances do not
have English translations.

Toshogu Shrine p151

Ueno & Yanaka

Ueno

Long before feng shui gained a foothold in the West, China's ancient rules of geomancy were being applied in feudal Japan. And it is thanks to feng shui that Ueno came into being. In the 17th century, as a one-time fishing village was developing into the administrative capital that would become Tokyo, shogun Tokugawa Hidetada was advised to build a great temple north-east of Edo Castle to guard against the evil spirits that were apt to enter from that inauspicious direction. So, in 1625, he duly installed a massive complex of 36 temples in Ueno.

Only a hint of his complex remains, but the land that the temples occupied is now Ueno's best-known feature – its park. **Ueno Koen** (Ueno Park) was Tokyo's first public park when it opened in 1873, but just five years earlier it had been the site of the bloody Battle of Ueno between supporters of the new Meiji government and warriors loyal to the Tokugawa shogun. The government won, but in the process much of the temple complex was destroyed. Nowadays the park is home to a zoo, a grand shrine and museums. It's also a prime cherry blossom spot in spring.

Ueno's other main attraction is the **Ameyoko** market, where more than 500 stalls are shoehorned into a 400-metre stretch. As well as fishmongers and fruit and veg stalls, there are scores of small shops selling cheap jeans, trainers and goods 'inspired' by international designers. It is also a reliable source of hard-to-find foods and spices.

Ueno & Yanaka

E 1 | 2 | 3
D
C
B
A

100 m
100 yds
© Copyright Time Out Group 2007

KOTOTOI DORI

Iriya Kishiboji'n Temple

NEGISHI

Uguisudani Station

Yamanote Line

Tokyo National Museum

National Science Museum 3

6

Nippori Station

Tenno-ji Temple

Yanaka Cemetery

TAITO-KU

Tokyo National University of Fine Arts & Music

Tokyo Metropolitan Art Museum 5

Kio-ji Temple

20

10

Enmei-in Temple 17

Kannon-ji Temple

Choan-ji Temple

Zuirin-ji Temple

19

Ueno Zoo

NEZU

Daien-ji Temple

Zenshoan Temple

Myoho-ji Temple

YANAKA

Nezu Station

18

KOTOTOI DORI

YANAKA GINZA

Sendagi Station

SHINOBAZU DORI

1 Sights & museums
1 Eating & drinking
1 Shopping
1 Nightlife
1 Arts & leisure

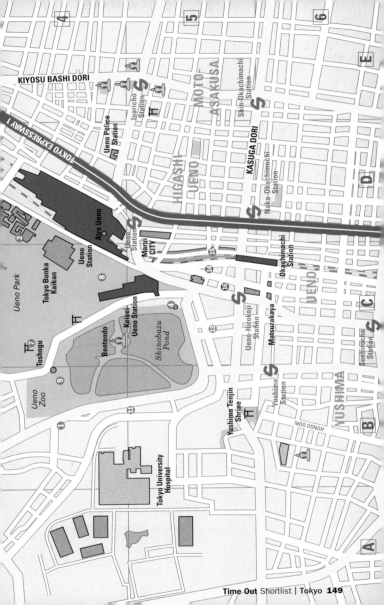

KIYOSU BASHI DORI

TOKYO EXPRESSWAY 1

MOTO-ASAKUSA

Shin-Okachimachi Station

KASUGA DORI

HIGASHI-UENO

Naka-Okachimachi Station

Ueno Police Station

Inaricho Station

Ueno Station

Atre Ueno

Marui CITY

Ueno Station

Okachimachi Station

Tokyo Bunka Kaikan

Ueno Park

Ueno Station

UENO

Toshogu

Keisei Ueno Station

Bentendo

Shinobazu Pond

Ueno-Hirokoji Station

Matsuzakaya

Suehirocho Station

Ueno Zoo

Yushima Tenjin Shrine

Yushima Station

YUSHIMA

HONGO DORI

Tokyo University Hospital

Sights & museums

Kyu Iwasaki-tei House & Gardens

1-3-45 Ikenohata, Taito-ku (3823 8033/www.tokyo-park.or.jp/english/ park/detail_06.html#kyuiwasakitei). Yushima station (Chiyoda line), exit 1. **Open** *9am-5pm daily.* **Admission** *¥400; free reductions. No credit cards.* **Map** *p149 B4* ❶

Built in 1896, this compound reveals the fin-de-siècle sheen beneath Ueno's grimy surface. Josiah Conder designed the recently renovated main residence – a two-storey wooden structure with Jacobean and Pennsylvanian country-house elements (and the first Western-style toilet in Japan) – and the adjacent billiards room in the form of a log cabin. Visitors can sip green tea in the large tatami rooms.

National Museum of Western Art (Kokuritsu Seiyo Bijutsukan)

7-7 Ueno Koen, Taito-ku (3828 5131/www.nmwa.go.jp). Ueno station (Yamanote line), park exit; (Ginza, Hibiya lines), Shinobazu exit. **Open** *9.30am-5.30pm Tue-Thur, Sat, Sun; 9.30am-8pm Fri.* **Admission** *¥420; free-¥130 reductions; additional charge for special exhibitions. Free 2nd & 4th Sat of mth. No credit cards.* **Map** *p149 D4* ❷

The core collection housed in this 1959 Le Corbusier-designed building, Japan's only national museum devoted to Western art, was assembled by Kawasaki shipping magnate Kojiro Matsukata in the early 1900s. For such a recent collection it is surprisingly good, ranging from 15th-century icons to Monet to Pollock.

National Science Museum

7-20 Ueno Koen, Taito-ku (3822 0111/www.kahaku.go.jp/english). Ueno station (Yamanote line), park exit; (Ginza, Hibiya lines), Shinobazu exit. **Open** *9am-5pm Tue-Thur; 9am-8pm Fri; 9am-6pm Sat, Sun.* **Admission** *¥500; free-¥70 reductions. No credit cards.* **Map** *p148 D3* ❸

At this museum inside Ueno Park, the exhibits of fossils, specimens and asteroids are enhanced by touchscreens that provide videos and multilingual explanations. After checking out dinosaur bones and a prehistoric house built with mammoth tusks, you may want to taste the speciality of the museum restaurant: a 'dinosaur's egg' croquette.

Shitamachi Museum (Shitamachi Fuzoku Shiryokan)

2-1 Ueno Koen, Taito-ku (3823 7451/ www.taitocity.net/taito/shitamachi). Ueno station (Yamanote, Ginza, Hibiya lines), Shinobazu exit. **Open** *9.30am-4.30pm Tue-Sun.* **Admission** *¥300; ¥100 reductions. No credit cards.* **Map** *p149 C5* ❹

A charming museum that recreates the lives of ordinary Tokyoites between the pivotal Meiji restoration of 1868 and the Great Earthquake of 1923. Take off your shoes and step into a merchant's shop, a coppersmith's workshop and a sweet shop. Everything has a hands-on intimacy: open a drawer and you'll find a sewing kit or maybe a children's colouring book.

Tokyo Metropolitan Art Museum

8-36 Ueno Koen, Taito-ku (3823 6921/www.tobikan.jp). Ueno station (Yamanote line), park exit; (Ginza, Hibiya lines), Shinobazu exit. **Open** *Main Gallery 9am-5pm Tue-Sun. Library 9am-5pm daily; closed 1st & 3rd Mon of mth.* **Admission** *Galleries free-¥1,500; free-¥500 reductions. Library free.* **Map** *p148 C3* ❺

Designed by Maekawa Kunio, this brick-faced art museum was largely constructed underground to remain unobtrusive, with limited success. Temporary shows in the main hall feature everything from traditional Japanese art to art nouveau.

Tokyo National Museum (Tokyo Kokuritsu Hakubutsukan)

13-9 Ueno Koen, Taito-ku (3822 1111/www.tnm.go.jp). Ueno station

Ameyoko Market p153

(Yamanote line), park exit; (Ginza, Hibiya lines), Shinobazu exit. **Open** 9.30am-5pm Tue-Sun. **Admission** ¥500; free-¥420 reductions; additional charge for special exhibitions. **Map** p148 D3 ⑥

If you have just one day to devote to museum-going in Tokyo and want to see some Japanese art, this is the place to visit. Japan's oldest and largest museum houses over 89,000 items. The 25 rooms regularly rotate their exhibitions of paintings, ceramics, swords, kimonos, sculptures and the like.

Toshogu Shrine

9-88 Ueno Koen, Taito-ku (3822 3455). Ueno station (Yamanote line), park exit; (Ginza, Hibiya lines), Shinobazu exit. **Open** 9am-sunset daily. **Admission** ¥200; ¥100 reductions. Garden ¥600. No credit cards. **Map** p149 C4 ⑦

Toshogu is dedicated to the first Tokugawa shogun, Ieyasu, and its style is similar to the shrine in Nikko where he is buried. It was built in 1627, then remodelled in 1651, and has withstood earthquakes and fires, as well as

the Battle of Ueno, to become one of Tokyo's oldest buildings. Karamon, the front gate of the temple, is famous for its dragon carvings.

Ueno Royal Museum (Ueno no Mori Bijutsukan)

1-2 Ueno Koen, Taito-ku (3833 4195/ www.ueno-mori.org). Ueno station (Yamanote line), park exit; (Ginza, Hibiya lines), Shinobazu exit. **Open** 10am-5pm daily (until 6pm during special exhibitions). **Admission** varies; usually free. No credit cards. **Map** p149 C4 ⑧

This medium-sized *Kunsthalle* in the woods of Ueno Park holds the annual VOCA exhibition of emerging Japanese artists, as well as touring shows from the likes of New York's MoMA and Barcelona's Picasso Museum. It has no permanent collection, and its temporary exhibitions are sporadic.

Ueno Zoo

9-83 Ueno Koen, Taito-ku (3828 5171/www.tokyo-zoo.net/english). Ueno station (Yamanote, Ginza,

Yanaka

paintings and photos. The large new building, opened in 1999, holds permanent collections but also hosts some temporary exhibitions.

Yokoyama Taikan Memorial Hall

1-4-24 Ikenohata, Taito-ku (3821 1017/www.tctv.ne.jp/members/taikan). Yushima station (Chiyoda line), exit 1. **Open** 10am-4pm Thur-Sun. **Admission** ¥500; ¥200 reductions. No credit cards. **Map** p149 B5 ⑪

One of Japan's great modern painters, Taikan Yokoyama, resided in this house overlooking Shinobazu Pond. Yokoyama practised *nihonga* (traditional Japanese painting), taking images from nature as his inspiration. If his paintings don't impress, his gardens certainly should. The house closes in bad weather and also occasionally during the summer.

Eating & drinking

Hantei

2-12-15 Nezu, Bunkyo-ku (3828 1440/ www.hantei.co.jp). Nezu station (Chiyoda line), exit 2. **Open** noon-2.30pm, 5-10pm Tue-Sat; 4-9.30pm Sun. ¥¥. No credit cards. **Japanese kebabs**. English menu. **Map** p148 B3 ⑫

Kushi-age (skewers of meat, fish or vegetables) is not gourmet fare, but Hantei almost makes it refined. There's no need to order: staff will bring course after course, stopping after every six to ask if you want to continue.

Ikenohata Yabu Soba

3-44-7 Yushima, Bunkyo-ku (3831 8977/www.yabu-soba.com). Yushima station (Chiyoda line), exit 2. **Open** 11.30am-2pm, 4.30-8pm Mon, Tue, Thur-Sat; 11.30am-8pm Sun. ¥¥. No credit cards. **Soba**. English menu. **Map** p149 C5 ⑬

Kanda Yabu Soba (p95) has spawned numerous shops run by former apprentices. This one does good noodles at reasonable prices in a simple Japanese setting. The menu also includes a range of snacks, and, in winter, offers warming *nabe* hot-pots.

Hibiya lines), park exit. **Open** 9.30am-5pm Tue-Sun (last entry 4pm). **Admission** ¥600; free-¥300 reductions. **Map** p149 B4 ⑨

Japan's oldest zoo, established in 1882, is also Tokyo's most popular, thanks mainly to its central location in Ueno Park and its range of beasts, including a giant panda and Sumatran tiger. You'll find the panda in the eastern section, along with elephants, lions, gorillas, sea lions and assorted bears.

University Art Museum

12-8 Ueno Koen, Taito-ku (5685 7755/ www.geidai.ac.jp/museum). Ueno station (Yamanote line), park exit; (Ginza, Hibiya lines), Shinobazu exit. **Open** 10am-5pm Tue-Sun. **Admission** ¥300; ¥100 reductions; additional charge for special exhibitions. No credit cards. **Map** p148 C3 ⑩

The museum connected to Japan's most prestigious national art and music school has an impressive collection of over 40,000 objects, ranging from Japanese traditional art to Western

Shopping

Ameyoko Plaza Food & Clothes Market

www.ameyoko.net. Ueno station (Yamanote, Ginza lines), Shinobazu exit; (Hibiya line), exits 6, 7. **Open** varies. No credit cards. **Map** p149 C5 ⑭
This maze of streets next to the railway tracks between Ueno and Okachimachi stations comprises two markets: the covered Ueno Centre Mall and open-air Ameyoko itself. The mall sells an array of souvenirs and clothes, while the 500 stalls of jam-packed Ameyoko – one of Tokyo's greatest street markets – specialise in fresh food, especially fish.

Hinoya

6-10-14 Ueno, Taito-ku (3831 9822/ www.rakuten.co.jp/hinoya/119784). Ueno station (Yamanote, Ginza lines), Shinobazu exit; (Hibiya line), exits 6, 7. **Open** 10am-8pm daily. **Map** p149 C5 ⑮
Heavyweight artisanal 'selvedge' denim from Japanese brands is gaining a global fashion fanbase, and Uneo is the place to pick it up. Hinoya stocks all the trendiest labels, including Evisu, Sugarcane and Tailor Toyo.

Nightlife

GH Nine

UNO Bldg 9F, 4-4-6 Ueno, Taito-ku (3837 2525/http://homepage1.nifty. com/ghnine). Okachimachi station (Yamanote line), north exit; or Ueno-Hirokoji station (Ginza line), exit 3. **Open** Shows from 8pm daily. **Admission** ¥3,000. **Map** p149 C5 ⑯
A rare beast indeed – a jazz spot in east Tokyo – this futuristic space at the top of a postmodern building is always a little eerie in feel, but the music is consistently high quality.

Yanaka

When the frantic pace of Tokyo starts to wear you down, come to Yanaka, a picturesque spot that has somehow survived many of the upheavals of the past century.

Although a geographical neighbour, low-key, low-rise Yanaka is a world away from the grand museums and huge, brash street market of Ueno. It survives as an endearing place where life seems to potter along more or less just as it did a century ago.

The area is also home to Tokyo's highest concentration of temples, ranging from the grand to the humble. The temples were moved here from elsewhere in Tokyo following the 1657 Long Sleeves Fire, which destroyed much of the city. Yanaka has led something of a charmed life ever since, escaping destruction in both the Kanto Earthquake of 1923 and the air raids in World War II.

Sights & museums

Asakura Choso Museum

7-18-10 Yanaka, Taito-ku (3821 4549/ www.taitocity.net/taito/asakura). Nippori station (Yamanote line), west exit. **Open** 9.30am-4.30pm Tue-Thur, Sat, Sun. **Admission** ¥400; ¥150 reductions. No credit cards. **Map** p148 B1 ⑰
This museum is the former house and atelier of Fumio Asakura, a leading figure in modern Japanese sculpture. The three-level building – designed by the artist in 1936 – melds modernism and traditional Japanese architecture. The centrepiece is a delightful rock and water garden, also designed by the artist. From the rooftop garden you can see just how low-rise Yanaka is compared with the rest of Tokyo.

Daimyo Clock Museum

2-1-27 Yanaka, Taito-ku (3821 6913). Nezu station (Chiyoda line), exit 1. **Open** 10am-4pm Tue-Sun. Closed July-Sept. **Admission** ¥300; ¥100-¥200 reductions. No credit cards. **Map** p148 B2 ⑱
Daimyo feudal lords were the only people who could afford the clocks on display here. Before Japan adopted the solar calendar in 1870, there was a set

number of hours between sunrise and sunset, with the result that an hour was longer in summer than in winter. This one-room museum displays dozens of other timepieces, from alarm clocks to watches worn with a kimono.

SCAI The Bathhouse

Kashiwayu-Ato, 6-1-23 Yanaka, Taito-ku (3821 1144/www.scaithebathhouse.com). Nippori station (Yamanote line), south exit. **Open** noon-7pm Tue-Sat. Closed 2wks Aug, 2wks Dec-Jan. **Map** p148 C2 ⑲

Formerly a bathhouse (the building is over 200 years old), this high-ceilinged space in a charming neighbourhood near Ueno Park features contemporary Japanese artists (Tatsuo Miyajima) and international practitioners (Lee Bul, Julian Opie).

Yanaka Cemetery

7-5-24 Yanaka, Taito-ku. Nippori station (Yamanote line), west exit. **Map** p148 C2 ⑳

One of Tokyo's largest graveyards and one of its most picturesque. It is the resting place of Japan's first great modernist writer Natsume Soseki, as well as of the last Tokugawa shogun, Yoshinobu, who surrendered power to the emperor in 1868. It's also a popular spot for a cherry blossom-viewing party in the spring.

Eating & drinking

Nezu Club

2-30-2 Nezu, Bunkyo-ku (3828 4004/www.nezuclub.com). Nezu station (Chiyoda line), exit 1. **Open** 6-10pm Wed-Sat. **¥¥¥. Traditional Japanese**. Map p148 A3 ㉑

Chef Yamada Etsuko's stylish Japanese cuisine is not as formal as *kaiseki*, but it is far more sophisticated than regular home cooking. She has a very creative modern touch that reflects the restaurant's innovative setting: a converted 30-year-old, metal-frame workshop tucked away down a narrow alley in this very traditional neighbourhood.

Sasanoyuki

2-15-10 Negishi, Taito-ku (3873 1145). Uguisudani station (Yamanote line), north exit. **Open** 11am-9.30pm Tue-Sun. **¥¥. Tofu**. English menu. **Map** p148 D2 ㉒

Tokyo's most famous tofu restaurant was founded way back in the Edo period by a tofu-maker who had been lured from Kyoto by the Kanei-ji temple's imperial abbot. Despite its illustrious past, Sasanoyuki is as down to earth as the Nippori neighbourhood it sits in, charging very reasonable prices for its food.

SCAI The Bathhouse

Sankeien p162

Neighbourhood Tokyo

Akihabara

'Electric Town' and geek culture hub, this is the place for manga and eight-foot anime robots. See box p156.

Eating & drinking

@home café

Mitsuwa Bldg 7F, 1-11-4 Soto-Kanda, Chiyoda-ku (5294 7707/www.cafe-athome.com). Akihabara station (Yamanote, Sobu lines), Electric Town exit; (Hibiya line), exit 3. **Open** 11.30am-10pm (last order 9pm) daily. **¥**. No credit cards. **Café**.
'Welcome home, master!' squeal the baby-faced servers as customers enter the original maid café. @home has everything a maid fetishist could desire: costumed girls serving heart-shaped food, who will, for a fee, play party games with you. Just the right side of creepy, @home draws a broader range of customers than its rivals, and women will feel welcome. See boxes p79 & p159.

Shopping

Laox: Duty Free Akihabara

1-15-3 Soto-Kanda, Chiyoda-ku (3255 5301/www. laox.co.jp). Akihabara station (Yamanote, Sobu lines), Electric Town exit; (Hibiya line), exit 3. **Open** 10am-9pm daily.
One of Japan's biggest suppliers of duty-free overseas-model electronics and appliances. There are English-language catalogues and instruction manuals for most products. This branch is near the station, with a huge sign outside, so it's hard to miss.

Geek wonderland

@home café

The area which began as a post-war electronics black market, and later blossomed into 'Electric Town', famed for its discount tech goods, has now been fully colonised by Tokyo's geek set. Akihabara still offers all the electronic goodies, but there's now also a multi-storey manga emporium, numerous porn shops and even schoolgirl uniform outlets that stock sizes as unlikely as 'Male XL'. The interests of the city's reclusive males have transformed 'Akiba' into one of the city's quirkiest neighbourhoods.

What piques the geek's interest most is maids. From the single café **@home** (p155), where socially awkward guys are served by costumed young ladies with extra-squeaky voices, the fun spread to around 50 rival cafés, as well as maid masseuses (**Moema**, 2F, 3-2-3 Soto-Kanda, 5294 0025),

maid beauticians (**Maid Beauty Salon Oave**, 4-8-3 Soto-Kanda, 5296 2006) and maid tour guides that help you navigate the whole Akiba fantasyland (http://akiba-guide.com). Even **Candy Fruit Optical** (3-16-3 Soto-Kanda, 3252 4902), an optician that's been in the same location for over five decades, now requires its staff to dress as maids.

And *otaku* obsessions don't stop there. For boys too shy to interact with a flesh-and-blood girl, there are doll-rental rooms where they can enjoy an hour or two of silicon companionship, or life-sized characters costing up to ¥600,000 which you can purchase in 60 easy instalments.

Nowadays the Akihabara experience has become such an institution for Tokyoites and visitors alike that the *otaku* have to share their hangouts with an ever-increasing number of sightseers. The government's Japanese National Tourist Organisation (p185) now offers free tours of Akihabara and information on how to 'immerse yourself in Japanese anime and comics'.

It's all quite a turnaround from the early 1990s. Then the term *otaku* connoted sinister sociopaths, after 27-year-old anime and manga obsessive Tsutomu Miyazaki kidnapped and murdered three young girls. It took more than a decade for obsessive, antisocial devotion to pop culture to become acceptable again, but the long, diverse queues at the leading maid cafés and the popularity of anime and manga across all demographics suggests the *otaku* tide has turned.

Takarada Musen

1-14-7 Soto-Kanda, Chiyoda-ku (3253 0101/www.takarada-musen.com). Akihabara station (Yamanote, Sobu lines), Electric Town exit; (Hibiya line), exit 3. **Open** 11am-8.30pm daily.
This small, busy shop has a number of bilingual staff to help you find what you want. It specialises in overseas models of Sony products – digital and video cameras, TVs, Walkmans and so on. English manuals are available.

Tora no Ana

B1F-4F, 4-3-1 Soto-Kanda, Chiyoda-ku (5294 0123/www.toranoana.co.jp). Akihabara station (Yamanote, Sobu lines), Electric Town exit; (Hibiya line), exit 3. **Open** 11am-9pm Mon-Thur; 10am-9pm Fri-Sun.
A giant cartoon mascot marks this six-floor hive of nerd activity. In addition to the nation's bestselling new comics, the shop offers a selection of *dojinshi*, fanzines created by devoted manga amateurs, showcasing everything from Disney-esque fantasies to hard-core porn, and plastic figures of all sizes.

Ebisu

One stop away from the rowdy youth centre of Shibuya lies Ebisu, renowned for its wealth of restaurants and bars, and regarded as Tokyo's number one spot for rowdy *go-kon* (group blind dates).

Sights & museums

Beer Museum Yebisu

B1F 4-20-1 Ebisu Garden Place, Shibuya-ku (5423 7255/www.sapporo beer.jp/brewery/y_museum). Ebisu station (Yamanote line), east exit; (Hibiya line), exit 1. **Open** 10am-6pm Tue-Sun. **Admission** free. *With beer* ¥200. No credit cards.
Where the Yebisu brewery once stood, Sapporo now runs a museum of photographs, beer labels, old posters and video displays. There's a virtual reality tour of the brewing process and, at last, a lounge. Alas, the beer's not free.

Tokyo Metropolitan Museum of Photography

Ebisu Garden Place, 1-13-3 Mita, Meguro-ku (3280 0099/www.syabi.com). Ebisu station (Yamanote line), east exit; (Hibiya line), exit 1. **Open** 10am-6pm Tue, Wed, Sat, Sun; 10am-8pm Thur, Fri. **Admission** free. No credit cards.
Tokyo's premier photography showcase has a large permanent collection and brings in star photographers for regular shows. The small Images & Technology Gallery in the basement presents a multimedia history of optics and occasional media art exhibitions.

Eating & drinking

Bistrot des Arts

4-9-5 Ebisu, Shibuya-ku (3447 0408). Ebisu station (Yamanote line), east exit; (Hibiya line), exit 1. **Open** 11.30am-3am Mon-Sat; 11.30am-11pm Sun. **¥¥. French.**
Forsaking the clichés of checked tablecloths and the like, Bistrot des Arts espouses a chic, modern look and has rotating contemporary art exhibitions. The food is well above the bistro norm, and late-night hours make this a great stop-off for some wine and a light meal.

Chibo

Yebisu Garden Place Tower 38F, 4-20-3 Ebisu, Shibuya-ku (5424 1011/www.chibo.com). Ebisu station (Yamanote line), east exit; (Hibiya line), exit 1. **Open** 11.30am-3pm, 5-10pm Mon-Fri; 11.30am-10pm Sat, Sun. **¥¥. Okonomiyaki.** English menu.
This branch of one of Osaka's top *okonomiyaki* restaurants replicates the original Kansai-style recipes. In addition to the usual meats and seafood, stuffings include asparagus, *mochi* (rice cakes), cheese and, of course, mayonnaise. Friendly staff, reasonable prices, a large menu and a gorgeous view make this a popular place.

Dagashi

1-13-7 Ebisu-Nishi, Shibuya-ku (5458 5150). Ebisu station (Yamanote, Hibiya lines), west exit. **Open** 6.30pm-4.30am Mon-Sat; 6pm-1am Sun. **¥. Izakaya.**

TOKYO BY AREA

A beautiful *izakaya* serving steaming versions of all the favourites. The twist is the all-you-can-eat candy (*dagashi*), offered free to every customer: sweet-toothed boozers can plunge their hand into the buckets of traditional Japanese sweets and crispy snacks. For an extra ¥500 you can take a bag home. The name outside is only in Japanese, so look for the blazing orange signs.

Ippudo

1-3-13 Hiroo, Shibuya-ku (5420 2225/www.ippudo.com). Ebisu station (Yamanote line), west exit; (Hibiya line), exit 1. **Open** 11am-4am daily. **¥**. No credit cards. **Ramen**.

Once you get past all the ordering choices – red or white pork broth; noodles soft-cooked, medium or al dente; with or without *chashu* pork – you can settle in and appreciate all the little touches that distinguish Ippudo from other ramen shops. The layout is simple and open, with lots of plain wood; you can add your own condiments (spicy beansprouts, sesame seeds and garlic that you grind yourself); and there are unlimited pots of *rooibos* (red bush) tea to quench your thirst.

Kissa Ginza

1-3-9 Ebisu-Minami, Shibuya-ku (3710 7320/www8.plala.or.jp/dj/index.html). Ebisu station (Yamanote, Hibiya lines), west exit. **Open** 10am-2am Mon-Sat. **Bar**.

Here's a recipe for postmodern kitsch, Tokyo-style. Take a 40-year-old coffee shop that hasn't seen a decorator in 30 years, install a glitter ball, two turntables and… absolutely nothing else. Result: the blue-rinse set still come for coffee in the daytime, but the evening brings lounge-loving urban hipsters drinking draft beer from narrow sundae glasses. Appalling value, but good fun the first time you see it.

Ricos Kitchen

4-23-7 Ebisu, Shibuya-ku (5791 4649). Ebisu station (Yamanote line), east exit; (Hibiya line), exit 1. **Open** 11.30am-3.30pm, 6-11pm Tue-Sun. **¥¥¥**. **International**. English menu.

Chef Natsume Haruki produces a suave and satisfying version of *cucina nueva americana*, served in a chic, airy space. This, and the place's location close to Ebisu Garden Place, is why Ricos has been full virtually every day since it opened. Definitely one worth seeking out.

Shopping

User's Side 2

K&S Ebisu Bldg 2F-4F, 1-16-2 Hiroo, Shibuya-ku (5447 7011/www.users-side.co.jp/2/index.php). Ebisu station (Yamanote line), west exit; (Hibiya line), exit 1. **Open** 11am-7pm Mon-Sat.

User's Side 2 sells export models of Japanese technology, with English software. It also has an affordable repair and troubleshooting service, with English-language technical support and bilingual shop staff.

Yebisu Garden Place

4-20 Ebisu, Shibuya-ku & 13-1/4-1 Mita, Meguro-ku (5423 7111/www. gardenplace.co.jp/english). Ebisu station (Yamanote line), east exit; (Hibiya line), exit 1. **Open** *Shops* 11am-8pm Mon-Sat; 11am-7.30pm Sun. *Restaurants* varies.

The shopping available in Garden Place is hardly dazzling by Tokyo standards, but the complex also houses a stylish cinema, an oyster bar and Joël Robuchon's palatial Taillevent Robuchon (5424 1338, www.taillevent. com/japon) housed in a bright-yellow, mock-French château.

Nightlife

Milk

Roob 6 Bldg B1F-B2F, 1-13-3 Ebisu-Nishi, Shibuya-ku (5458 2826/ www.milk-tokyo.com). Ebisu station (Yamanote line), west exit; (Hibiya line), exit 2. **Open** 10pm-5am; days vary. **Admission** from ¥2,500. No credit cards.

This dingy two-floor basement regularly plays host to Tokyo's rock, punk and hardcore bands, but more recently has succumbed to the ubiquitous clubland sounds of techno and house.

Despite a capacity of around 400, the venue has neglected to devote much space to one essential amenity: on busy nights there is often a longer queue for the toilet than the bar.

Odaiba

You'll either love or hate Odaiba. Its wide avenues give a spacious feel, and with entertainment galore and the water of Tokyo Bay just a couple of streets away, it's a popular dating spot. But this pristine playground on reclaimed land can also feel sterile, artificial and just a little bit tacky.

Sights & museums

Fuji TV Building

2-4-8 Daiba, Minato-ku (5500 8888/ www.fujitv.co.jp). Odaiba Kaihin-Koen station (Yurikamome line). **Open** 10am-8pm Tue-Sun. **Admission** *Studios & observation deck* ¥500.
The headquarters of the Fuji TV corporation, one of Japan's nationwide commercial channels, has exhibitions (mostly in Japanese with occasional English subtitles) on popular programmes and guided studio tours.

Mega Web

1 Aomi, Koto-ku (3599 0808/test drive reservations 0070 800 489 000/www. megaweb.gr.jp/english/index.html). Aomi station (Yurikamome line); or Tokyo Teleport station (Rinkai line). **Open** *Toyota City Showcase* 11am-9pm daily. *History Garage* 11am-9pm Mon-Fri, Sun; 11am-10pm Sat. **Admission** free.
Part of the huge Palette Town development, Mega Web certainly lives up to its name. Its giant Ferris wheel – at 115m (383ft) one of the tallest in the world – is visible for miles. Beneath it is the world's largest car showroom, the Toyota City Showcase, where you can take a test drive (¥300) on the two-lap track (Japanese or international driver's licence required) or be ferried around in the self-driving electric town-car prototypes (¥200).

National Museum of Emerging Science & Innovation (Nihon Kagaku Miraikan)

2-41 Aomi (Odaiba), Koto-ku (3570 9151/www.miraikan.jst.go.jp). Fueno-Kagakukan station or Telecom Center station (Yurikamome line). **Open** 10am-5pm Mon, Wed-Sun. **Admission** ¥500; free-¥200 reductions. No credit cards.
The entrance is dominated by a globe measuring 6.5m (22ft) in diameter, with 851,000 LEDs on its surface showing real-time global climatic changes. The museum holds interactive displays on robots, genetic discoveries and space travel and, perhaps most bizarre of all, a model using springs and ball bearings to explain the operating principle of the internet. There are ample explanations in English.

Oedo Onsen Monogatari

2-57 Omi, Koto-ku (5500 1126/www. ooedoonsen.jp). Telecom Center station (Yurikamome line). **Open** 11am-9am daily (last entry 2am). **Admission** 11am-6pm ¥2,800; 6pm-2am ¥1,900; from 2am ¥3,400.
This hot-spring theme park does a pretty good job of recreating an Edo-period bathhouse, with numerous bathing areas, indoor and out, plus hot-sand baths and saunas. The admission fee includes *yukata* and towels.

Shopping

Venus Fort

Palette Town, 1 Aomi, Koto-ku (3599 0700/www.venusfort.co.jp). Aomi station (Yurikamome line); or Tokyo Teleport station (Rinkai line). **Open** *Shops* 11am-9pm Mon-Fri, Sun; 11am-10pm Sat. *Restaurants* 11am-11pm daily.
Touted as the 'first theme park exclusively for women', this unusual mall is decorated in a faux-classic Graeco-Roman style designed to evoke the feeling of strolling through Florence or Milan (it even has an artificial sky that changes colour with the time of day outside). It contains mainly European-style boutiques and pâtisseries.

Arts & leisure

Joypolis

Decks Tokyo 3F-5F, 1-6-1 Daiba, Minato-ku (5500 1801/www.sega.co.jp/joypolis/tokyo_e.html). Odaiba Kaihin-Koen station (Yurikamome line); or Tokyo Teleport station (Rinkai line). **Open** 10am-11pm daily (last entry 10.15pm). **Admission** *1-day passport* ¥3,300; ¥3,100 reductions.

Simulate snowboarding in the half-pipe canyon, ride a virtual hang-glider over tropical islands or whirl round the rollercoaster at this indoor fun park.

Naka-Meguro

The closest thing Tokyo has to bohemia, funky Naka-Meguro is the favourite haunt of artists, designers and musicians. The Meguro river is lined with cafés, boutiques and interior outfitters, almost all owned and run by entrepreneurs rather than big corporations.

Sights & museums

Mizuma Art Gallery

Fujiya Bldg 2F, 1-3-9 Kami-Meguro, Meguro-ku (3793 7931/www.mizuma-art.co.jp). Naka-Meguro station (Hibiya, Toyoko lines). **Open** 11am-7pm Tue-Sat. Closed 2wks Dec-Jan.

This gallery presents some of Japan's hottest contemporary artists, including Makoto Aida and Muneteru Ujino.

Museum of Contemporary Sculpture

4-12-18 Naka-Meguro, Meguro-ku (3792 5858/www.museum-of-sculpture.org). Naka-Meguro station (Hibiya, Toyoko lines), central exit. **Open** 10am-5pm Tue-Sun. **Admission** free.

The Watanabe Collection includes more than 200 pieces by 56 contemporary Japanese artists. Three outdoor areas filled with large, mostly conceptual works complement two storeys of figurative studies. The marble tombstones in the adjacent graveyard provide an interesting counterpoint.

Eating & drinking

Combine

NEW *103 Riverside Terrace, 1-10-23 Naka-Meguro, Meguro-ku (3760 3939). Naka-Meguro station (Toyoko line).* **Open** noon-4am Mon-Sat; noon-2am Sun. ¥. **Café**.

With an airy interior, riverside location and bookshelves holding hundreds of art books, Combine is a great spot to pass some time daytime or evening.

Higashi-yama

1-21-25 Higashiyama, Meguro-ku (5720 1300). Naka-Meguro station (Hibiya, Toyoko lines). **Open** 6pm-1am Mon-Sat. ¥¥¥. **Traditional Japanese**.

Inventive traditional cuisine from a team of gifted chefs, matched by a beautifully sleek, modern interior (the creation of Ogata Shinichiro: this is Japanese contemporary designer dining at its best. The staff are friendly and reservations essential.

Junkadelic

4-10-4 Kami-Meguro, Meguro-ku (5725 5020/http://junkadelic.jp). Naka-Meguro station (Hibiya, Toyoko lines). **Open** 6pm-2am daily. ¥¥. No credit cards. **Mexican**. English menu.

Day of the Dead figurines, primitive murals and junk-shop furniture set the scene here. The frozen Margaritas are large and lurid. The kitchen turns out a strange Japanese hybrid of Tex-Mex cantina food that's always tasty. Later in the evening it segues into a DJ bar.

Makani & Lanai

2-16-11 Aobadai, Meguro-ku (5428 4222/www.zetton.co.jp/aloha/ml/index.htm). Naka-Meguro station (Hibiya, Toyoko lines). **Open** 11.30am-3am Mon-Sat; 11.30am-midnight Sun. ¥¥. **Hawaiian**. English menu.

The food here, which with names like *pupu* and *ahi poke* won't mean much unless just you've just flown in from Hawaii, is distinctly lightweight. But it's the location, right on the cherry-lined Meguro river, that establishes M&L's credentials. An ideal spot for chilling with a Kona beer or three.

Cow Books

Nakame Takkyu Lounge

1-3-13 Naka-Meguro, Meguro-ku (5722 3080/www.mfs11.com). Naka-Meguro station (Hibiya, Toyoko lines). **Open** 6pm-1am daily. **Bar**.

Famous for its semi-secret location and full-size ping-pong table, this bar is a Naka-Meguro highlight. See box p79.

Shopping

Cow Books

1-14-11 Aobadai, Meguro-ku (5459 1747/www.cowbooks.jp). Naka-Meguro station (Hibiya, Toyoko lines). **Open** 2pm-9pm Tue-Sun.

This riverside book shop sells rare, out-of-print books and vintage magazines in English and Japanese. It specialises in art, the Beat Generation and counter culture in general.

Nightlife

Ovo

NEW *Wada Bldg B1F, 1-20-5 Kami-Meguro, Meguro-ku (3791 8065/www. clubovo.com). Naka-Meguro station (Hibiya, Toyoko lines).* **Admission** ¥2,500-¥3,000.

This basement bar-cum-club was reborn in revamped form in 2007, and now attracts the Naka-Meguro late-nighters. It's more than intimate – there's barely room for 30 people – but it's a friendly spot with quality music and a strong sound system.

Further afield

Sights & museums

Edo-Tokyo Open-Air Architectural Museum (Edo-Tokyo Tatemono-en)

3-7-1 Sakuracho, Koganei Ishi (042 388 3300/www.tatemonoen.jp). Musashi Koganei station (Chuo line), north exit then any bus from bus stops 2 or 3 to Koganei Koen Nishi-Guchi. **Open** *Apr-Sept* 9.30am-5.30pm Tue-Sun. *Oct-Mar* 9.30am-4.30pm Tue-Sun. **Admission** ¥400; free-¥200 reductions. No credit cards.

TOKYO BY AREA

Tokyo's architectural heritage is well preserved at this picturesque branch of the Edo-Tokyo Museum. Swanky private residences, quaint old town shops, an ornate bathhouse and a mausoleum built for a shogun's wife are among the imports that grace the spacious, verdant grounds.

Ghibli Museum

1-1-83 Shimo-Renjaku, Mitaka-shi (0570 05 5777/www.ghibli-museum.jp). Kichijoji station (Chuo line), north exit then 15mins walk or Mitaka station (Chuo line), south exit then community bus. **Open** (tours only) 10am, noon, 2pm, 4pm Mon, Wed-Sun. **Admission** ¥1,000; ¥400-¥700 reductions.

It's not easy gaining access to the museum devoted to Miyazaki Hayao's studio (responsible for anime classics such as *Princess Mononoke* and *Spirited Away*). You need to purchase tickets in advance (check the website for details), then show up at the prescribed time on the prescribed day with your ticket and ID. You will be escorted into another world where you can view original prints, play in rooms with painted ceilings and walls, and watch short animations. The gift shop sells original animation cels.

Sankeien

58-1 Honmoku-Sannotani, Naka-ku (045 621 0635/www.sankeien.or.jp). Yokohama station, east exit then bus 8 or 125 from bus stop 2 to Honmoku Sankeien-mae. **Open** *Outer Garden* 9am-5pm daily. *Inner Garden* 9am-4.30pm daily. **Admission** ¥500; ¥200 reductions. No credit cards.

Sankeien is a beautiful, traditional Japanese garden about an hour's trek from the city. When religious relics were being torn down in the Meiji era, a local merchant decided it would be a good idea to save the treasures and began importing them from across Japan. The grounds now house a three-storey pagoda from Kyoto and a feudal lord's residence, among many other priceless structures. The park opens in the evening for cherry-blossom season (April) and Moon Viewing (September).

Tokyo Disney Resort

1-1 Maihama, Urayasu-shi, Chiba (English information 045 683 3333/ www.tokyodisneyresort.co.jp/tdr/ index_e.html). Maihama station (Keiyo, Musashino lines), south exit. **Open** varies. **Admission** (per park) 1-day passport ¥5,500; ¥3,700-¥4,800 reductions. Off-peak passport available.

The resort comprises two adjacent but separate theme parks: Disneyland and DisneySea. The latter, opened in 2001, has given the place a huge shot in the arm, since the park was starting to show its age. Disneyland's seven main zones have 43 attractions; another 23 water-based ones are at DisneySea. As always with Disney, the queues can be horrendous. Go on a weekday.

Nightlife

Ageha

2-2-10 Shinkiba, Koto-ku (5534 2525/ www.ageha.com). Shinkiba station (Rinkai, Yurakucho lines). **Open** 11pm-5am Thur-Sat. **Admission** usually ¥4,000. No credit cards.

Tokyo's biggest club suffers from a far-flung location and huge dimensions. But on a busy night, it's one of the city's best clubbing experiences, with three dancefloors, a pool, numerous bars and chill-out spaces, and the best sound system in town. A free bus runs from the bottom of Roppongi Dori in Shibuya every half hour; you'll need photo ID with your birth date on it.

Air

Hikawa Bldg B1F-B2F, 2-11 Sarugakucho, Shibuya-ku (5784 3386/ www.air-tokyo.com). Daikanyama station (Toyoko line). **Open** 10pm-5am Mon, Thur-Sat. **Admission** ¥2,500-¥3,500. No credit cards.

One of Tokyo's best-designed clubs. Large but intimate, stylish but never flash, and run by staff without the snootiness that seems de rigueur for major venues, Air draws big-name international DJs, as well as the best local talent. Hungry clubbers can pop upstairs for some decent late-night food in the stylish Frames café.

Essentials

Mandarin Oriental Tokyo p168

Hotels

Fearsome room rates were once a major tourist deterrent for Tokyo, but those days are long gone. The capital still isn't a backpacker destination, but it does offer the full spectrum of accommodation, from dormitories (**Sakura Hotel**) to luxury suites in the sky (for ¥2 million per night at the **Ritz-Carlton**). At the top end, the two most conspicuous newcomers to the city – the **Ritz-Carlton** and the **Peninsula** – join a suddenly crowded field of five-star international chains that already included the **Park Hyatt**, **Grand Hyatt**, a pair of **Four Seasons** hotels and a **Mandarin Oriental**. All this activity at the top-end of the market has had a trickle-down effect, with many mid-range hotels indulging in makeovers.

Ryokan

Many hotels in all price brackets offer Japanese-style rooms, but for a truly traditional experience the *ryokan* is a must. Everything from service to decor to dining options is distinctly Japanese, and if you don't mind sleeping on a futon or taking a communal bath these inns are highly recommended. They tend to be found in the older parts of town, such as Asakusa or Yanaka, and consequently are easier on the wallet than many hotels. On the downside, some *ryokan* impose curfews, so be certain to check the rules when you book your room.

The quirky stuff

Though not recommended for extended stays, Tokyo's capsules and love hotels promise an experience to remember. Neither are really geared to peaceful slumber, but for single men or amorous couples, these are cheap and unforgettable options. To find a love hotel, head for Shinjuku or Shibuya and look for the gaudiest sign. Capsule hotels are more dispersed, but we've listed one for Shinjuku (**Shinjuku Kuyakusyo-Mae Capsule Hotel**). In either case, you'll be kicked out each morning with your luggage.

Where to stay

For access to everything, Shinjuku is hard to beat. It's the largest public transport hub in the city and boasts numerous impressive hotels on its west side, plus plenty of dining, dancing and shopping options on the east side. If you're in town for nightlife, Shibuya or Roppongi are your best bets. In Roppongi you'll also be on the doorstep of top-class restaurants, bars, galleries and shops. For calm and culture, head north-west to Ueno, Yanaka or Asakusa.

Sales tax

All room rates are subject to Japan's usual five per cent sales tax, but if your bill climbs to the equivalent of over ¥15,000 per night (including service charges), you will be liable to pay an additional three per cent tax. Then there's a flat-rate surcharge of ¥100 per night for rooms costing ¥10,000-¥14,999, rising to ¥200 for rooms costing ¥15,000 or over. This money goes to help the metropolitan government promote Tokyo as a tourist destination.

No tipping is expected in any Tokyo hotel, although most high-end places include a standard service charge of 10-15 per cent in their room rates. Ask when booking.

SHORTLIST

Best new faces
- Peninsula Tokyo (p170)
- Ritz-Carlton (p172)

Authentic Japanese
- Ryokan Katsutaro (p177)
- Ryokan Ryumeikan Honten (p170)
- Sukeroku No Yado Sadachiyo (p166)

Easy on the wallet
- Hotel Edoya (p176)
- Hotel New Koyo (p177)
- Hotel Nihonbashi Saibo (p168)
- Ryokan Sawanoya (p177)

Designer digs
- Claska (p177)

For peace and quiet
- Four Seasons Hotel Tokyo at Chinzan-so (p177)

Heart of the action
- Excel Hotel Tokyu (p174)
- Granbell Hotel (p174)
- Hotel Arca Torre Roppongi (p171)
- Star Hotel Tokyo (p176)

Rooms with a view
- Cerulean Tower Tokyu Hotel (p172)
- Mandarin Oriental Tokyo (p168)

The classics
- Hilltop Hotel (p168)
- Hotel Okura Tokyo (p172)
- Imperial Hotel (p167)

Fine dining
- Conrad Tokyo (p166)
- Grand Hyatt Tokyo (p171)
- Park Hyatt Tokyo (p174)

For a night to remember
- P&A Plaza (p174)
- Shinjuku Kuyakusyo-Mae Capsule Hotel (p174)

ESSENTIALS

Asakusa

Asakusa View Hotel

3-17-1 Nishi-Asakusa, Taito-ku (3847 1111/fax 3842 2117/www.viewhotels. co.jp/asakusa). Tawaramachi station (Ginza line), exit 3. ¥¥¥.
The only luxury hotel in this working-class neighbourhood lives up to its name with great river views from the upper floors. For a traditional experience befitting the area, book one of the sixth-floor Japanese-style rooms, complete with their own garden.

Ryokan Shigetsu

1-31-11 Asakusa, Taito-ku (3843 2345/fax 3843 2348/www.shigetsu. com). Asakusa station (Asakusa line), exit A4; (Ginza line), exits 1, 6. ¥¥.
Barely 30 seconds from Asakusa's market and temple complex, yet surprisingly peaceful, the Shigetsu offers comfortable rooms in Japanese and Western styles. All rooms have en suite bathrooms, but there is also a Japanese-style communal bath on the top floor. Booking is recommended and can be made through www.jpinn.com.

Sakura Ryokan

2-6-2 Iriya, Taito-ku (3876 8118/fax 3873 9456/www.sakura-ryokan.com). Iriya station (Hibiya line), exit 1. ¥.
Ten minutes' walk north of Asakusa's temple complex, in the traditional downtown area of Iriya, the Sakura is friendly, traditional and family-run. Not all rooms have en suite bathrooms, but there is a communal bath on each floor.

Sukeroku No Yado Sadachiyo

2-20-1 Asakusa, Taito-ku (3842 6431/fax 3842 6433/www.sadachiyo. co.jp). Asakusa station (Asakusa line), exit A4; (Ginza line), exits 1, 6; or Tawaramachi station (Ginza line), exit 3. ¥¥.
This smart, modern *ryokan* is situated five minutes' walk from Asakusa's temple. The façade resembles a cross between a European chalet and a Japanese castle, but inside it's pure Japan, with kimono-clad receptionists who speak only minimal English. All rooms are Japanese-style and the communal baths add to the authenticity.

Ginza

Conrad Tokyo

Tokyo Shiodome Bldg, 1-9-1 Higashi-Shinbashi, Minato-ku (6388 8000/fax 6388 8001/www.conradtokyo.co.jp). Shinbashi station (Yamanote, Asakusa lines), exit 1; (Ginza line), exit 2; or Shiodome station (Oedo, Yurikamome lines), exit 9. ¥¥¥¥.
The Conrad opened in July 2005 with spacious rooms in a modern Japanese design. Extras include a 25m pool, ten-room spa, floor-to-ceiling windows, plasma-screen TVs and wireless internet. The hotel is also home to a pair of eateries by Brit chef Gordon Ramsay.

Dai-ichi Hotel Tokyo

1-2-6 Shinbashi, Minato-ku (3501 4411/fax 3595 2634/www.daiichi hotels.com/hotel/tokyo). Shinbashi station (Yamanote, Asakusa, Ginza lines), Hibiya exit. ¥¥¥¥.
This 1993 tower, a ten-minute walk from Ginza, appears to be losing out to the hotels in nearby mini metropolis Shiodome City. The interior is a strange mix of styles: the entrance hall is a self-conscious echo of the grandeur of old European luxury hotels, while the restaurants cram a multitude of interior styles into one building. Rooms, however, are beautifully furnished.

Ginza Mercure

2-9-4 Ginza, Chuo-ku (4335 1111/ fax 4335 1222/www.mercureginza. com). Ginza-Itchome station (Yurakucho line), exit 11. ¥¥¥.
This French-owned hotel opened in autumn 2004 in a great central location. The converted office building now has the feel of a European boutique hotel, featuring smart cherry-wood furniture, stylish wallpaper and black-and-white photos of old Paris. There are 18 special 'ladies' rooms', with feminine decor, additional security and female-oriented amenities. A good choice for business and independent travellers.

ESSENTIALS

Granbell Hotel p174

Hotel Ginza Daiei

3-12-1 Ginza, Chuo-ku (3545 1111/ fax 3545 1177). Higashi-Ginza station (Asakusa line), exits A7, A8; (Hibiya line), exit 3. **¥¥**.

A well-situated, no-frills hotel that's well past its prime, the Ginza Daiei does at least offer decent-sized rooms with plain, functional pine furniture and inoffensive decor. Services are minimal, but high-speed internet has been installed in recent years. The top-price 'Healthy Twin' room also boasts a jet bath.

Hotel Seiyo Ginza

1-11-2 Ginza, Chuo-ku (3535 1111/ fax 3535 1110/www.seiyo-ginza.com). Ginza-Itchome station (Yurakucho line), exits 7, 10. **¥¥¥¥**.

Rosewood Hotels took over the Seiyo in 2000 and elevated the already upscale boutique property to unrivalled heights of fancy. The 77 rooms have all been refurbished, each in its own distinct style, to recreate a 'personal residence' away from home.

Hotel Villa Fontaine Shiodome

1-9-2 Higashi-Shinbashi, Minato-ku (3569 2220/fax 3569 2111/www. villa-fontaine.co.jp). Shiodome station (Oedo line), exit 10. **¥¥**.

The great value Villa Fontaine chain has mushroomed across the city in the last few years. This branch, opened in 2004, sits in the gleaming Shiodome complex. With a funky interior design, its well-designed rooms make the most of their small size. Free broadband internet access is a bonus, but buffet breakfast was disappointing.

Imperial Hotel

1-1-1 Uchisaiwaicho, Chiyoda-ku (3504 1111/fax 3581 9146/www.imperial hotel.co.jp). Hibiya station (Chiyoda, Hibiya, Mita lines), exits A5, A13; or Yurakucho station (Yamanote, Yurakucho lines), Hibiya exit. **¥¥¥¥**.

There has been an Imperial Hotel on this site overlooking Hibiya Park since 1890. This 1970 tower block replaced the glorious 1923 Frank Lloyd Wright

ESSENTIALS

creation that famously survived the Great Kanto Earthquake on its opening day. A five-year renovation plan, overhauling the lobby and all guest rooms, concludes in 2008.

Marunouchi

Four Seasons Hotel Tokyo at Marunouchi

Pacific Century Place, 1-11-1 Marunouchi, Chiyoda-ku (5222 7222/ fax 5222 1255/www.fourseasons.com/ marunouchi). Tokyo station (Yamanote, Marunouchi lines), Yaesu south exit. **¥¥¥¥**.

Unparalleled luxury and style in the heart of the city's business district, the Four Seasons is decorated in cool, modern timber and is beautifully lit. The rooms are among the biggest in any Tokyo hotel; some have great views. Service is multilingual and impeccable, as you'd expect for the price. Each room comes with high-speed internet access, a 42in plasma-screen TV with surround sound and a DVD player.

Hilltop Hotel

1-1 Kanda-Surugadai, Chiyoda-ku (3293 2311/fax 3233 4567/www. yamanoue-hotel.co.jp). Ochanomizu station (Chuo, Marunouchi lines), Ochanomizubashi exit. **¥¥¥**.

The Hilltop deserves praise for retaining its old-fashioned charm, with antique writing desks and small private gardens for the more expensive suites. That said, its seventh storey, called the Art Septo Floor, offers funky furniture and decor. Known as a literary hangout, the Hilltop tries to boost the concentration of scribes by pumping ionised air into every room.

Hotel Kazusaya

4-7-15 Nihonbashi-Honcho, Chuo-ku (3241 1045/fax 3241 1077/www. h-kazusaya.co.jp). Kanda station (Yamanote, Ginza lines), east exit; Mitsukoshimae station (Ginza, Hanzomon lines), exit A10. **¥¥**.

There has been a Hotel Kazusaya in Nihonbashi since 1891, but you'd be hard pushed to know it from the modern exterior of the current building, in one of the last *shitamachi* areas of Tokyo's business district. The rooms are reasonably sized and functionally furnished, with one Japanese-style tatami room for three to four guests. Service is obliging, although only minimal English is spoken.

Hotel Nihonbashi Saibo

3-3-16 Nihonbashi-Ningyocho, Chuo-ku (3668 2323/fax 3668 1669/www. hotel-saibo.co.jp). Ningyocho station (Asakusa, Hibiya lines), exit A4. **¥**.

The Saibo became a great choice when it remodelled its rooms but retained the bargain rates. Good for solo travellers.

Kayabacho Pearl Hotel

1-2-5 Shinkawa, Chuo-ku (3553 8080/ fax 3555 1849/www.pearlhotel.co.jp/ kayabacho). Kayabacho station (Hibiya, Tozai lines), exit 4B. **¥¥**.

An upmarket canalside business hotel, the Pearl has good-sized, well-furnished rooms and reasonable service. Staff speak some English.

Mandarin Oriental Tokyo

2-1-1 Nihonbashi-Muromachi, Chuo-ku (3270 8800/fax 3270 8828/www.mandarinoriental.com/ tokyo). Mitsukoshimae station (Ginza line), exit A7. **¥¥¥¥**.

The Mandarin exploits its location in the historic Nihonbashi area by sourcing art and furnishings from local artisans. The lobby and rooms all hint at traditional Japanese motifs, from the *torii* shrine gates and *washi* paper lanterns to the fabric stencils that hang in place of paintings. The view trumps those of most top-end rivals, taking in a mosaic of lights from the business district and Mount Fuji.

Marunouchi Hotel

1-6-3 Marunouchi, Chiyoda-ku (3217 1111/fax 3217 1115/www. marunouchi-hotel.co.jp). Tokyo station (Yamanote line), Marunouchi north exit; (Marunouchi line), exit 12. **¥¥¥**.

The Marunouchi's seventh-floor lobby features a spectacular atrium that soars through the centre of the hotel. Rooms (which vary considerably in

The Peninsula Tokyo

Despite the city's legendary appetite for luxury, it's only in the 21st century that Tokyo has been accruing the kind of high-end hotels that most metropolises take for granted. With its economic malaise firmly in the past, the city has welcomed a Who's Who of hospitality giants to town – Conrad, Four Seasons, Mandarin Oriental, Ritz-Carlton.

Now there's a Peninsula too. With the Hong Kong flagship often cited as one of the world's best hotels, the arrival of a Tokyo sister in September 2007 is yet another sign that the capital has come of age as a Great Global Destination.

The Peninsula has picked an impressive plot within sight of the Imperial Palace and an easy stroll from the free-spending, big-brand swank of Ginza or Marunouchi. But spendthrifts don't even have to leave the hotel. Jewellery brands de Grisogono, Chantecler and Graff will all have their first Japanese outlets here, and Kyoto's renowned *kaiseki* restaurant Tsuruya has a spot in the basement. The truly extravagant can be ferried to the ¥850,000 per night, 3,730sq ft (350sq m) Peninsula Suite, the second biggest in the city, in a 1934 Rolls-Royce Phantom II.

Local star Yukio Hashimoto, designer of Azumitei (p62), was given the brief 'international in design but Japanese by inspiration', and has produced suitably deluxe rooms in the de rigueur earth tones, with plenty of wood and stone, and eastern-style layouts with boundary-free living spaces flowing into each other. Dominating the lobby, meanwhile, is a stunning bamboo creation from Keisen Hama, one of over 900 pieces by local creators. Among the innovative tech luxuries are portable room phones that operate as hotel lines while on the premises, and convert to mobile phones when roaming the city.

In a now bustling luxury hotel market, with several of its biggest rivals within easy walking distance, the Peninsula can at least claim to be the freshest hotel in Tokyo – the freshest, that is, until the Shangri-La arrives in 2009.

ESSENTIALS

Ryokan Shigetsu p166

size) are decorated in sumptuous materials in a palette of browns and golds. Japanese and French restaurants and good business facilities help make this a classy joint.

Peninsula Tokyo

NEW *1-8-1 Yurakucho, Chiyoda-ku (6270 2288/fax 6270 2000/www. peninsula.com/tokyo.html). Hibiya station (Chiyoda, Hibiya lines), exit A6.* **¥¥¥¥**.
The world's eighth Peninsula was due to open in Tokyo in September 2007. See box p169.

Ryokan Ryumeikan Honten

3-4 Kanda-Surugadai, Chiyoda-ku (3251 1135/fax 3251 0270/www.ryumeikan.co.jp/honten.html). Ochanomizu station (Chuo, Marunouchi lines), Hijiribashi exit. **¥¥**.
A modern and clean *ryokan* with helpful staff and decent-sized Japanese rooms. The interior shows how ingeniously the Japanese can disguise a

dour building, but you still might find yourself wishing you'd stayed somewhere a little more traditional.

Sakura Hotel

2-21-4 Kanda-Jinbocho, Chiyoda-ku (3261 3939/fax 3264 2777/www.sakura-hotel.co.jp). Jinbocho station (Hanzomon, Mita, Shinjuku lines), exits A1, A6. **¥**.
The most central of Tokyo's budget hotels and *ryokan*, this is located in the Jinbocho district just a mile or so north of the Imperial Palace. Small groups can use the dorm rooms, which sleep six. Rooms are tiny but clean, and all are no-smoking. Staff are on duty 24 hours a day and speak good English. Book well in advance.

Sumisho Hotel

9-14 Nihonbashi-Kobunacho, Chuo-ku (3661 4603/fax 3661 4639/www.sumisho-hotel.co.jp). Ningyocho station (Asakusa, Hibiya lines), exit A5. **¥¥**.
Guests cross a small pond to reach to the foyer of this charming Japanese-style hotel, helping them forget that it sits in an ugly modern Tokyo building. It's a pleasant enough place to stay, with good facilities and a high level of service, though non-Japanese speakers may need to work hard.

YMCA Asia Youth Centre

2-5-5 Sarugakucho, Chiyoda-ku (3233 0611/fax 3233 0633/www.ymcajapan.org/ayc). Suidobashi station (Chuo line), east exit; (Mita line), exit A1. **¥**.
Part of the Korean YMCA in Japan, this centre offers many of the same facilities and services you'd expect at a regular hotel, which is reflected in its relatively high prices. The smallish rooms are Western in style, with their own bathrooms.

Roppongi

ANA Intercontinental Tokyo

1-12-33 Akasaka, Minato-ku (3505 1111/fax 3505 1155/www.anahotel tokyo.jp/e). Tameike-Sanno station (Ginza, Nanboku lines), exit 13. **¥¥¥¥**.

In 2007 owners All Nippon Airways teamed up with the Intercontinental chain and rebranded this 29-storey hotel. Its airy lobby has been redone in gleaming marble and cherry wood, with the modern space broken up by cascading waterfalls and artworks. Spacious, well-equipped rooms have all been recently renovated. The open-air rooftop pool offers a view of Mount Fuji on a clear day.

Asia Center of Japan

8-10-32 Akasaka, Minato-ku (3402 6111/fax 3402 0738/www.asiacenter. or.jp). Nogizaka station (Chiyoda line), exit 3. ¥.
Founded by the Ministry of Foreign Affairs in the 1950s as a cheap place for visiting students to stay, this has long since outgrown its origins and offers comfortable, no-frills accommodation to all visitors on a budget. A good choice for those who don't want to sacrifice location in favour of price, the Asia Center of Japan is conveniently situated for Roppongi and Aoyama.

Grand Hyatt Tokyo

6-10-3 Roppongi, Minato-ku (4333 1234/fax 4333 8123/www.tokyo. grand.hyatt.com). Roppongi station (Hibiya line), exit 1C; (Oedo line), exit 3. ¥¥¥¥.
The effortlessly sleek Grand is pleasingly low key. Located in the upmarket Roppongi Hills complex, the high-end shops and restaurants, a 53-floor panorama and world-class art on your doorstep can be considered quite an amenity. Its palette is taupe and cream, marble and wood, and though not flashy, the rooms are extremely comfortable and well thought out, including a tub you could park your car in.

Grand Prince Hotel Akasaka

1-2 Kioi-cho, Chiyoda-ku (3234 1111/ fax 3262 5163/www.princehotelsjapan. com/akasakaprincehotel). Akasaka-Mitsuke station (Ginza, Marunouchi lines), exit D; or Nagatacho station (Hanzomon, Nanboku, Yurakucho lines), exit 7. ¥¥¥¥.

Situated to the west of the Imperial Palace complex and designed by award-winning architect Kenzo Tange, the 40-storey Prince is part of a complex that includes a convention centre, European-style guesthouse, banqueting hall and numerous restaurants. Inside the main tower it's all glittering marble and bright lights. Rooms are clean and simple.

Hotel Arca Torre Roppongi

6-1-23 Roppongi, Minato-ku (3404 5111/fax 3404 5115/www.arktower. co.jp). Roppongi station (Hibiya, Oedo lines), exit 3. ¥¥.
Arca Torre is a smart, bright, high(ish)-rise business hotel sandwiched between the adults' playground of Roppongi and the Roppongi Hills complex. Rooms are small and functional with a vaguely Italian vibe. For nightlife lovers, the hotel's location is hard to beat, but light sleepers will bemoan the noisy streets.

Hotel Avanshell

2-14-4 Akasaka, Minato-ku (3568 3456/fax 3568 3599/www.avanshell. com). Akasaka station (Chiyoda line), exit 2; or Tameike-Sanno station (Ginza, Nanboku lines), exit 10. ¥¥¥.
The Avanshell is the latest incarnation of a one-time serviced apartment building on a side street in Akasaka, a fact that's reflected in the mini kitchens and other apartment-style touches. Long-term stays are encouraged, with a range of electronics and other items available to rent. Rooms are designed around five themes, with names like Zen, Primo and Ultimo, and are pleasingly spacious, with large living and work areas plus separate bedrooms.

Hotel Ibis

7-14-4 Roppongi, Minato-ku (3403 4411/fax 3479 0609/www.ibis-hotel. com). Roppongi station (Hibiya, Oedo lines), exit 4A. ¥¥.
With all the new Roppongi competition, Hotel Ibis is looking a little worn, and customers may well be enticed elsewhere. But it's clean, functional and

good value, and no other hotel can claim to embody Roppongi more effectively, with a gentlemen's club off the front desk, a karaoke lounge downstairs, plus Italian and Vietnamese restaurants thrown into the mix.

Hotel New Otani Tokyo

4-1 Kioi-cho, Chiyoda-ku (3265 1111/ fax 3221 2619/www1.newotani.co.jp/ en/tokyo). Akasaka-Mitsuke station (Ginza, Marunouchi lines), exit D; or Nagatacho station (Hanzomon, Nanboku, Yurakucho lines), exit 7. **¥¥¥¥**.

The New Otani sprawls over a vast area ten minutes' walk west of the Imperial Palace. The building bears the unattractive hallmarks of its 1969 construction, but inside, the dim lighting and spacious foyers produce the feeling of a luxury cruise ship. The beautifully laid-out and tended Japanese garden hosts several of the hotel's numerous restaurants.

Hotel Okura Tokyo

2-10-4 Toranomon, Minato-ku (3582 0111/fax 3582 3707/www.okura.com/ tokyo). Tameike-Sanno station (Ginza, Nanboku lines), exit 13. **¥¥¥¥**.

The Okura, next door to the US Embassy, doesn't appear to have changed much in the last half century. The huge wooden lobby's gold-and-beige decor evokes a bygone era, while the guest rooms offer an antiquated fusion of European and Japanese styles. But the Okura is taking steps to modernise itself, beginning with two 'Relaxation Floors' that feature jet baths, saunas and massage services in plush new rooms.

Ritz-Carlton

NEW *Tokyo Midtown, 9-7-1 Akasaka, Minato-ku (3423 8000/fax 3423 8001/ www.ritzcarlton.com/en/Properties/ Tokyo). Roppongi station (Hibiya, Oedo lines), exit 8.* **¥¥¥¥**.

Occupying 12 floors of Tokyo's tallest skyscraper, the Ritz-Carlton arrived in spring 2007, signalling its clear intent to top Tokyo's luxury lists. The largest suite clocks in at ¥200,000 per night,

the amenities come from Bulgari, and the bar's priciest cocktail? Just ¥1.8 million (for a vodka martini – although it does come with a Bulgari diamond in it).

Tokyo Prince Hotel Park Tower

3-3-1 Shibakoen, Minato-ku (3432 1111/fax 3434 5551/www.prince hotels.co.jp/parktower-e). Akabanebashi station (Oedo line), Akabanebashi exit. **¥¥¥¥**.

Occupying the corner of Shiba Park next to the Tokyo Tower, this 33-storey luxury hotel opened in spring 2005, offering everything from a jazz bar to a natural hot-spring spa. All rooms have internet service, jet baths and balconies with views across the park and as far as Mount Fuji. The Royal Suite comes with a full-time butler.

Shibuya

Arimax Hotel Shibuya

11-15 Kamiyamacho, Shibuya-ku (5454 1122/fax 3460 6513/www. arimaxhotelshibuya.co.jp). Shibuya station (Yamanote, Ginza, Hanzomon lines), Hachiko exit. **¥¥¥**.

Modelled on European boutique hotels, the Arimax offers a choice of English or neo-classical rooms and exudes the atmosphere of a long-established gentlemen's club, with warm, dim lighting and dark wood panelling. The only drawback is the location, about 15 minutes' walk from the centre of Shibuya.

Cerulean Tower Tokyu Hotel

26-1 Sakuragaoka-cho, Shibuya-ku (3476 3000/fax 3476 3001/www. ceruleantower-hotel.com). Shibuya station (Yamanote line), south exit; (Ginza, Hanzomon lines), Hachiko exit. **¥¥¥¥**.

It may be outshone in the luxury market by the myriad new entrants, but the Cerulean is Shibuya's lone top-end establishment, offering grandstand views of the area. In addition to the usual restaurants and bars, it also has

P&A Plaza p174

a Noh theatre (p132) and jazz club (p129). Room furnishings are a step down from luxury competitors like the Grand Hyatt, but so is the price.

Excel Hotel Tokyu

Shibuya Mark City, 1-12-2 Dogenzaka, Shibuya-ku (5457 0109/fax 5457 0309/www.tokyuhotels.co.jp/en/ TE/TE_SHIBU). Inside Shibuya station. **¥¥¥**.

Situated in the Mark City complex attached to Shibuya station, the Excel is popular with domestic visitors on weekend retreats. Pleasant and clean, with spacious rooms and decent views, it also offers two women-only floors with added security.

Granbell Hotel

NEW *15-17 Sakuragaoka-cho, Shibuya-ku (5457 2681/fax 5457 2682/www. granbellhotel.jp). Shibuya station (Yamanote line), south exit; (Ginza, Hanzomon lines), Hachiko exit.* **¥¥**.

This small and welcoming hotel a few blocks from Shibuya station offers minimalist rooms with a big splash of pop art. The single rooms are small, but for the price, there's no better place.

P&A Plaza

1-17-9 Dogenzaka, Shibuya-ku (3780 5211/www.p-aplaza.com). Shibuya station (Yamanote, Ginza lines), south exit; (Hanzomon line), exit 5. **¥¥¥**.

A top-end love hotel near Shibuya station, the P&A offers a peculiarly kitsch version of luxury. One room comes with its own swimming pool, and the eighth-floor Moroccan-style suites are so lavish you'll be reluctant to leave when they kick you out at 10am.

Shinjuku

Hilton Tokyo

6-6-2 Nishi-Shinjuku, Shinjuku-ku (3344 5111/fax 3342 6094/www. hilton.com/hotels/TYOHITW). Nishi-Shinjuku station (Marunouchi line), exit C8; or Tochomae station (Oedo line), exit C8. Free bus from Keio department store (bus stop 21), Shinjuku station, west exit. **¥¥¥**.

Rooms here are spacious but the views, often blocked by other towers in the area, can be disappointing. As you'd expect, the standard of service is high. For business travellers, the hotel offers five executive floors, with separate check-in, a fax machine in each room and guest relations officers on hand to help out and advise. The Hilton is also one of the few Tokyo hotels to have its own tennis courts.

Keio Plaza Hotel

2-2-1 Nishi-Shinjuku, Shinjuku-ku (3344 0111/fax 3345 8269/www. keioplaza.com). Shinjuku station (Yamanote line), west exit; (Marunouchi line), exit A17; (Shinjuku line), exit B1. **¥¥¥**.

The lavish decor that once made this Tokyo's most prestigious hotel now looks dated, but the rooms are being refurbished. The location is great – a stone's throw from the world's busiest train station – and the upper floors offer superlative views of the metropolis.

Park Hyatt Tokyo

3-7-1-2 Nishi-Shinjuku, Shinjuku-ku (5322 1234/fax 5322 1288/http:// tokyo.park.hyatt.com). Shinjuku station (Yamanote, Marunouchi lines), west exit; (Shinjuku line), exit 6. Free shuttle bus from in front of Shinjuku L Tower, Shinjuku station, west exit. **¥¥¥¥**.

For a long time the standout luxury hotel in town, the Park Hyatt has become 'the one from *Lost in Translation*'. By Tokyo standards, it's a small, intimate establishment, a feeling emphasised by the well-lit decor. The reception is on the glass-walled 41st floor, with stunning views over the whole of the city. Service is attentive but not overly fussy, and the rooms are immaculately equipped but unremarkable to look at.

Shinjuku Kuyakusyo-Mae Capsule Hotel

1-2-5 Kabuki-cho, Shinjuku-ku (3232 1110/www.toyo-bldg.ne.jp/hotel). Shinjuku station (Yamanote line), east exit; (Marunouchi line), exit B7; (Shinjuku, Oedo lines), exit 1. **¥**.

Rooms with a brew

Tokyo's best hotel bars.

With over 300,000 other hostelries, and booze on sale everywhere from local temples to the Tokyo Tower, it isn't as though anyone needs to hit their hotel bar, but some of the best new drinking spots happen to have hotels attached.

The Mandarin Oriental's **Mandarin Bar** (p95) offers impeccable design from local hotshot Ryu Kosaka who was asked to create 'something sexy, but like nothing you've seen before'. His spacious layout, incorporating a Zen pool and a mishmash of designer furnishings, succeeds on both counts. The view of Nihonbashi's business district is impressive, but you might not even notice. The inventive drinks include house speciality the '88', comprising sake, chestnut liqueur and maple syrup or, for the less sweet-toothed

drinker, the Glorious Martini (pictured), with Grand Marnier, Galliano and rose syrup.

The **Lobby Lounge** on the 45th floor of the Ritz-Carlton (p172) also has a serene interior with flickering pool, but it's the drink menu that grabbed headlines. Martinis come with puréed watermelon, blue cheese or, for just ¥1,798,000 more, a 1-carat Bulgari diamond. If you remember to fish the gem out, the local Bulgari outlet will fit a ring for free.

The latest luxury option is the Peninsula's 24th-floor **Rooftop Restaurant & Bar** (see box p169), designed by Yabu Pushelberg, the Toronto duo also responsible for the interior of the Four Seasons, Marunouchi (p168). Once again, there's Tokyo's skyline to remind you why the prices are so high, and – being the new kid in town – Rooftop is bustling with the see-and-be-seen set.

Lest we seem to be suggesting that only the top-end spots are worth a look, Shibuya's Granbell Hotel has the delightfully named **Plate of Pie.Pop** (p123). The narrow standing bar and stern seating area are a world away from the swish destinations above, but it's licensed 24 hours a day, stocks 16 varieties of beer and serves a truly extensive range of snacks, from jambalaya or oven-baked snails to the pies that inspired the name. Extensive beer list aside, Plate of Pie.Pop's signature drink is the Pop Panic - frozen tequila, guava and strawberry, served by the jug. It's far from chic, but it's definitely open.

ESSENTIALS

Keio Plaza Hotel p174

A step down in price and luxury from other west Shinjuku hotels, rooms are small and blandly furnished, but the service is spot on. There is now a women-only floor, and a newer annex which offers more modern decor.

Star Hotel Tokyo

7-10-5 Nishi-Shinjuku, Shinjuku-ku (3361 1111/fax 3369 4216/www. starhotel.co.jp/city/tokyo.html). Shinjuku station (Yamanote line), west exit; (Marunouchi, Shinjuku lines), exit D4; or Shinjuku-Nishiguchi station (Oedo line), exit D4. ¥¥.
A frill-free option with tiny rooms, the Star nevertheless offers decent value with a location in sight of so many upscale rivals on the west side of Shinjuku. The hotel has made some cosmetic upgrades, but choose this for location rather than comfort.

Ueno & Yanaka

Homeikan Honkan/ Daimachibekkan

5-10-5 Hongo, Bunkyo-ku (Honkan 3811 1181/Daimachibekkan 3811 1186/fax 3811 1764). Hongo-Sanchome station (Marunouchi line), Hongo-Nichome exit; (Oedo line), exit 2. ¥¥.
This wonderful old *ryokan* in the sleepy streets of Hongo looks just like a Japanese inn ought to: wooden, glass-fronted and with an ornamental front garden. And its owners plan to keep it that way following the *ryokan*'s designation as an important cultural property by the Ministry of Education. Homeikan's cordial, English-speaking manager can help you choose a room away from the rowdy Japanese students who often lodge here. The only drawback is its location: the *ryokan* is around 20 minutes' walk from the nearest real action around Ueno or Ochanomizu stations.

Hotel Edoya

3-20-3 Yushima, Bunkyo-ku (3833 8751/fax 3833 8759/www.hoteledoya. com). Yushima station (Chiyoda line), exit 5. ¥.

For a place to flop after a night out in Shinjuku, or to experience a unique stay in coffin-like conditions, the men-only Kuyakusyo-Mae Hotel offers little more than a sauna and a sleeping slot. It should prove an unforgettable experience nonetheless.

Shinjuku Palace Hotel

2-8-12 Kabuki-cho, Shinjuku-ku (3209 1231). Shinjuku station (Yamanote line), east exit; Shinjuku-Sanchome station (Marunouchi, Shinjuku lines), exit C7. ¥.
A palace in name only, this hotel in the heart of Kabuki-cho offers basic, no-frills Japanese or Western-style rooms aimed primarily at local businessmen. Rooms are small, but how much time are you really going to spend here?

Shinjuku Washington Hotel

3-2-9 Nishi-Shinjuku, Shinjuku-ku (3343 3111/fax 3342 2575/www. wh-rsv.com/english/shinjuku). Shinjuku station (Yamanote, Marunouchi lines), south exit; (Oedo, Shinjuku lines), exits 6, 7. ¥¥.

This mainly Japanese-style *ryokan*, not far from Ueno Park, offers good value at the budget end of the spectrum. There's a small Japanese tearoom and garden on the first floor, and the roof has an open-air hot bath for both men and women.

Ryokan Katsutaro

4-16-8 Ikenohata, Taito-ku (3821 9808/fax 3821 4789/www.katsutaro. com). Nezu station (Chiyoda line), exit 2. ¥.

In a backstreet on the northern side of Ueno Park, Katsutaro is a small, friendly *ryokan* with the atmosphere of a real family home (which it is). Rooms can hold up to four people, at an extra charge of roughly ¥4,000 per person. The owner does speak a little English, but you'll need to have a phrasebook handy if you want the conversation to progress. Just a short walk away is the more modern Annex.

Ryokan Sawanoya

2-3-11 Yanaka, Taito-ku (3822 2251/fax 3822 2252/www.tctv.ne.jp/ members/sawanoya). Nezu station (Chiyoda line), exit 1. ¥.

One of the only *ryokan* exclusively targeting foreign visitors, Sawanoya's rooms are small but comfortable, and there are signs in English reminding you how to behave and explaining bathroom etiquette. More expensive rooms have en suite baths; cheaper ones have access to the communal tub. The friendly couple who own the place help make this great value.

Further afield

Claska

1-3-18 Chuo-cho, Meguro-ku (3719 8121/fax 3719 8122/www. claska.com). Gakugei-Daigaku station (Tokyu line). ¥¥¥.

Nine rooms occupying two floors: hotels don't get any more exclusive than the Claska. Add the funky designer vibe and you have one of the trendiest spots in the city, albeit one of the least accessible – ten minutes walk from an obscure station. Each room is styled differently, with the most expensive boasting a 41sq m (441sq ft) terrace. The building also features a hip bar/restaurant, a gallery and a dog-grooming salon.

Four Seasons Hotel Tokyo at Chinzan-so

2-10-8 Sekiguchi, Bunkyo-ku (3943 2222/fax 3943 2300/www.fourseasons. com/tokyo). Mejiro station (Yamanote line), then 61 bus; or Edogawabashi station (Yurakucho line), exit 1A. **¥¥¥¥**.

Inconveniently located in the wilds of northern Tokyo, this is a breath-takingly opulent and beautiful hotel popular with locals on weekend escapes and celebrities seeking privacy away from the bright lights of the city. Take a stroll around the Japanese garden – which has its own firefly population, as well as ancient statues that come from Nara and Kamakura.

Hotel Monterey Hanzomon

NEW *23-1 Ichibancho, Chiyoda-ku (3556 7111/fax 3556 7199/www. hotelmonterey.co.jp/hanzomon/index. html). Hanzomon station (Hanzomon line), exit 5.* **¥¥¥**.

Opened in the middle of 2006, the latest Monterey is a stylish place with rooms decorated in what they describe as 'Edo taste'. In practice, this means colourful rooms of pinks and yellows, with touches of classic Japanese design. This isn't designer living to the degree offered at Claska, Grand Hyatt Tokyo or the Mandarin Oriental, but it's a comfortable, peaceful option.

Hotel New Koyo

2-26-13 Nihonzutumi, Taito-ku (3873 0343/fax 3873 1358/www.newkoyo.jp). Minowa station (Hibiya line), exit 3. ¥.

A backpacker joint with facilities that put more expensive places to shame (kitchens on each floor, laundry machines, a Japanese-style bath), the New Koyo may offer the cheapest overnight stay in Tokyo. The rooms are tiny, however, and the hotel is a long way away from the action.

Getting Around

Arriving & leaving

By air

Two airports serve Tokyo. Most overseas flights arrive at **Narita International Airport**, which is nearly 70 kilometres (45 miles) from Tokyo and well served by rail and bus links to the city. It's less likely that you'll arrive at **Haneda International Airport**, closer to the city and to the south, which handles mainly internal flights.

Narita International Airport

Flight information 0476 34 5000/ www.narita-airport.jp/en/index.html.
The **Narita Express train** (050 2016 1603, www.jreast.co.jp/e/nex), run by Japan Railways (JR), is the fastest way to get into Tokyo from Narita, but it's also the most expensive. All trains go to Tokyo station (¥2,940), with some also serving Shinjuku (¥3,110), Ikebukuro (¥3,110), Omiya (¥3,740) and Yokohama (¥4,180). Trains depart every 30 to 40 minutes, and seats can be reserved up to a month in advance.

The **Keisei Skyliner** (Narita 0476 32 8505, Ueno 3831 0989, www.keisei.co.jp/keisei/tetudou/keisei_us/top.html), operated by a private rail company, is a cheaper option. Trains on this line will take you into Ueno or Nippori station (¥1,920) in around an hour. Even cheaper is a Keisei limited express (*tokkyu*), a regular train that makes a few stops on its 75-minute route to Ueno station (¥1,000).

Limousine buses (3665 7220, www.limousinebus.co.jp) also run regularly to various key points and certain hotels in the city. There are

ticket counters inside the arrivals halls near the exits of terminals 1 and 2; buses depart from just outside. Fares are ¥3,000.

Taxis are recommended only for those with bottomless wallets: they cost from ¥30,000 and are often slower than the train.

Haneda International Airport

Flight information 5757 8111/ www.tokyo-airport-bldg.co.jp.
Haneda is served by the **Tokyo Monorail** (www.tokyo-monorail.co.jp), which leaves every five to ten minutes from 5.01am to 11.50pm, linking up to Hamamatsucho station (¥470) on the Yamanote line in a little over 20 minutes. The Keikyu line (5789 8686, www.keikyu.co.jp) can take you to Shinagawa, also on the Yamanote line, in 19 minutes (¥400). From here you can link up with major JR lines.

Limousine buses to central Tokyo cost in the region of ¥1,000, depending on which part of the city you want to go to. A taxi will cost a minimum of ¥6,000.

By train

Most of Japan's vast and efficient rail network is run by **Japan Railways** (JR). One of the fastest but most expensive ways to travel Japan's elongated countryside is by *shinkansen* (bullet train), which travels at speeds up to 270 kilometres (168 miles) per hour. Tickets can be purchased at JR reservation 'Green Window' areas or travel agents, or online at www.world.eki-net.com. Call the **JR East Infoline** (p179) for information in English.

ESSENTIALS

Trains depart from different stations depending on destination; most leave from Tokyo or Ueno stations. Slower, cheaper trains go to many destinations. Marks on the train platforms show where the numbered carriages will stop. Most carriages have reserved seats only (reservations cost extra), but some carriages are set aside for unreserved seating. Arrive early if you want to sit down.

By coach

Long-distance buses are a cheaper option, although anyone over 5ft 6in (1m 68cm) may find the seats small. Most of these buses leave at midnight and arrive early the next morning; all are air-conditioned and have ample luggage space. Seats can be reserved through a travel agent. Long-distance buses are run by the railway companies; for information, refer to our sections on **JR trains** (below) and **Private train lines** (p180).

Public transport

Tokyo has one of the most efficient train and subway systems in the world: in the rare event of delays in the morning rush, staff give out apology slips for workers to show their bosses. Services are fast, clean, reliable and remarkably easy to use. Almost all stations have signs in English and signs telling you which exit to take. Subways and train lines are colour-coded.

Subways and trains operate from 5am to around midnight (JR lines slightly later). Rush hours are roughly 7.30-9.30am and 5-7pm; the last train of the day can be extremely uncomfortable.

Tokyo's rail network is run by several different companies, but a Pasmo or Suica magnetic rail pass gives access to almost all routes.

The user-friendly **Jorudan** website (www.jorudan.co.jp) is in English. You can type in your starting point and destination to get routes, times and prices.

JR trains

Overland trains in Tokyo are operated by **Japan Railways East** (www.jreast.co.jp/e). Their **Yamanote line** is the loop that defines the city centre – all other subway and rail lines link to it. JR's other major lines in Tokyo are: **Chuo** (orange), **Sobu** (yellow), **Saikyo** (turquoise) and **Keihin Tohoku** (blue). Because of its notoriety for gropers, the insanely crowded Saikyo line offers women-only cars during peak hours.

JR East Infoline
050 2016 1603. **Open** 10am-6pm daily.

Subways

There are 12 subway lines in Tokyo. Most are run by **Tokyo Metro** (3941 2004, 9am-9pm daily, www.tokyometro.jp/e), formerly the Teito Rapid Transit Authority (Eidan). Its eight colour-coded lines are: **Chiyoda** (dark green), **Ginza** (orange), **Hanzomon** (purple), **Hibiya** (grey), **Marunouchi** (red), **Nanboku** (light green), **Tozai** (turquoise) and **Yurakucho** (yellow), which includes **New Yurakucho** (brown), called Shin-Sen in Japanese.

Four – slightly pricier – subway lines are run by the metropolitan government, **Toei** (3816 5700, 9am-7pm daily, www.kotsu.metro. tokyo.jp). They are: **Asakusa** (pale pink), **Mita** (blue), **Oedo** (bright pink) and **Shinjuku** (green). If transferring from Tokyo Metro to Toei trains, buying a transfer ticket is ¥70 cheaper than buying separate tickets.

ESSENTIALS

Private train lines

Tokyo's private railway lines mainly ferry commuters to the outlying districts of the city. Most were founded by companies that also run department stores, so they usually terminate inside, or next to, one of the branches.

You can pick up a full map showing all lines and subways from the airport information counter on arrival. Keio lines offer women-only cars during peak hours: look for the pink window stickers (or the hundreds of grinning faces in the train if you've entered by mistake).

Tokyo's major private lines are:

Keio
www.keio.co.jp

Keisei
www.keisei.co.jp

Keikyu
www.keikyu.co.jp

Odakyu
www.odakyu.jp

Seibu
www.seibu-group.co.jp/railways

Tobu
www.tobuland.com

Tokyu
www.tokyu.co.jp

Tickets & passes

Standard tickets

Single tickets for adults (under-12s pay half-price, under-6s travel free) are available at automatic ticket machines at any station. Touch-screen ticket machines can display information in English, but should you be unsure of the fare, buy the cheapest ticket and settle up at a fare adjustment machine (or window) at your destination. These machines, usually bright yellow, are found just before the exit barriers of all stations. Travellers with incorrect tickets do not have to pay punitive fines.

Transferring from one line to another, provided it is run by the same operator, will be covered by the price of your ticket. If your journey involves transferring from one network to another, you will have to buy a transfer ticket (if available) or buy another ticket at the transfer point.

If you're in town for any length of time, buy a travel pass.

Pasmo/Suica

The Pasmo card launched in spring 2007 as the first travel card to cover buses, trains and the metro network. Containing an IC chip, the cards are swiped over screens at the ticket gate, where the minimum fare is automatically deducted, with the balance being picked up on exit at your destination. The cards can be purchased at JR 'Green Window' areas or at ticket machines in train or subway stations. Credits can be added at most ticket machines. The Suica card, once exclusively for JR lines, now functions identically to Pasmo cards.

JRPasses

The **Japan Rail Pass** (www.japanrailpass.net) allows virtually unlimited travel on the entire national JR network, including *shinkansen* and all JR lines in Tokyo, including the Yamanote line. It cannot, however, be used on the 'Nozomi' super-express *shinkansen*. It costs from ¥28,300 for seven days, about the same price as a middle-distance *shinkansen* return ticket. It's essential if you're planning to travel much around Japan.

The JRPass is available only to visitors from abroad travelling under the entry status of 'temporary

ESSENTIALS

visitor', and must be purchased *before* coming to Japan. You buy an Exchange Order abroad, which is then changed into a pass on arrival in Japan at an exchange office (you'll need to show your passport).

JR East, which runs trains in and around Tokyo, has its own version of the pass (www.jreast. co.jp/e/eastpass), which costs from ¥20,000 for five days. If you are not intending to travel beyond the JR East area (Tokyo and the area to the north and east), this makes a sensible choice. The same conditions apply.

Exchange Orders can be bought at overseas offices of the Japan Travel Bureau International, Nippon Travel Agency, Kinki Nippon Tourist, Tokyu Tourist Corporation and other associated local travel agents, or at an overseas Japan Airlines office if you're travelling by Japan Airlines. Check the Japan Rail Pass website for overseas locations.

Buses

Like the trains, buses in Tokyo are run by several companies. Travel by bus can be confusing if you're new to Japan, as signs are rarely in English. Toei and Keio bus fares cost ¥200, other buses are ¥210 (half-price for kids) – no matter what the distance. Get on the bus at the front and off at the back. If you aren't using a Pasmo card, drop the exact fare into the slot in front of the driver. If you don't have it, a change machine, usually to the right, will deduct your fare from the money. Fare machines accept ¥50, ¥100 and ¥500 coins and ¥1,000 notes. Stops are usually announced by a pre-recorded voice. A Toei bus route guide in English is available at Toei subway stations and hotels.

Tokyo Bus Association
5360 7111/www.tokyobus.or.jp

The website and phone line provide information on all bus routes within and leaving Tokyo, in Japanese only.

Cycling

The bicycle remains the most common form of local transport in Tokyo, and therefore the most commonly stolen form of transport, so get a strong lock. Areas in and around stations are usually no-parking zones for bikes, a rule that locals gleefully ignore, but which can result in your bike being impounded. Some hotels will loan bicycles to guests.

Driving

If you rent a car, expect to pay astronomical parking fees (usually around ¥100 for 30 minutes, more in the centre). If you do decide to hire a car, you'll need an international driving licence backed up by at least six months' driving experience. English-speaking rental assistance is available at many of the large hotels as well as at the airport.

The **Japan Automobile Federation** (www.jaf.or.jp) publishes a 'Rules of the Road' guide (¥1,000) in English. Request one from their Shiba branch office: 2-2-17 Shiba, Minato-ku (6833 9100). A Metropolitan Expressway map in English is available from the **Metropolitan Expressway Public Corporation** (www.shutoko.jp).

If you want to drive outside the capital (which is definitely a much safer option), JR offers rail and car rental packages. Call the **JR East Infoline** (p179) for details.

Toyota Rent-a-lease
Narita International Airport Terminals 1 & 2 (0476 32 1020/ fax 0476 32 1088/http://rent.toyota. co.jp). **Open** 7am-10pm daily.

Resources A-Z

Accident & emergency

The following hospitals and medical centres offer regular appointments, deal with 24-hour emergencies and have English-speaking staff.

Japan Red Cross Medical Centre

4-1-22 Hiroo, Shibuya-ku (3400 1311/www.med.jrc.or.jp). Hiroo station (Hibiya line), exit 3. **Open** 8.30-11am Mon-Fri.

St Luke's International Hospital

9-1 Akashicho, Chuo-ku (3541 5151/www.luke.or.jp). Tsukiji station (Hibiya line), exits 3, 4. **Open** 8.30-11am Mon-Fri; appointments only from noon.

Seibo International Catholic Hospital

2-5-1 Naka-Ochiai, Shinjuku-ku (3951 1111/www.seibokai.or.jp). Shimo-Ochiai station (Seibu Shinjuku line), north exit. **Open** 8-11am Mon-Sat; appointments only from 12.30pm. Closed 3rd Sat of month.

Tokyo Medical Clinic & Surgical Clinic

Mori Bldg 32 2F, 3-4-30 Shiba-koen, Minato-ku (3436 3028/www.tmsc.jp). Shiba-Koen station (Mita line), exit A2. **Open** 8.30am-5.30pm Mon-Fri; 8.30am-noon Sat.

Doctors hail from the UK, America, Germany or Japan, and all speak English. The clinic also has a pharmacy on the first floor.

ATMs

Japan is still a society that mainly uses cash, and restaurants and bars may refuse credit cards.

Larger shops, restaurants and hotels accept major cards, but always carry cash.

ATMs are located inside banks so most are closed overnight (times vary) and all day Sundays. Larger branches, close to major stations, do however stay open 24 hours. Citibank and Shinsei Bank ATMs are all open around the clock and have English instructions.

Post offices are also convenient for cash: their ATMs allow you to withdraw money using most foreign credit cards and have instructions in English. Some of their ATMs open 24 hours a day.

The ATMs at Narita Airport only work during banking hours. Ensure you have some Japanese cash if arriving early in the morning or late at night.

Credit cards

To report lost or stolen credit cards, dial one of these 24-hour freephone numbers:

American Express

0120 020 120.
English message follows Japanese.

Diners Club

0120 074 024.

MasterCard

00531 11 3886.

Visa

00531 44 0022.

Customs

The duty-free allowances for non-residents entering Japan are: 400 cigarettes or 100 cigars or 250g of tobacco; three 750ml bottles of spirits; 57g (20oz) of perfume;

gifts or souvenirs up to a value of ¥200,000. There is no limit on importing currency. For more information, visit Japan Customs at www.customs.go.jp.

Dental

Both of the following have English-speaking staff.

Dr JS Wong

1-22-3 Kami-Osaki, Shinagawa-ku (3473 2901). Meguro station (Yamanote, Mita, Nanboku lines), east exit. **Open** by appointment only Mon-Wed, Fri, Sat.

Tokyo Clinic Dental Office

Mori Bldg 32 2F, 3-4-30 Shiba-Koen, Minato-ku (3431 4225). Kamiyacho station (Hibiya line), exit 1; or Akabanebashi station (Oedo line), Tokyo Tower exit. **Open** by appointment only Mon-Thur, Sat.

Disabled

Information for disabled visitors is available at http://accessible.jp.org. Club Tourism Division Barrier-free Travel (www.club-t.com) organises tours that cater for disabled travellers.

Electricity

Electric current in Japan runs at 100V AC. Plugs have two flat-sided prongs. If bringing electrical appliances from Europe, you need to purchase an adaptor.

Embassies

Embassies are usually open 9am to 5pm Monday to Friday; opening times for visa sections may vary.
Australian Embassy *2-1-14 Mita, Minato-ku (5232 4111/www.australia.or.jp). Azabu-Juban station (Nanboku, Oedo lines), exit 2.*
British Embassy *1 Ichibansho, Chiyoda-ku (5211 1100/www.uknow.*

or.jp). Hanzomon station (Hanzomon line), exit 4.
Canadian Embassy *7-3-38 Akasaka, Minato-ku (5412 6200/www.canadanet.or.jp). Aoyama-Itchome station (Ginza, Hanzomon, Oedo lines), exit 4.*
Irish Embassy *2-10-7 Kojimachi, Chiyoda-ku (3263 0695/www.embassy-avenue.jp/ireland). Hanzomon station (Hanzomon line), exit 4.*
New Zealand Embassy *20-40 Kamiyamacho, Shibuya-ku (3467 2271/www.nzembassy.com/japan). Yoyogi-Koen station (Chiyoda line), exit 2.*
US Embassy *1-10-5 Akasaka, Minato-ku (3224 5000/http://tokyo.us embassy.gov). Tameike-Sanno station (Ginza, Nanboku lines), exit 13.*

Internet

Most of Tokyo's 24-hour manga coffee shops (*manga kissa*) offer cheap internet services. They are usually clustered around train stations. For a list of internet cafés ordered by station, visit www.tcvb.or.jp/en/guide/09cafe.html. Wi-Fi hotspots are sporadic, with hotel lobbies the best bet.

Opening hours

Department stores and larger shops in Tokyo are open daily from 10am or 11am to around 8pm or 9pm. **Smaller shops** are open the same hours six days a week. Mondays and Wednesdays are the most common closing days; Sunday is a normal shopping day. **Convenience stores** offer 24-hour shopping at slightly higher prices than supermarkets and can be found all over the city.

Most **restaurants** open at around 11am and close around 11pm, though some **bars** and *izakaya* are open until 5am. **Banks** are open 9am to 3pm Monday to Friday. Main **post offices** are open 9am to 7pm weekdays and often on Saturdays

ESSENTIALS

(usually 9am-3pm) or even Sundays; smaller post offices close at 5pm Monday to Friday and at weekends.

Police

For emergencies, call **110**. If you are using a green public phone, press the red button.

Post offices

Post offices (*yubin-kyoku*) – indicated by a red-and-white sign like a letter 'T' with a line over it – are plentiful. Local post offices open from 9am to 5pm Monday to Friday, and are closed at weekends and on public holidays. Larger post offices close at 7pm on weekdays, and may open on Saturdays (usually 9am-3pm) or even Sundays. Post office ATMs accept foreign bank and credit cards.

Smoking

Many wards have banned public smoking, but there are designated smoking areas near, and inside, many stations. The legal age for smoking is 20.

Telephones

Dialling & codes

The country code for Japan is **81**. The area code for Tokyo is **03**. Throughout this guide, we have omitted the 03 from the beginning of Tokyo telephone numbers, as you don't need to dial it when calling from within the city. If you're phoning from outside Japan, dial the international access code plus 81 plus 3, followed by the main eight-digit number. Numbers that start with 0120 are freephone.

For the operator, dial **100**; for directory enquiries, dial **104**. Both services are Japanese-language only.

International calls

Dial 001 (KDDI), 0041 (Japan Telecom), 0061 (Cable & Wireless IDC) or 0033 (NTT Communications), followed by your country's international code, area code (minus any initial zero) and the phone number. The cheapest time to call is between 11pm and 8am, when an off-peak discount of 40 per cent applies.

To use a public phone you need to buy a prepaid card or have a lot of change (some old phones refuse all prepaid cards). Find a booth with 'ISDN' or 'International' on the side – usually a grey phone.

Public phones

Green phones take flexible phone cards and ¥10 and ¥100 coins, but don't allow international calls; grey phones are the same, but usually allow international calls; grey and orange phones only take IC cards (snap off the corner before use) and coins, but you can always make international calls; the blue credit phones require a credit card to make international calls and are hard to find.

Prepaid phone cards

The KDDI 'Super World' prepaid card for international phone calls is sold at most major convenience stores in denominations of ¥1,000, ¥3,000 or ¥5,000 and can be used with any push-button phone.

Mobile phones

You can rent a mobile phone from Softbank stands at the airport. Otherwise, try:

DoCoMo Shop *Shin-Otemachi Bldg 1F, 2-2-21 Otemachi (freephone 0120 680 100/http://www.docomosentu.co.jp/ Web/product/rental/index.html). Tokyo station (Yamanote, Marunouchi lines), north exit.* **Open** 10am-7pm Mon-Fri; 10am-5pm Sat.

Tickets

The largest ticket agency is **Ticket Pia** (0570 029 111, http://t.pia.co.jp), which has outlets throughout the city, often in department stores. Convenience store chain **Lawson** (www2.lawsonticket.com) has ticket vending machines in most stores, but navigation is in Japanese.

Time

Japan is nine hours ahead of Greenwich Mean Time (GMT). Daylight Saving Time is not used.

Tipping

Tipping is not expected in Japan and people will often be embarrassed if you try. At smart establishments, a service charge is often included.

Tourist information

The **Japan National Tourist Organisation (JNTO)** is the national English-language tourist service for visitors coming to Japan. It has offices abroad, plus a Tourist Information Centre (TIC) next to Yurakucho station. Its website, www.jnto.go.jp, is packed with useful information.

There's also the **Tokyo Tourist Information Centre**, run by the Tokyo Metropolitan Government in its headquarters in Shinjuku.

Tokyo TIC

Tokyo Kotsu Kaikan 10F, 2-10-1 Yurakucho, Chiyoda-ku (3201 3331). Yurakucho station (Yamanote line), *Kyobashi exit; (Yurakucho line), exit A8.* **Open** 9am-5pm daily.
Friendly, multilingual staff and a wealth of information are on offer here: there are maps, event booklets, books on Japanese customs, even NTT English phonebooks, plus a useful budget hotel booking service via the Welcome Inn Reservation Centre. There's nothing on the outside of the building to indicate the tourist office is here – just take the lift to the tenth floor, where there is a sign. The Narita Airport outposts open 8am-8pm daily. **Other locations** Arrival floor, Terminal 1, Narita Airport (0476 30 3383); Arrival floor, Terminal 2, Narita Airport (0476 34 6251).

Tokyo Tourist Information Centre

Tokyo Metropolitan Government Bldg No.1 1F, 2-8-1 Nishi-Shinjuku, Shinjuku-ku (5321 3077, www. kanko.metro.tokyo.jp/public/center. html). Tochomae station (Oedo line), exit 4. **Open** 9.30am-6.30pm daily.
If you're visiting the observation deck in the Tokyo Metropolitan Government Building, pop into this ground-floor office.

What's on

If you read Japanese, there's a wealth of what's-on details in weekly publications such as **Pia** and **Tokyo Walker** (both ¥320). For English listings, see:

Metropolis

www.metropolis.japantoday.com
Tokyo's biggest and best free weekly magazine, with listings galore. It's distributed at foreigner-friendly bars, clubs, shops and hotels every Friday.

Tokyo Art Beat

www.tokyoartbeat.com/index.en
Comprehensive listings of upcoming art events.

Higher Frequency

www.higher-frequency.com
Upcoming clubbing highlights.

ESSENTIALS

Vocabulary

Japanese pronunciation presents few problems for native English speakers, but you must split the syllables: *made* (until) is 'ma-de', not the English 'made', and *shite* (doing) is 'shi-te', rather than anything else. When a 'u' falls at the end of the word, it is barely spoken: 'desu' is close to 'dess'.

Consonants are the same as in English, but always hard ('g' as in 'girl', not 'gyrate'), except for the 'l/r' sound, which falls halfway between the English pronunciation of the two letters. As for vowels, **a** is as in 'car', **e** as 'bed', **i** as 'feet', **o** as 'long', and **u** as 'flu'. Elongated vowels are the same, but longer – an easy distinction to Japanese ears, less so for English speakers!

Numbers

1 *ichi;* **2** *ni;* **3** *san;* **4** *yon;* **5** *go;* **6** *roku;* **7** *nana;* **8** *hachi;* **9** *kyuu;* **10** *juu;* **11** *juu-ichi;* **12** *juu-ni;* **100** *hyaku;* **1,000** *sen;* **10,000** *man;* **100,000** *juu-man*

Days, months, times

Monday *getsu-yoobi;* **Tuesday** *ka-yoobi;* **Wednesday** *sui-yoobi;* **Thursday** *moku-yoobi;* **Friday** *kin-yoobi;* **Saturday** *do-yoobi;* **Sunday** *nichi-yoobi;* **January** *ichi-gatsu;* **February** *ni-gatsu;* **March** *san-gatsu;* **April** *shi-gatsu;* **May** *go-gatsu;* **June** *roku-gatsu;* **July** *shichi-gatsu;* **August** *hachi-gatsu;* **September** *ku-gatsu;* **October** *juu-gatsu;* **November** *juu-ichi-gatsu;* **December** *juu-ni-gatsu;* **excuse me, do you have the time?** *sumimasen, ima nan-ji desu ka?* **it's ... o'clock** *... ji desu;* **noon/midnight** *shougo/mayonaka;* **this morning/this afternoon/**

this evening *kesa/kyoo no gogo/konban;* **yesterday/tomorrow/today** *kinoo/ashita/kyoo;* **last week/this week/next week** *sen-shuu/kon-shuu/rai-shuu;* **the weekend** *shuumatsu*

Basic expressions

yes/no *hai/iie;* **please (asking a favour)** *onegai shimasu;* **please (offering a favour)** *doozo;* **thank you (very much)** *(doomo) arigatoo;* **good morning** *ohayoo gozaimasu;* **good afternoon** *kon nichi wa;* **good evening** *kon ban wa;* **goodnight** *oyasumi nasai;* **how are you?** *ogenki desu ka?* **excuse me (getting attention)** *sumimasen;* **excuse me (may I get past?)** *shitsurei shimasu;* **sorry** *gomen nasai;* **it's okay** *daijoobu desu;* **my name is...** *...desu;* **what's your name?** *o namae wa nan desu ka?* **pleased to meet you** *doozo yoroshiku;* **cheers!** *kampai!* **do you speak English?** *eigo o hanashi masu ka?* **I don't speak (much) Japanese** *nihongo o (amari) hanashi masen;* **could you speak more slowly?** *yukkuri itte kudasai;* **could you repeat that?** *moo ichido itte kudasai;* **do you understand?** *wakari masu ka?* **I understand/don't understand** *wakari mashita/masen;* **where is it?** *doko desu ka?* **when is it?** *itsu desu ka?* **what is it?** *nan desu ka?*

Hotels

do you have a room? *heya wa arimasu ka?* **I'd like a single/double room** *shinguru/daburu no heya o onegai shimasu;* **I'd like a room with...** *...tsuki no heya o onegai shimasu;* **a bath/shower**

furo/shawaa; **I've a reservation** yoyaku shite arimasu; **is there…** **in the room?** heya ni… wa arimasu ka? **air-con** eakon; **TV/telephone** terebi/denwa; **we'll be staying…** …tomari masu; **one night only** ippaku dake; **a week** isshuu-kan; **I don't know yet** mada wakari masen; **how much is…?** …ikura desu ka? **does the price include…?** kono nedan wa… komi desu ka? **sales tax (VAT)** shoohi zee; **breakfast/ meal** chooshoku/shokuji; **could you wake me up at…?** …ji ni okoshite kudasai; **bathtowel/ blanket/pillow** basu taoru/moofu/ makura; **what time do we have to check out by?** chekkuauto wa nan-ji made desu ka? **could I have my bill, please?** kaikei o onegai shimasu; **could I have a receipt, please?** reshiito o onegai shimasu; **would you order me a taxi, please?** takushii o yonde kudasai

Shopping & money

I'd like… …o kudasai; **do you have…?** …wa arimasu ka? **how much is that?** ikura desu ka? **could you help me?** onegai shimasu; **can I try this on?** kite mite mo ii desu ka? **I'm looking for…** …o sagashite imasu; **I'll take it** sore ni shimasu; **that's all, thank you** sore de zenbu desu; **currency exchange** ryoogae-jo; **I'd like to change pounds into yen** pondo o en ni kaetain desu ga; **could I have some small change, please?** kozeni o kudasai

Health

where can I find a hospital/ dental surgery? byooin/hai-sha wa doko desu ka? **I need a doctor** isha ga hitsuyoo desu; **is there a doctor/dentist who speaks English?** eego ga dekiru isha/ ha-isha wa imasu ka? **what are** the surgery hours? shinryoo jikan wa nan-ji desu ka? **could the doctor come to see me here?** ooshin shite kuremasu ka? **could I make an appointment for…?** …yoyaku shitain desu ga; **it's urgent** shikyuu onegai shimasu; **I'm diabetic** watashi wa toonyoobyoo desu; **I'm asthmatic** watashi wa zensoku desu; **I'm allergic to…** …arerugii desu; **contraceptive pill** hinin yoo piru; **I feel faint** memai ga shimasu; **I have a fever** netsu ga arimasu; **I've been vomiting** modoshi mashita; **I've got diarrhoea** geri shitemasu; **it hurts here** koko ga itai desu; **I have a headache** zutsuu ga shimasu; **I have a sore throat** nodo ga itai desu; **I have a stomach ache** onaka ga itai desu; **I have a toothache** ha ga itai desu; **I've lost a filling/tooth** tsumemono/ha ga toremashita

Sights & transport

gallery bijutsukan; **hot springs** onsen; **mountain** yama; **museum** hakubutsu-kan; **palace** kyuuden; **park** kooen; **shrine** jinja; **temple** tera; **where's the nearest underground station?** chikatetsu no eki wa doko desu ka? **a map of the underground, please** chikatetsu no rosenzu o kudasai; **to…, please** …made onegai shimasu; **single/return tickets** katamichi/oofuku kippu; **where can I buy a ticket?** kippu wa doko de kaemasu ka? **how much…?** …wa ikura desu ka? **when does the train for… leave?** …iki no densha wa nan-ji ni demasu ka? **can you tell me when we get to…?** …ni tsuitara oshiete kudasai; **ticket office** kippu-uriba; **ticket vending machines** kenbai-ki; **bus** basu; **train** densha; **bullet train** shinkansen; **subway** chikatetsu; **taxi** takushii

ESSENTIALS

Menu Reader

寿司屋 **sushi-ya**
sushi restaurants
いくら *ikura* salmon roe
たこ *tako* octopus
まぐろ *maguro* tuna
こはだ *kohada* punctatus
とろ *toro* belly of tuna
ほたて *hotate* scallop
うに *uni* sea urchin roe
えび *ebi* prawn
ひらめ *hirame* flounder
あなご *anago* conger eel
いか *ika* squid
たまご *tamago* sweet egg omelette
かっぱ巻き *kappamaki* rolled cucumber
鉄火巻き *tekkamaki* rolled tuna
おしんこ巻き *oshinkomaki* rolled pickles

そば屋 **soba-ya**
noodle restaurants
そば *soba*
thin, buckwheat noodles
うどん *udon*
thick, white, wheat-flour noodles
天ぷらそば／うどん *tempura soba/udon*
noodles in hot broth with prawn tempura
ざるそば／うどん *zaru soba/udon*
noodles served on a bamboo rack in
a lacquer box
きつねそば／うどん *kitsune soba/udon*
noodles in hot broth topped with spring
onion and fried tofu
たぬきそば／うどん *tanuki soba/udon*
noodles in hot broth with tempura batter
月見そば／うどん *tsukimi soba/udon*
raw egg broken over noodles in hot broth

居酒屋 **izaka-ya**
Japanese-style bars
Literally 'a place where there is sake'.
An after-work drinking den frequented
by Japanese businessmen, usually
serving reasonably priced food
日本酒 *nihon-shu* sake
冷酒 *rei-shu* cold sake
焼酎 *shoochu* barley or potato spirit
チュウハイ *chuuhai*
shoochu with juice or tea

生ビール *nama-biiru* draught beer
黒ビール *kuro-biiru* dark beer
梅酒 *ume-shu* plum wine
焼き魚 *yakizakana* grilled fish
刺身 *sashimi*
raw fish in bite-sized pieces, served
with soy sauce and wasabi
枝豆 *edamame*
green soy beans boiled in the pod
and sprinkled with salt
おにぎり *onigiri*
rice parcel with savoury filling
焼きおにぎり *yakionigiri*
grilled rice balls

焼き鳥屋 **yakitori-ya**
yakitori restaurants
焼き鳥 *yakitori*
barbecued chicken pieces seasoned
with sweet soy sauce
つくね *tsukune* minced chicken balls
タン *tan* tongue
ハツ *hatsu* heart
シロ *shiro* tripe
レバー *rebaa* liver
ガツ *gatsu* intestines
鳥皮 *tori-kawa* skin
ねぎま *negima* chicken with leek

おでん屋 **oden-ya**
oden restaurants
Winter food, simmered in pots of *dashi*
(a traditional stock). *Oden* can be found
on street stalls and in convenience stores
さつま揚げ *satsuma-age* fishcake
昆布 *konbu* kelp rolls
大根 *daikon*
long, white radish (aka mooli)
厚揚げ *atsu-age* fried tofu

Other types of restaurant
料亭 *ryootei*
high-class, traditional restaurants
ラーメン屋 *ramen-ya*
ramen (Chinese-style noodles) shop
天ぷら屋 *tempura-ya*
restaurants serving fish, shellfish or
vegetables dipped in a light batter and
deep-fried, served with soy or mirin dips
to which you add finely grated daikon
and fresh ginger

すき焼き屋 *sukiyaki-ya*
restaurants where pieces of thinly
sliced beef and vegetables are simmered
in a sweet soy-based sauce at the table
on a portable stove, then taken out and
dipped in raw egg (which semi-cooks
on the hot food) to cool them for eating

とんかつ屋 *tonkatsu-ya*
restaurants serving breaded and
deep-fried pork

お好み焼き屋 *okonomiyaki-ya*
restaurants serving the Japanese
equivalent of filled pancakes or a
Spanish omelette, with ingredients
added to a batter and usually cooked on
a tabletop hot plate in front of diners

Essential vocabulary

a table for one/two/three/
four, please
*hitori/futari/san-nin/yo-nin
onegai shimasu*

is this seat free?
kono seki aite masu ka?

outside *soto*

non-smoking area *kin-en-seki*

by the window *madogiwa*

excuse me *sumimasen*

may I see the menu, please?
menyuu o onegai shimasu

do you have a set meal?
setto menyuu/teishoku wa arimasu ka?

I'd like… …*o kudasai*

I'd like a bottle/glass of…
…*o ippon/ippai kudasai*

I can't eat food containing…
…*ga haitte iru mono wa taberare masen*

do you have vegetarian meals?
bejitarian no shokuji wa arimasu ka?

do you have a children's menu?
kodomo-yoo no menyuu wa arimasu ka?

the bill, please
o-kanjyoo onegai shimasu

that was delicious, thank you
gochisou sama deshita

we'd like to pay separately
betsubetsu ni onegai shimasu

it's all together, please
issho ni onegai shimasu

is service included?
saabisu-ryoo komi desu ka?

can I pay with a credit card?
kurejitto caado o tsukae masu ka?

could I have a receipt, please?
reshiito onegai shimasu

Common Signs

General

左 *hidari* left
右 *migi* right
入り口 *iriguchi* entrance
出口 *deguchi* exit
トイレ／お手洗い *toire/o-tearai* toilets
男／男性 *otoko/dansei* men
女／女性 *onna/jyosei* women
禁煙 *kin-en* no smoking
危険 *kiken* danger
立ち入り禁止 *tachiiri kinshi* no entry
引く／押す *hiku/osu* pull/push

Hotels/restaurant

フロント *furonto* reception
予約 *yoyaku* reservation
非常口 *hijyoo guchi* emergency/fire exit
湯 *yu* hot (water)
冷 *ree* cold (water)

Shops

営業中 *eegyoo chuu* open
閉店 *heeten* closed
エレベーター *erebeetaa* lift ('elevator')

エスカレーター *esukareetaa* escalator
会計 *kaikee* cashier

Sightseeing

入場無料 *nyuujoo muryoo*
free admission
大人／子供 *otona/kodomo*
adults/children
割引（学生／高齢者）
waribiki (gakusei/koureisha)
reduction (students/senior citizens)
お土産 *o-miyage* souvenirs
手を触れないでください
te o furenai de kudasai do not touch
撮影禁止 *satsuei kinshi* no photography

Public buildings

病院 *byooin* hospital
交番 *kooban* police box
銀行 *ginkoo* bank
郵便局 *yuubinkyoku* post office
プール *puuru* swimming pool
博物館 *hakubutsu-kan* museum
美術館 *bijutsukan* art museum

ESSENTIALS

Index

ESSENTIALS

ESSENTIALS